Speak with Confidence

A PRACTICAL GUIDE

Fifth Edition

Albert J. Vasile
Bunker Hill Community College

Harold K. Mintz
Bunker Hill Community College

Scott, Foresman and Company
Glenview, Illinois
Boston
London

Literary Credits

page 49   Table of interaction from *The Silent Language* by Edward T. Hall. Copyright © 1959 by Edward T. Hall. Reprinted by permission of Doubleday, a division of Bantam, Doubleday, Dell Publishing Group, Inc.

page 110   From *Readers' Guide to Periodical Literature*, May 1987. Copyright © 1987 by the H. W. Wilson Company. Reprinted by permission.

page 111   From *Business Periodicals Index*, April 1987. Copyright © 1987 by the H. W. Wilson Company. Reprinted by permission.

page 222   From "Exercise" by Deidre Wallace in *Winning Orations*, 1985. Copyright © 1985 by the Interstate Oratorical Association. Reprinted by permission.

page 251   "Good News About Failure: To Fail Is Not to Be Defeated" given by Eugene W. Brice to the Downtown Rotary Club, Kansas City, Missouri, January 6, 1983. Reprinted by permission.

page 309   Taken from the "Dear Abby" column by Abigail Van Buren. Copyright © 1983 by Universal Press Syndicate. Reprinted with permission. All rights reserved.

Credits continue on page 383, which is a legal extension of the copyright page.

Library of Congress Cataloging-in-Publication Data

Vasile, Albert J.
   Speak with confidence: a practical guide/Albert J. Vasile,
Harold K. Mintz.—5th ed.
   400 pp.
   Includes bibliographical references and index.
   ISBN 0-673-38222-2
   1. Oral communication.   2. Public speaking.   I. Mintz, Harold K.
II. Title.
PN4121.V35 1989
808.5'1—dc19   88-18232
                                                            CIP

1 2 3 4 5 6–RRC–94 93 92 91 90 89 88

To my wife, Evelyn, for her patience and understanding. And our two sons:

To Wally, who is sure to set the world afire, at least while practicing his culinary art in some of the finest kitchens of the world . . . and

To Albie and Barbara, who will soon start writing their first chapter of life—together . . . and

To my Mom and Dad.

AJV

To our children Andrea and Lloyd and to Edith, their late beloved Mom.

HKM

Preface

A hearty welcome to the Fifth Edition of *Speak with Confidence!* This text began, more than a decade ago, with a new philosophy for a basic speech guide. It was nurtured and developed, and it blossomed through continuous concern and meticulous attention to that philosophy.

Speak with Confidence is basic in that it is designed for students who are taking a speech course for the first and perhaps the only time. This book includes what we think should be covered in one semester: from a detailed guide for planning and putting together your very first talk to informative, persuasive, and social speechmaking. Our aim has been to incorporate practicality, human interest, currency, easy-to-understand language, and a conversational style. That is why practically all of the footnotes cite newspapers, magazines, and books readily accessible to the public, rather than scholarly journals and abstruse tomes.

We are pleased and proud that so many professors and students have embraced our text as their primary medium for an introductory course in oral communication. *Speak with Confidence* has been adopted by educational institutions in two thirds of all of the states—from community colleges and two-year business and vocational schools to four-year colleges and universities.

So that we might match this Fifth Edition to your needs as closely as possible, detailed questionnaires were sent to ninety-four professors who were using the Fourth Edition of this book. We hold our heads high, because forty-four of those professors responded to the questionnaires. And while dozens of their suggestions are incorporated, we have not only preserved but enhanced the strengths of earlier editions.

A unique feature of *Speak with Confidence* is its method of equal treatment of the sexes. Throughout the book, the pronouns he/his and she/her are used in alternate chapters. In our combined teaching experience of some forty years, we have never seen this feature in any other textbook.

MAJOR IMPROVEMENTS AND ADDITIONS IN THE FIFTH EDITION

In every chapter of this Fifth Edition, both the language and the content have been sharpened in terms of clarity, conciseness, and relevance to student needs. New photographs of great speakers are included, and many cartoons have been updated, replaced, or dropped. Also in every chapter, more student exercises have been added. In addition, there are dozens of new topics for informative, persuasive, and demonstration talks, both in the text itself and in Appendix C. Specifically, the major additions and improvements in this edition are, by chapter number:

Chapter	Changes and Additions
1	A listing of situations in which the ability to *Speak with Confidence* is more important than ever before. Opinions from students who have taken this course. Expanded treatment of shyness.
2	Earlier placement of this important material on giving the first talk (formerly Chapter 4). More suggested topics for the first talk. Expanded treatment of nervousness.

3   A new table listing nine attitudes and the ways in which they may be communicated nonverbally, either intentionally or not.
    A new table enumerating the various distances (intimate, personal, social, and public) that may separate people in communication situations.
    Chapter-end vocabulary section now including antonyms as well as synonyms.
    New sequence in text (formerly Chapter 2).

4   New sequence in text (formerly Chapter 3).

5   Expanded material on articulation problems.

6   Revised material on doing research, specifically on summarizing, paraphrasing, and quoting source material.
    New coverage of plagiarism.

7   Revised section on planning and outlining a talk, with two new sample outlines.

8   Greatly expanded section on audience analysis.
    New sequence in text (formerly Chapter 9).

9   Increased emphasis on speaking with enthusiasm.
    Many suggestions on coping with nervousness before speaking and while speaking.
    New sequence in text (formerly Chapter 8).

10 Revised and expanded material on using audiovisual aids and equipment.
    Many new topics for demonstration talks.
    New chapter-end section on mass communications and telecommunications.

11 New examples showing the powerful effect of dramatizing statistics.
    An award-winning speech by a college student and its outline.
    More topics for informative talks.

12 Up-to-date example of perceived credibility achieved "overnight" during the Iran-Contra hearings.
    Revised material on persuasion.
    More topics for persuasive talks.

13 New examples of speeches to introduce a speaker and to present an award.

14	Revised material on panel discussions. New chapter-end vocabulary section on computers and data processing.
15	Real-life anecdotes emphasizing the importance of conversational skills, both on the job and in interpersonal situations.
16	Revised and sharpened chapter-opening materials.

Like its predecessors, this Fifth Edition is directed to all who want to sharpen their ability to converse, to listen, and to speak before a group—in short, to communicate and to *Speak with Confidence* now.

ACKNOWLEDGMENTS

For the fifth time it's a pleasure to acknowledge the unique talents of Steve Miles, who created all of the cartoons in this Fifth Edition.

Special appreciation and gratitude are extended to four professors who carefully reviewed chapters of the manuscript and offered a multitude of suggestions and recommendations, many of which appear in this edition. They are: Julie McNellis, Saint Xavier College; Bob Sampson, Central Piedmont Community College; Merle H. Smith, Oakland Community College; and D. G. Wilson, Mt. San Antonio College.

We sincerely thank the professors—users of our text—who took the time and effort to respond to our in-depth questionnaire regarding this edition. Their comments provided many positive and practical suggestions that strengthen the text throughout. They are: John B. Baird, Tricia Hays, and Lynne E. Lichtenstein, Catawba Valley Technical College; Carol H. Adams and Sara N. Lewis, Delaware Technical and Community College; Judith T. Hudson and Margaret Lawing, Central Piedmont Community College; Barbara Mase, Lima Technical College; Ruth F. Hutton, Houghton College; Jonathan Dewberry, The Interboro Institute; Denise A. Martini, Community College of Beaver County; Marietta Vaughn, Merritt College; Jo Thornton, Cape

Fear Technical Institute; Mary Jeanne Wolf, Ivy Tech.; Steve Millnitz, Central Community College; Dan Martin, Lockyear College; Larry Newman, Keystone Junior College; D. Donald Fitzgerald, Springfield Technical Community College; Dr. Celia Miles, Asheville-Buncombe Technical College; Dorothy Hardman, The Fort Valley State College; Elaine M. Denman, Terra Technical College; Pamela Perkins, Bunker Hill Community College (formerly at Hostos Community College); James L. Brother, Hartford State Technical College; Jack D. Cook, Robeson Technical College; Carol R. Davenport, Jefferson State Junior College; Nancy Potts, Davidson County Community College; David L. Murphy, Sandhills Community College; Martie Erne, Loma Linda University; Audrey Simmons, Mankato Technical Institute; Eddie Smith, Tri County Technical College; Mary S. Barrett, Edgecombe Technical College; Clement Howton, John C. Calhoun Community College; Vicky Ryan, Davis College; Mona Colson, Dalton Junior College; Don Barnes, Nash Technical College; Cheryl E. Martin, Roanoke-Chowan Technical College; Marjorie Wallem Rowe, Daniel Webster College; Dr. Fred Sokol, Ashuntuck Community College; Paul A. Hutchins, Cooke County College; and Dr. Harold Cantor, Mohawk Valley Community College.

We would also like to thank three colleagues from Bunker Hill Community College for their important contributions: Herb Gross, Jim McCann, and Jim O'Brien. Special thanks go to two people who are highly responsible for this final product and who were deeply influential in helping set this book's tone and direction: Barbara Muller, Acquisitions Editor, and Louise Howe, Developmental Editor. Working very closely with Louise was an enjoyable experience that evolved into an extremely productive relationship. Her many excellent suggestions, recommendations, and contributions appear throughout the text. And finally, our sincerest thanks and appreciation to our Project Editor, Debra DeBord, for her many solid contributions as she guided us down the final stretch and across the finish line.

AJV
HKM

Contents

1

More men have talked their way up the ladder of success than have climbed it in any other way.[1]

Me Study Speech? You've Got to Be Kidding

Chapter Objectives

After reading and understanding this chapter, you should know:

- The importance of this course in enriching your personal life and your career.
- The benefits you will get from working at this course.
- Ways to conquer your shyness.
- The importance of making business and social contacts.

Chapter Digest

Assuming that you do the assigned work, you will gain substantial benefits from this course: self-confidence; the ability to communicate one to one, within a group, and to a group; conquering shyness; a keen sense of personal accomplishment; and a heightened ability to listen. These benefits can help you attain your full potential in the career and life-style you seek. In other

---

1. Bruce Barton, best-selling author, advertising pioneer, and lecturer.

words, as many former students have said, this course may well turn out to be the most important one of your college years.

The authors find it difficult to recall any era in our history more inundated with controversial issues impacting on most, if not all, Americans than today—our trillion-dollar federal budget, gay rights, nuclear energy, the AIDS epidemic, test-tube conception, surrogate motherhood, political crises in Central America and the Persian Gulf, and the soaring costs of a college education, to name a handful. Such areas of concern have motivated thousands of otherwise inactive Americans to become "activated," from writing to their local newspapers to joining and, in some cases, organizing groups and movements to express their views in order to exert their influence. Your time to speak up may be at hand. Are you prepared?

Let's face it, you're taking this basic course in speech, or oral communication, for one of two reasons:

1. You *want* to.
2. You *have* to.

If you *want* to take the course, you have nothing to worry about. Apparently, you appreciate the importance of oral communication and the boost that this course can contribute to the career and lifestyle you want. If you simply exert the effort, you will develop into a self-confident communicator whom people will listen to and respect.

If you've been "drafted" into the speech course, this is a different ballgame. To most Americans, the idea of compulsion is self-defeating, destructive, and, in many instances, antilearning. Yet, during college or after college, we sometimes have to do things that we don't want to do.

For example, if we decided to obey traffic lights and speed limits only at our own convenience, what would happen? If pilots decided not to abide by their pre-established flight patterns and procedures from takeoff to landing, what would happen?

If this course is required and you're not really ecstatic about taking it, try to control your enthusiasm by accepting this experience with an open mind. Who knows, you may enjoy the course. You may find yourself warming up to the challenge and even thriving on the zestful give-and-take of verbal jousting in class. Take the plunge on a positive note. Remember, you'll never know what you're capable of doing until you try.

HOW IMPORTANT IS THIS COURSE TO YOU?

Every day you communicate orally without giving it a thought. You greet people. You express opinions and desires. You ask questions and you answer them. You agree with people and you disagree. Sometimes you try to influence them.

Have you ever envied someone for his ability to express thoughts and opinions authoritatively? Have you ever experienced a situation in which you wished you had had the confidence and ability to communicate ideas and opinions? Do you have problems meeting people and making new friends? Have you ever wished you were a better conversationalist? If you answered "yes" to all or some of these questions, then get set for one of the most important courses of your life.

Talking, listening, writing, and reading are acts of communication that you perform throughout your life. Of these four acts, there's no question that talking and listening predominate in business, social, and political relationships. For every word you write, you may speak thousands of words to carry you through a typical day. Consider the following circumstances in which effective oral communication may be crucial to you:

- Being able to disagree with your boss or immediate supervisor without being disagreeable.
- Being able to express your feelings and file a grievance rather than suppressing your feelings and being miserable.
- Wanting some time off from your job without having to call in sick.
- Handling a delicate situation like being sexually harassed on the job (male or female).
- Evaluating and selecting courses with your faculty adviser. In order to receive maximum benefit from the consultation, you must be able to express your course selections in the light of your long- or short-range goals.
- Voicing your opinions at home, in classes, in politics, at the office, and at weekend orientations.
- Interviewing for a job or seeking a raise or promotion. Unless

People listen to and respect a self-confident talker.

you express yourself knowledgeably and confidently, what would your chances be?

- Participating in community, business, or political action groups. Consumer, taxpayer, environmental,and labor organizations, women's and men's liberation groups, and PTA's, for example, need people who have ideas and the ability to communicate as well as to execute them. How many of us shy away because we lack confidence in our ability to champion our beliefs?

- Trying to break the news gently to your parents that you've decided to move out of your home and into an apartment . . . with your boyfriend or girlfriend.

These represent only a few situations that require clear, confident talking.

An ability to communicate orally will be crucial in your chosen career, whether you're interacting with a doctor or patient as a nurse, explaining a design or decision in engineering, asking for specific instructions in electronics or accounting, preparing and giving a report

A delicate situation—like being sexually harassed on the job . . .

to your superiors or peers in the business world, or explaining a process in computer technology. No matter what your vocation—sales, education, marketing, advertising, administration—being able to speak with confidence will be an invaluable asset to your personal development.

Since these experiences will confront you throughout life, you should prepare yourself to cope with them to your advantage. No matter who you are, the keys to achieving your lifetime goals are your competence on the job and your ability to communicate effectively with your fellow humans.

We thought that you might be interested in some opinions of your peers who have completed this course. Here are some representative quotations:

- "I liked this course very much, even though I was going to drop it because I didn't have confidence in myself to get up in front of people. I have that confidence now and I think it's great."

"Mom and Dad, I'm going to live with Endicott."

- "My initial reaction to this course, at the beginning, was utter panic. Needless to say, however, by the end of the semester this course turned out to be the best I ever had."
- "The course was terrific. I received confidence, warmth, and a real feeling of belonging."
- "This course has helped me tremendously, not only to be able to better communicate in my other classes but also on the job when communicating with my peers and superiors. Thank you."
- "Not only has this course taught me a great deal about myself, but I learned a lot from and about my classmates."
- "This course gave me the courage and confidence that I needed to be able to stand and give a talk in front of an audience. The book helped me to learn and understand the proper ways to address a group of people. I never thought that a textbook could be so much fun to read."

There's Nothing Wrong with Being Shy—But . . .

There's nothing wrong with being shy—if that is what you want. Please read the preceding sentence again, especially the last six words. These words—"if that is what you want"—say it all. If you're shy and you feel comfortable with your shyness, it's because you *choose* to be that way, but you don't *have* to be. Although you weren't born shy, there may be a multitude of reasons, especially during your adolescent years, for your development in that direction. One valid reason might be that you were never encouraged to participate in conversation or in other activities involving social exchanges. Another reason might be that you allowed people to make you feel inferior or inadequate.

Whatever the reason for your shyness, the vital point is that if you don't want to be shy, you don't have to be. You must decide, and it could be one of the most crucial decisions you'll make during your lifetime. If you should decide that you would rather be able to greet people, speak with them, socialize more, and cultivate new friendships, then you've taken a giant step forward.

If you're shy, we strongly believe that it is not due to your physical appearance or to a lack of talent, but rather to your own low estimation of yourself. You must constantly strive to think about yourself in a positive manner. You can reinforce this principle by first deciding that you're going to change and then by repeating to yourself dozens of times daily such positive thoughts as:

"I'm no longer going to be shy."

"I am an attractive person."

"I am going to be more friendly to people."

"People are going to like me."

"I can contribute to a conversation as well as any of my friends."

"I am a good person and I have a lot to offer."

By reiterating such statements, you will help raise your levels of self-esteem and self-confidence. At the same time, your degree of shyness

You allowed other people to make you feel inferior.

should gradually diminish. You should already start to feel positive about yourself because you've made an important decision—independently. You must constantly remind yourself that you're no longer going to accept your shyness, and you must constantly visualize yourself as being more gregarious. It's a very important beginning.

This course will present you with many opportunities to develop ways to overcome your diffidence, and your class environment will provide you with the necessary encouragement. Your most important mentor at this stage will be your speech professor, who will, most likely, be supportive, understanding, and sympathetic. Make an appointment to see him as soon as possible and explain your decision and goal. As your speech course progresses, listen carefully to your classmates and ask questions after their talks.

In addition, before and after class, make an effort to talk to a classmate, even if you start with a simple greeting such as "Good morning," "Hi, how are you doing?" or "I enjoyed your talk today. You know what I'd like to ask you?" Every day, try to start a con-

"I'm no longer going to be shy . . .
I'm no longer going to be shy . . .
I'm no longer going . . ."

versation with a different classmate, and always try to remember names. It will be difficult at first but will become easier as the days pass.

When you begin to feel more self-confident and relaxed, expand this new approach to people in your other classes, at home, at work, and at social gatherings. If you notice someone at a social occasion whom you would like to meet or who appears alone, go out of your way to strike up a conversation. Take a deep breath, smile, and confidently approach that person. Extend your hand and introduce yourself. Often you'll be pleasantly surprised with the results. That person may be grateful to meet and talk with someone who is friendly. You may even discover that that person is shy.

Remember, there's nothing wrong with being shy, but being friendly and outgoing could open new vistas for a more meaningful, interesting, and exciting personal, as well as professional, life for you. It's your *choice*. Good luck!

MAKING BUSINESS AND SOCIAL CONTACTS

Almost everyone would agree that making contacts and knowing the "right people" are invaluable aids in moving ahead. Making contacts can help you move ahead in your career and in many other ways. Perhaps your son, daughter, or other relative is looking for summer or part-time work; perhaps you want a favor from a politician—a letter of recommendation or introduction; perhaps you are seeking college admission or membership in a prestigious organization. Your chances of obtaining these favors will be immensely improved if you know people in a position to help you.

You should realize that it's no shame to ask for a favor. What is a shame is to need something and not get it because you don't know anyone who could possibly open some doors for you. (This topic is discussed further in Chapters 15 and 16.)

Since knowing the right people may make a significant impact on your life, you should strive to meet and interact with as many people as possible. You never know when they may be able to "come through" for you. By the same token, you should be helpful to others whenever you can, because helping is a two-way street.

Your sincere desire and ability to meet people should become an integral part of your daily life. The way to include them in your life is to communicate orally—speak, listen, question, answer, and get involved.

WHAT THIS COURSE CAN DO FOR YOU

Provided that you expend the effort—and it is vital that you do—this course will enable you to:

- Develop more self-confidence when interacting with people, one to one, within a group, and to a group.
- Be more **assertive.**
- Improve your ability to listen.

- Learn how to present your ideas more clearly, logically, and forcefully.
- Acquire a sense of accomplishment.
- Learn the secrets of meeting and being accepted by people.
- Be more convincing.
- Develop a more positive self-image.
- Sell yourself to an employer, a group, or friends.

You can develop these abilities and reap the advantages by exerting yourself in the following ways:

1. By giving many talks on various topics. In this way you'll communicate your views, experiences, and feelings to your colleagues.

2. By responding to questions from the audience after your talk. The key to performing well in a question-and-answer period is to know your subject thoroughly. If you've done your homework, you will, like most people, be exhilarated by your effort. The adrenalin racing through your veins could produce a new "high" for you. As a result, you will speak more forcefully and fluently than ever before.

3. By asking questions after others have spoken. Listening intently and having some knowledge of the subject under discussion will enable you to ask interesting and penetrating questions. Perhaps you will disagree with the speaker or perhaps you can shed light on a questionable point; in that case, think first and then speak your mind. Your self-confidence will grow once you notice that others listen to you. Remember, the more often you speak, the more self-confident you'll become.

4. By talking or debating with fellow students. The question-and-answer session after a talk often triggers discussion among class members, sometimes without involving the original speaker. Someone may ask a question or present an opinion that incites others to reply. This may result in a sizzling, crackling demonstration of the power of the spoken word to move people.

After each talk, you'll feel a sense of accomplishment, and rightfully so. Even after your first effort, you'll admit not only to great relief

"And then I should've said . . ."

(which you've earned) but, far more important, to a feeling of tremendous satisfaction. With each talk you give, you can only become more confident, and that glow of achievement will intensify.

Keep in mind that this course will not only teach you how to research, prepare, and deliver an effective speech in public or private, but will help you develop your self-confidence whether you are interacting one to one, participating in a small group, or speaking before a large gathering. Remember, once you achieve self-confidence, you will be able to do almost anything you want, provided, of course, that you prepare properly.

Developing self-confidence will enable you to stand up for yourself when someone treats you condescendingly. Congresswoman Geraldine Ferraro showed the nation how to cope with that kind of situation. During a television debate in October 1984, Vice-President Bush said, "Let me help you with the differences, Mrs. Ferraro, between Iran and Lebanon." In a flash, the congresswoman charged at him: "Let me say, Mr. Bush [note that she did not address him as Vice-President Bush], I resent your patronizing attitude that you have to *teach* me about foreign policy." Then she attacked his version of her opinion on the deaths of 241 Marines in Beirut.[2]

Nothing is more frustrating than having something to contribute to a discussion at school, at home, at work, or at a social affair—but not doing so for lack of self-confidence. "To sin by silence," said Abraham Lincoln, "when they should protest makes cowards of men." This course will help you make your contribution.

Things to Discuss in Class

1. List a few topics that you can talk about for at least three minutes.

2. How would speech training help you in your current occupation or in one that you plan to enter?

3. Name a few benefits that you hope to gain from this course.

4. Which public figure do you consider an excellent speaker? Why?

5. Which public figure do you consider a poor speaker? Why?

6. Can you recall any times when you wanted to express your viewpoints and didn't? Why?

7. Do you ever envy friends because they express themselves better than you do?

8. Have you ever started to express yourself, then suddenly stopped for some reason?

9. Do you feel more confident when speaking to one person than to a group?

10. Do you have more (less) difficulty speaking to people of the opposite sex?

---

2. *Boston Globe*, 14 October 1984, A21.

2

The first time I
attempted to
make a public
talk . . . I was in
a state of misery
. . . my tongue
clove to the roof
of my mouth,
and, at first, I
could hardly get
out a word.[1]

Your First Talk: Getting to Know You

Chapter Objectives

After reading and understanding this chapter, you should be able to:

- Appreciate the importance of knowing your subject well.
- Prepare a short, interesting talk about yourself.
- Deliver the talk about yourself.
- Grasp the importance of eye contact and gestures.
- Realize the importance of good posture, some movement, and the limited use of notes.
- Understand that nervousness strikes everybody.

Chapter Digest

This chapter will introduce you to some of the ways of giving a good, stimulating talk. Since it's easier to talk with people you know, the sooner you get to know each other, the better. That's why your first talk will probably be an autobiographical sketch from four to five minutes long.

---

1. David Lloyd George, Prime Minister of England from 1916 to 1922 and one of the most eloquent speakers in this century.

Thorough knowledge of a subject gives speakers more self-confidence than does anything else. Since you know yourself best, you should be able to talk for at least three or four minutes about yourself.

All of us like attention and respect. When you're "front and center," you're the focus of attention. If you follow the suggestions in this chapter and those in later chapters, you will earn the respect of your peers and other listeners.

Everybody, including professional speakers and actors, gets nervous before a performance. It's a normal reaction that usually diminishes soon after you get involved in your message. Since it's almost impossible to eliminate all **nervousness,** you should strive to control it. Suggestions are offered for that purpose.

Eye contact with your listeners is vital, so look them right in the eye. This arouses them initially and gives you the momentum to keep them interested. Eye contact also provides you with feedback on how you're doing.

Gestures support and dramatize your ideas. As long as your gestures are spontaneous and vigorous, use them. In addition, they're an excellent outlet for your nervous energy.

Other nonverbal elements touched on briefly are movement, posture, facial expression, and appearance. This vital area, nonverbal communication, is discussed in depth in Chapter 3.

If using notecards will give you confidence, use them; professional speakers often do. Just don't read so much from the cards that you disrupt eye contact with your listeners.

This first talk will probably be the toughest one of all. Remember that giving good talks requires that you do your homework beforehand. Homework includes rehearsing, preferably with at least one listener.

If you've never addressed a group before, this will be an exciting and memorable experience. Although your talk will probably be short, it could provide you with the challenge and motivation that could exert a positive influence on your life. Your professor may either ask you to talk about yourself or ask you to interview a classmate and then give a talk about her. No matter which talk you give, this chapter will guide you in how to plan and present it.

Since most of you are more relaxed when communicating with people you know, your instructor may feel that it's a good idea for everyone to give a brief autobiographical sketch. In this way you'll learn to know each other sooner and "get the feel" of giving a prepared talk before a group.

This short autobiographical talk will afford you an opportunity to listen to everyone in the class introduce herself. What an excellent chance to find out which classmates have the same interests as yours! Perhaps, while listening to someone interesting, you'll look forward to the class break or a chance to meet at the cafeteria to develop a more personal relationship on a one-to-one basis. So prepare yourself to absorb what your classmates have to say and listen carefully for possible clues of mutual interest or concern. This talk is an important first step in developing new friends. In addition, this will be your introduction to a critical aspect of speech communication—audience analysis. (See Chapters 8 and 12.)

The distance from your seat to the speaker's stand may be only fifteen feet, but it may seem like a mile to you. This is understandable because of your anxiety about what's to come. Many things will zip through your mind, like "I wonder if I'll be able to move when I'm called. I'll just play dead—on second thought, who'll be playing?" or "What am I doing here?" Believe it or not, you're here to give your first talk.

KNOW YOUR SUBJECT

Most speech professors agree that *knowing your subject* is about 50 percent of presenting an effective talk and that *delivery* is the other 50 percent. No one knows you better than you do, and no other topic should interest you more or provide you with more material, so your own life is an excellent topic for your first talk.

You shouldn't let this talk upset you because, in all probability, you won't be graded or critiqued. Your professor may only wish to introduce you to how it feels to stand up and speak before a group— and to convince you that there's nothing mysterious about doing so.

Preparing your first talk should be a simple exercise. With paper and pencil at hand, conduct a self-inventory and make notes. Think about your childhood, parents, and relatives. Where were you born and raised? Which schools did you attend? What made you decide to go to college? Why this one? Has any one person had a strong influence on you? Why did you select your major area of study?

Were you in the service? If so, what branch and what rank did you hold? How was basic training and where did you take it? What type of work did you do in the military and where were you stationed? Did you have any spine-tingling encounters?

"What am I doing here?"

Maybe you're working. Do you like your job—why or why not? How long have you worked there?

Did you ever travel? Where have you been and with whom? How long were you there? Would you like to return—why or why not?

Don't overlook your hobbies or other interests. Do you play a musical instrument? Perhaps you play for a group. If so, where and how often? Maybe you're into karate, automobile repair, ceramics, exercising, or gourmet cooking. Share your experiences.

Are you married or single? Do you have children? If so, how old are they? Maybe you're a grandparent. What made you decide to return to school? How much of a challenge is it? Are you a full-time or part-time student? What are your plans when you graduate?

Have you met any unusually interesting people or celebrities? Tell us about them. When and where did you meet them and under what circumstances? What were your impressions of them? If you've never met a celebrity but wanted to, who would it be and why?

You should now have some ideas on how to prepare for your first talk. Go over the preceding questions again and use them as a guide. We're sure you can expand on them.

Remember, you can be an interesting person. You have something to say: you do things; you have likes and dislikes; you have opinions, dreams, and ambitions. Here is your chance to express them. Good luck.

For your first talk you might choose to use the following format as a guide.

My name is ————————————————————————————.
My friends call me ——————————————————————.
I live at ——————————— and my family consists of ——————————.

I attended the following schools: ————————————————.
My favorite subject(s) were ——————————————————.
My extracurricular activities consisted of ——————————.

I am presently employed at ——————————————— and my responsibilities are ——————————————————————.
The days and hours I work are —————————————————.
What I like best about my job is ——————————————.
What I don't like about my job is ——————————————.

I've decided to come to this college because ———————————.
My major is ————————————————————————————.
My plans after I graduate are ——————————————————.
I participate in the following college activities: ——————————.
I am a full-time/part-time student and I'm taking courses in
——————————————————————————————————————.

My biggest obstacle in coming to college is ————————————.
As far as what my family thinks about my coming to college, ——————————————————————————————————.
I decided to return to college because ———————————————.

I enjoy traveling and have visited ——————————————————.
Of all the places I visited, I enjoyed ————————————— the most because ——————————————————————————.
I was a member of the Armed Forces (mention branch, length of service, duty stations, and occupational specialty):
——————————————————————————————————————.

My short-term goal is ——————————————————————.
My long-term goal is ——————————————————————.

Some of the things I enjoy doing are ————————————.
Some of the things I don't enjoy are ————————————.
My biggest gripe is ————————————————————.
The one thing that gives me great pleasure is ——————————.
I think the biggest problem facing our society is ———————.

Your answers to such statements as these should give your class-mates a handle on who you are and where you come from and could lead to some stimulating relationships.

After you've finished your talk, you might answer questions from the class. This question-and-answer session (further discussed at the end of this chapter), more than any other exercise, will help you develop self-confidence because you'll have completed your formal talk, and you will be able to relax and answer questions on a subject that you thoroughly know—you.

Question-and-answer sessions have uncovered some unusual experiences, including the following:

- A young woman in the class appeared on TV programs several times a week and communicated to deaf viewers in sign language.
- A mother and her son and daughter attended this school at the same time. Each was enrolled in a separate section of my speech classes (AJV).
- A young man enrolled in the course because he wanted to enter politics. He did, and he won his campaign.
- A student told the class she signed up for this course to meet a prospective husband. You guessed it; a year later she was married.
- During semester breaks and summer vacations a student works at Disneyworld in Florida.
- A student told the class of her two hobbies—sky diving and hang gliding.
- A mother of two children worked one summer driving a cab. She was robbed twice and shot at once. She no longer drives a cab.

Here are some topics you might consider if your professor chooses not to assign an autobiographical talk. Remember, your first talk, if you have a choice, should be on a topic that you know very well.

1. The lack of day-care centers
2. How to buy a good used car
3. How to select a reliable baby-sitter
4. The importance of a college degree
5. Searching for your first apartment
6. Working and going to school
7. Being a single parent
8. Microwave cooking
9. A person who has greatly influenced me
10. A person I greatly admire (living or dead)
11. Some problems of being a parent today
12. My biggest gripe
13. Parent(s) should be more selective of their children's viewing habits
14. The increasing number of homeless people
15. Every American should have some type of health insurance
16. The government should allocate more funds for AIDS research
17. There should be tougher penalties for convicted drunken drivers
18. The value of a foreign car versus the value of a domestic one
19. The need for a longer school year

ICE CUBES IN THE STOMACH

Suddenly the professor calls your name—it's your turn to address the class. Your heart pounds with such force that you think it can be heard across the room, your forehead breaks out with beads of perspiration, your mouth goes dry, and your stomach quivers.

You're experiencing an attack of nerves—**stage fright**—that is not unique to you. Most people get it, whether they admit it or not. This sensation, in varying degrees, occurs thousands of times daily: on an individual's first day on a new job, on a first date, and on a student's first day at a new school. It happens to actors and actresses just before the curtain goes up or the camera starts to roll, to students in other speech classes throughout the country ready to give their first talks, and to your own classmates who have spoken before you and to those who will follow you. Even professors aren't immune.

For example, the week before each semester begins, the thought of facing four classes, each of approximately thirty strangers, rattles me (AJV). The thought of walking alone into each classroom, with students staring and trying to assess their "prof," and knowing that this first encounter is crucial in establishing respect and rapport for the entire semester, leads to many anxious moments. But once I start two-way communication and break the ice, the problems melt away. Then, when the first class ends, I enjoy a tremendous feeling of relief and accomplishment.

Nervousness can be a form of positive energy that will keep you on your toes. If you accept it as normal, which it is, it will help you do your best. In a new environment, there is no stigma to feeling nervous or even frightened before speaking. It is a normal reaction, and its intensity will lessen the more you speak.

Even the great and the powerful suffer from nervous attacks. In a talk before London journalists years ago, a famous British cartoonist, David Low, said that every time he had to make a speech he felt as if he had a block of ice, nine inches by nine inches, in the pit of his stomach. Later he was approached by a member of the audience, Winston Churchill, one of the greatest speakers of this century. "Mr. Low," asked Churchill, "how large did you say that block of ice is?"

"Nine inches by nine inches," replied Low.

"What an amazing coincidence," said Churchill, "exactly the same size as mine."

There's no cure for nervousness, but to help control it, you should admit that you're nervous, a bit uptight, queasy, even petrified; some textbooks call it **speaking apprehension.** You should be greatly relieved to learn how many of your peers share your feelings, and things don't seem quite that bad if you're able to talk freely about them. Discuss them at home, at school, at work, with other members of your class, and certainly with your professor.

Even royalty suffers from pangs of nervousness. At her royal wedding in July 1981, the bride, Lady Diana Spencer, called the groom "Philip Charles Arthur George" instead of Charles Philip Arthur George. He, in turn, omitted (or forgot?) the word "worldly" in pledging to share all his worldly goods with her.[2]

---

2. *New York Times*, 30 July 1981, 1.

While there's no simple antidote for nervousness, there are steps you can take to help control this unwanted, involuntary behavior. The first remedy is to be totally prepared; this includes planning your presentation, researching and outlining your topic, and practicing your talk several times. No single action is more important in helping you develop self-confidence and in allaying that uptight feeling than knowing your subject cold. Chapter 9 contains further suggestions on what you can do, both before and during your talk, to relieve tension and to diminish your nervousness.

FRONT AND CENTER

When the initial shock of hearing your name has subsided, slowly draw a few deep breaths. This should help ease that uptight feeling. Walk to the front of the classroom with purpose and confidence. Don't shuffle your feet, don't look at the floor, and don't make any remarks to class members. Once you begin your talk, all of their attention will be riveted on you.

Before starting to speak, you may find it reassuring to look around the classroom. You may sense encouragement from familiar faces. You may also observe a look of genuine understanding from those who appreciate your feelings because it will soon be their turn. You now realize that you're not alone. The preceding speakers sweated through the same experience, and the following speakers will do the same. The quicker you appreciate this, the more relaxed you'll become.

As soon as you get wrapped up in what you're saying, perhaps twenty to thirty seconds into your talk, your nervousness should diminish. This is why we emphasize knowing your subject thoroughly. (In this regard, it may be helpful to memorize the first few sentences, and perhaps even the closing one, to avoid the hesitant and awkward, "Well, I guess that's just about it.")

SAY IT WITHOUT WORDS

First impressions are crucial to communicators, and all of you are communicators. Every day you see people, you greet people, and you meet people—at work, at school, and at social or business functions. Before you even say a word, you transmit impressions,

Keep your cool.

favorable or not, through **nonverbal communication,** the conscious or subconscious transmission and reception of unspoken messages. (You are being introduced to this topic because it will be an integral part of your autobiographical talk. Chapter 3 is devoted entirely to this subject.) Some features of nonverbal communication include:

- *Your walk:* Is it slow, fast, listless, jerky, confident, or hesitant? Do you march, saunter, strut, shuffle, or stalk?
- *Your posture:* Are you straight as a drill sergeant? Do you slump, shift from one leg to the other, droop, or lean on the **lectern?**
- *Your facial expressions:* Do you smile, frown, or smirk? Do you look condescending, absorbed, disappointed, or troubled?
- *Your eyes:* Are they expressive, twinkling, shifty, piercing, friendly, cold, or penetrating?
- *Your dress:* Are you neat or sloppy? Is your hair combed? Are your colors coordinated or clashing?
- *Your cosmetics:* Odors from aftershave lotion, cologne, perfume,

hairspray, antiperspirant (or lack of it), as well as the amount and application of other cosmetic aids, transmit messages.

- *Your **gestures:*** What you do with your hands, head, and shoulders also conveys impressions. A firm handshake or a listless one, a nod of your head or a shrug of your shoulders all carry messages, and you must be aware of them.

First impressions are usually long lasting. How many times have you prejudged a person by any of the above criteria, only to change your assessment after she has spoken or you've become better acquainted? How many times have you reached a negative opinion of a person before she has had the opportunity to communicate orally?

Indeed, nonverbal communication can often influence your opinions more forcefully than the spoken word. The old aphorism that actions speak louder than words is more than mere rhetoric.

In all communication you don't always have to say it to convey it, and in nonverbal communication you may often transmit messages entirely different from what you think you're transmitting. Call it what you like—**body language,** the **silent language, soundless speech,** or nonverbal communication—it is an eloquent form of message transmission and reception. (For more on nonverbal communication, refer to Chapter 3.)

Importance of Eye Contact

Perhaps you know the feeling of approaching several of your friends who are involved in a discussion. When you join the group, you notice that the speaker doesn't look at you but continues looking at the others. She doesn't even acknowledge your presence, and you feel left out.

Eye contact with your audience is extremely important. Without it you will have immense difficulty conveying interest and sincerity. What is your reaction when you listen to someone who doesn't look you in the eye, at least occasionally? The speaker's believability is seriously impaired. When you appear before a group, you should remember that they are not only listening to you, they are also looking at you.

As tempting as it is, don't gaze out windows, at notes, or at the floor or walls. Some speakers, by looking at people in the last row of a large audience, can give the impression that they're looking at

It's OK to relax, but . . .

everyone in front of them. In a smaller group, however, look at the students to your left, then to your right, then in between. Don't make the mistake of some beginning speakers who focus their eyes solely on the professor. Just remember that people like to be talked to and looked at simultaneously.

Making eye contact means that you, the sender, are making a connection with your audience, the receiver. You're transmitting a message, and without eye contact the transmission is broken and communication is disrupted.

By maintaining eye contact with your audience you can receive visual feedback. Your listeners' eyes can tell you if they're getting your message. Do they look confused, bored, doubting, satisfied, or interested? Do they seem to enjoy and understand what you're saying? Do they look drowsy? As long as you're aware of telltale signals from your audience, the communication cycle can be complete. You have a message to communicate with your mind, your voice, your body, and your eyes—you maintain eye contact with your audience and you receive messages in response to your spoken thoughts. If

Eye contact with your audience is extremely important.

you fail to look at your audience, you can't receive any reaction from them. (For more on eye contact, see Chapter 3.)

What About Gestures?

Many people gesture as naturally as they breathe. Perhaps you know people who would be speechless if their hands were tied behind their backs. If you find it natural to move your hands and arms while communicating, continue to do so. If, however, you tend to be carried away by gestures, don't be too concerned about them now because you'll learn to control them as the course progresses.

Your professor will make suggestions as to the degree and effectiveness of your gestures. One practical exercise is to speak before a mirror and watch your body movements, while being videotaped is the best way to see yourself exactly as you appear to others.

Gestures can be natural.

Try to become more aware of how people gesture (nonverbal communication is also discussed in Chapters 3, 5, and 16) when they talk—for example, groups of students, your teacher, friends, family members, your boss, and performers on TV. Are their gestures meaningful and expressive or do they look awkward and meaningless?

Hands always seem to be a problem for inexperienced speakers, but they don't have to be. Putting one hand in a pocket is permissible, and many experienced speakers do it. In his early days of public speaking, the late President John F. Kennedy used to jingle coins in his pocket. He was "cured" by the constant criticism of his mother. His favorite position, when addressing either a press conference or a large gathering, was to keep one hand in his jacket pocket; it contained no coins.

On occasion you may clasp your hands behind your back and, if there's no **lectern,** you may hold notes in them. Be sure to keep your hands away from your face, hair, neck, ears, and nose. Also, if you wear necklaces, pendants, earrings, or bracelets, leave them alone. Fiddling with them distracts people.

Moving Around

As far as movement is concerned, many speakers feel that they must stay in one place and remain completely motionless. Not so. You should feel free to move around. Taking a few steps in either direction from the stand is desirable as long as you move smoothly, not jerkily like a puppet.

However, avoid perpetual motion, for example, swaying back and forth or from side to side, crossing and uncrossing your feet, or fidgeting with your hands and fingers. Movement can be effective when done in moderation, with purpose and naturalness. It helps you develop poise and confidence, and it constructively channels your nervous energy.

Standing Tall

Good posture—standing straight, but not like a ramrod, and squarely on both feet—conveys an impression of confidence and alertness. Your posture communicates attitude, just as your face and voice do. Don't slouch, lean against a table, or drape yourself over the speaker's stand. These actions detract from your overall appearance and create a negative effect on your audience.

Perhaps the best way to improve your posture is to observe yourself on videotape or in a full-length mirror. Then you can see if you're standing tall or hunched over, if your head is held high or drooping, and if your weight is equally distributed on both feet.

There's no question about it—erect posture helps you look sharper and feel more alert.

TAKE NOTE

Using notes is recommended because it can give you a feeling of confidence and security. In fact, many professional speakers use them. Just be careful not to rely on them to the point that you read the entire talk and do not look at your audience.

If there is no lectern, 3-by-5 cards can fit comfortably in the palm of your hand without annoying the audience. If your classroom is equipped with a lectern, 4-by-6 cards (or even standard-sized 8½-

by-11-inch paper) may rest on it without being noticed. Try to keep your cards lying flat so they won't distract your audience, and, as you finish with one, simply slide it to the side unobtrusively. If you have more than two cards, number them in case you drop or misplace them.

QUESTION-AND-ANSWER SESSION

As you conclude your talk, don't lower your voice so that it becomes almost inaudible. Keep it strong and confident until you finally ask, "Are there any questions?" Some of your classmates and even your professor may have a few. If they do, you should feel complimented and, by this time, relaxed enough to answer them easily and naturally.

While you're answering questions, try not to focus your attention solely on the questioner. If the answer is long, you may glance around the class, but when you're concluding your reply, look again at the questioner. Pause a second or two as if to ask, "Did I answer you satisfactorily?" Then field the next inquiry.

When you've handled all of the questions, breathe deeply and return to your seat confidently. Don't rush. Don't crumple your notes and stuff them into your pocket, and don't collapse into your chair. Just sit down quietly.

Congratulations! You've given your first talk. Was it as difficult as you thought it would be? Was it as traumatic an experience as you envisioned? Of course it was. But you did it, and this was the most difficult talk you'll ever make—your toughest obstacle course. Your other talks will be easier and more enjoyable.

NOTE:
You don't look even half as nervous as you feel inside.

Things to Discuss in Class

1. Be aware of eye contact among your friends, colleagues, speakers, and TV performers. When you are personally involved, observe the importance and effect of eye contact among your associates.

2. Using the format presented in this chapter as an aid, prepare and rehearse a four- to five-minute autobiographical talk.

3. Notice how people gesture when they speak. Do the gestures of anyone in particular impress you? Why or why not?

4. Watch speakers on TV, especially religious personalities, and observe their physical movements while speaking. Do they move at all? Do their movements coincide with their message? Are their movements distracting? Prepare to discuss your answers in class.

5. When you meet an individual for the first time, what determines your first impression of that person?

6. What are your personal feelings about judging an individual solely on the basis of physical appearance?

7. Do you have friends who never look directly at you when they talk with you? How do you feel about this behavior?

What Do You Remember from This Chapter?

1. What two elements in speaking do more than anything else to help you acquire self-confidence?

2. Is getting nervous before speaking uncommon? Explain.

3. Why is eye contact so vitally important?

4. When you speak before a group, why is it important to constantly look around at individuals in the audience rather than to focus on a limited area?

5. Do gestures enhance your ability to communicate? Why?

6. What must you be aware of when you use notes?

7. What are two things you can do to help control nervousness?

8. Explain why good posture is important to a public speaker.

Vitalize Your Vocabulary

You can have a clear, musical voice; an attractive appearance; good eye contact; and a solid knowledge of your subject; but if your vocabulary is weak and vague, your presentation will also be weak and vague. Whether you're communicating with one or two people or a group of thirty, a strong vocabulary is a major asset. That is why, starting now and continuing with each succeeding chapter, we include a list of words (and their most basic meanings) that educated people should not only understand but be able to use.

The lists of words vary considerably. Some lists contain families of words that relate to the same subject, for example: government and politics, court and law, business and finance, computers and data processing. Other lists consist of synonyms and antonyms, words based on Latin and Greek roots, words from American Indians, and words from Japan that have entered our language.

We hope that these brief glimpses into the intriguing world of words will galvanize you into exploring deeper into that world.

English words derive from countless languages, principally from Latin and Greek, and from other sources such as literature, art, and science. Among the most fascinating words are *eponyms*—words based on the names of real or mythical people who have accomplished something unusual.

Eponyms

babbitt (n.)   a conventional person interested chiefly in business and social success and indifferent to cultural values. Based on the title character of a 1922 novel by Sinclair Lewis.

boycott (v.)   to join together in refusing to buy, sell, use, or deal with; (n.) the act of boycotting. Derived from Captain Charles C. Boycott (1832–97), a landlord's agent, whose job was to collect high rents from impoverished Irish tenant farmers.

cardigan (n.)   a sweater or jacket that opens full length down the front, usually long-sleeved and collarless. Named after the seventh earl of Cardigan (1799–1868), an English general.

casanova (n.)   a man who has a reputation for being a promiscuous lover, with many female conquests. After Giovanni Casanova, an Italian adventurer and writer of the eighteenth century.

chauvinist (n.)   an extremist in any cause, often militaristic or patriotic. Derived from Nicolas Chauvin, one of Napoleon's most fanatic followers.

gerrymander (v.)   to rearrange a voting district so as to favor the party in power. After Massachusetts Governor Elbridge Gerry, who in 1812 carved out a district whose shape resembled a salamander.

hooker (n.)   a prostitute. During the Civil War, General Joseph Hooker's troops were encamped for a time in Washington. Prostitutes who "serviced" them became known as "Hooker's Division." After the troops moved out, the women were then called "hookers."

leotard (n.)   a one-piece, tight-fitting garment that covers the torso and is now worn by dancers and acrobats. Named for Jules Leotard, a nineteenth-century French trapeze artist.

levis (n.)   blue jeans. Named after Levi Strauss, a Texas merchant who popularized them in the 1800s.

machiavellian (adj.)   deceitful, unscrupulous, crafty. In accordance with the political ideas explained in *The Prince*, a book written by Niccolo Machiavelli (1469–1527), Italian statesman, political philosopher, and author.

nicotine (n.)   a poisonous substance that is the chief active ingredient in tobacco. From Jean Nicot, a seventeenth-century French diplomat who introduced Turkish tobacco into France.

pasteurize (v.)   to destroy disease-producing bacteria and to stop fermentation in milk, beer, cider, and wine by heating the liquid to high temperatures. From Louis Pasteur (1822–95), French chemist and bacteriologist.

sadist (n.)   a person who enjoys inflicting pain on another. Named after the Marquis de Sade (1740–1814), French soldier and novelist who conducted experiments on pain and wrote about them.

sandwich (n.)   two or more slices of bread with a filling of cheese, meat, jam, or fish between them; (v.) to squeeze between two persons, places, things, etc. After John Montagu (1718–92), the fourth earl of Sandwich, who ate this way so as not to leave the gambling table for meals.

saxophone (n.)   a woodwind instrument with a curved metal body. Invented by Antoine Sax (1814–94), Belgian maker of musical instruments.

3

He that has eyes to see and ears to hear may convince himself that no mortal can keep a secret. If his lips are silent, he chatters with his fingertips; betrayal oozes out of him at every pore.[1]

You Don't Have to Say It to Convey It

After reading and understanding this chapter, you should be able to:

- Define nonverbal communication.

- Explain the vital role that nonverbal communication performs in the daily verbal messages we transmit and receive.

- Observe and explain the various modes that communicate nonverbal messages.

- Explain the role of objects, time, space, and environment in nonverbal communication.

Chapter Digest

This chapter deals with nonverbal language—the language without words that you use throughout life, consciously or subconsciously, to convey and receive messages. This language is often termed body language, face language, silent

---

1. Sigmund Freud (1856–1939), founder of psychoanalysis.

language, and silent messages. You may, in fact, depend more on this wordless language than you do on words.

Some personal elements of nonverbal language include posture, eye contact, facial expressions, tone of voice, body movement and gestures, clothes, smell, taste, and touch. Some impersonal elements are environment, weather, lighting, objects (artifacts), space, and time.

Your appearance, for example, creates powerful first impressions, even before you utter a word. How often have you misjudged someone initially because he wore a beard or she exuded a perfume that you couldn't stomach? On the job and in your social life, your appearance can help you or hurt you—tremendously.

Impersonal aspects of nonverbal communication also create impressions about you. Time and how you use it in relation to others tells something about you. If you're a high-ranking manager, for instance, you can keep your employees waiting. Space, or turf as it is sometimes called, is another impersonal element that denotes your status and authority. As a manager, you probably have an office with a large desk, windows, a rug, extra furniture, air conditioning, recessed lighting, plants, and paintings on the walls. All of these artifacts represent power, prestige, and prosperity.

Our personal lives are influenced by our use of nonverbal language. Depending on how we control it, career decisions may be positively or negatively affected.

WHAT IS NONVERBAL COMMUNICATION?

As you learned in Chapter 2, nonverbal communication is the conscious or subconscious transmission and reception of unspoken messages. An authority on nonverbal communication concludes from his research that 93 percent of the meaning we receive from another's message derives from the nonverbal part of the communication—facial expression and tone of voice—and only 7 percent from the words.[2]

One immediate observation comes to mind: what we *do* say may not be as important as what we *don't* say or as important as *how* we say it. Since so much of our message's impact depends on nonverbal aspects, how much more effectively would we communicate if we could become more proficient in this vital form of communication?

---

2. Albert Mehrabian, "Communication Without Words," *Psychology Today*, (September 1968): 53.

Nonverbal communication is a vast and ever-growing field for further study and research. Some elements of this type of communication include: environment, weather, lighting, objects, space, time, sight, taste, smell, touch, clothes, color, and sound. Other elements include facial expressions, eye contact, gestures, other body movements, and **paralanguage**—laughing, coughing, throat clearing, vocal pitch, and pauses. This is just a partial list of nonverbal elements, and we will discuss only those over which you may have some control and which you may find important in your daily lives.

VERBAL REMARKS WITH NONVERBAL MEANINGS

We have all heard any number of sayings and phrases that clearly demonstrate the importance of nonverbal communication, such as:

> "Actions speak louder than words." Perhaps you can recall, as a child, the number of times you were told (verbal) not to do something, but you persisted to the point that the only "language" you really understood was a slap (nonverbal) on the hand or rear.
>
> "It wasn't so much *what* he said, but *how* he said it." Try to recall a number of situations that this statement applies to.
>
> "She had a look that could kill." If your mate discovers you where you shouldn't be, with someone you shouldn't be with, you'll appreciate this remark.

The nonverbal elements of communication are extremely important and in some instances more so than the spoken words. In fact, when a person's actions and words appear contradictory, the actions often communicate the true feelings.[3]

Nonverbal communication is often referred to by other terms, such as the silent language, body language, face language, silent messages, and beyond words. No matter what it is called, it means the conscious or subconscious transmission and reception of messages, other than spoken words.

---

3. Albert Mehrabian, *Silent Messages* (Belmont, CA: Wadsworth, 1971), 56.

HOW WE COMMUNICATE WITHOUT WORDS

We cannot NOT communicate. Our very presence or absence "says something." If, for example, you had registered for a certain course and then cut several classes, what messages might your absence transmit to the professor? He might think you were ill, or that you were still vacationing, or that you had changed your mind and signed up for another course. In fact, maybe you had changed jobs and your new hours prevented you from going to that first class, or perhaps you had to stay home with an ill child. The professor, though, might interpret your absence as apathy.

If you sign up for a course and attend from day one, your presence alone would transmit some of the following messages to your professor: He would know your sex, approximate height and weight, and probably your taste in clothes or makeup. He may even know your socioeconomic background and your general health, or, from the way you dress, whether you're a conservative or a moderate. Your facial expressions may announce that you're happy, sad, nervous, friendly, shy, frightened, or restless. Where you sit in class (front row, back row, near the door) and how you sit (straight up, slouched, feet resting on the chair in front of you) are other nonverbal signs that communicate messages to your professor. Such messages are transmitted by your presence—and even before you speak a word.

We communicate nonverbally by who we are; our appearance; the way we walk and stand; our facial expressions and eye contact; the way we move, gesture, and touch; and our **vocalics,** or paralanguage.

Who We Are

We communicate simply by being alive. Messages are received and transmitted by such bodily qualities as our sex; bodily frame; scars, birthmarks, and other visible features; hair color and style; skin and eye color, as well as the quality of our complexion. How many of us have made initial judgments of people from a superficial first glance—and been wrong?

Our **self-image** is crucial not only to us personally, but to how others perceive us. More and more people, regardless of age, are spending thousands of dollars for plastic surgery simply to look and feel more appealing or to change their image. Vive la sex appeal!

Our Appearance

Before we even open our mouths, we make an impression, favorable or unfavorable. The clothes we wear often communicate our status in life and our degree of self-confidence. Just from observing a person's apparel, you may have said that the person "has class" or "has no class." Author Alison Lurie, in her book *The Language of Clothes*, mentions that even before she's close enough to talk to a person, she knows that individual's sex, approximate age, and social status and has a fairly good idea of that person's occupation, ethnic origin, personality, opinions, tastes, sexual desires, and current mood.

Regarding what America wears, a survey of over one hundred top executives of major corporations showed:

- 96 percent said that their employees had a better chance of getting ahead if they knew how to dress.
- 72 percent said they would stall the promotion of a person who didn't dress properly.
- 84 percent turned down people who dressed improperly for job interviews.[4]

An authority on apparel writes, "When you step into a room, even though no one in that room knows you or has seen you before, they will make ten decisions about you based solely on your appearance." He further states: "To be successful in almost any endeavor, you must be sure that these decisions about you are favorable, because in that first impression you make—*you are what you wear.*"[5]

For example, what impression would you make if you appeared before a group impeccably dressed but with messy hair and dirty fingernails? Your perfume, cosmetics, aftershave lotion, and deodorant (or lack of it) convey messages. Is your breath always fresh and your body clean? If not, it will be no secret.

Posture often reflects your attitude, pride, confidence, and general

---

4. John T. Molloy, *Dress for Success* (New York: Warner Books, 1975), 36.

5. William Thourlby, *You Are What You Wear* (New York: New American Library, 1978), 1.

health. If your professor observes—and he's adept at this—that you're sitting erect and looking at him, he'll probably conclude that you're alert and interested in his lecture. If, on the other hand, you're drooping in your chair, he'll conclude that you're tired, bored, or daydreaming.

At the next chance, notice the way people walk. You can almost tell a person's mission by his posture and stride: Is he fast-paced, slow-paced, skipping, ambling, hunched over, or walking tall? Is he in a hurry? Perhaps he's late for a date. Is he slouching along? Maybe he's dreading a dental appointment. Good posture projects a positive image.

Our Facial Expressions

There is, perhaps, no nonverbal code which can be so easily misread as facial expressions, because so many people control them so well. Controlling these expressions can camouflage true feelings. We are better prepared to lie with our face than with any other nonverbal cue. Perhaps you can recall a situation when you were eating something you really didn't like but, so as not to offend the cook, you said it was "delicious" and your remark was reinforced by your feigned facial expression. You've heard the saying "He lied through his teeth." This is understandable when you consider that facial muscles can create thousands of different expressions.

To ensure credibility, we should strive to have our facial expression and verbal message coincide. Imagine the reaction if you smiled at a funeral or flashed an expression of indifference while congratulating someone on a happy occasion. Conversely, crying at a wedding is acceptable because, presumably, these would be tears of joy.

Research tells us that facial expressions can communicate the following meanings: surprise, fear, happiness, sadness, contempt, disgust, anger, interest, determination, and bewilderment.[6] The following quote is appropriate: "A man finds room in the few square inches of his face for the traits of all his ancestors, for the expression of all his history, and his wants."[7]

---

6. Paul Ekman, W. V. Friesen, and P. Ellsworth, *Emotion in the Human Face* (New York: Pergamon Press, 1972), 57–65.

7. Ralph Waldo Emerson, "Behavior," *The Conduct of Life* (1860).

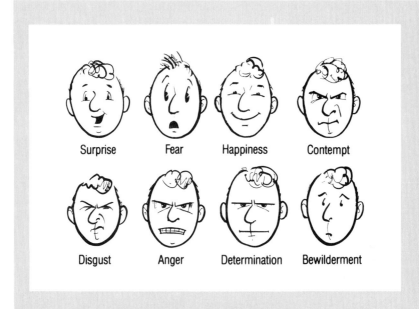

Surprise   Fear   Happiness   Contempt

Disgust   Anger   Determination   Bewilderment

Our Eyes

Eye contact is necessary to establish and maintain a beam of communication. If you're listening to a lecture and suddenly the speaker starts reading a long passage verbatim, the chances are that he has disrupted this strong line of communication and may lose your attention.

Eyes can convey approval or disapproval; they can include or exclude a person during a conversation; they transmit happiness, sadness, confusion, and even terror. Eyes tell us if someone is interested or bored. Eyes can communicate at a glance. If you've ever visited a singles bar, you've probably experienced the dynamics of communication via glances, winks, and stares.

Our culture teaches us that it's impolite to stare. The next time you're on a bus or a train, single out a person and stare at him. See how long it takes before the situation becomes awkward. When children are being scolded, they try to avoid eye contact but are ordered to "Look at me when I talk to you."

The next time you're in an elevator, notice how little eye contact takes place because of the occupants' proximity to each other. They will stare at the flashing floor numbers, the floor, or the ceiling, but seldom at each other unless, of course, they're seeking contact. Most people tend to increase eye contact with those from whom they seek approval or recognition.[8]

Our Body Movement

To appreciate the almost total power of nonverbal communication, watch a professional pantomimist perform—it is sheer artistry. Some of the classic characterizations in show business belong to such superstars as Red Skelton, Marcel Marceau, Lucille Ball, Jerry Lewis, and the late Jackie Gleason and Charlie Chaplin. Their artful use of apparel, movement, eye contact, gestures, and facial expressions brings laughter and tears to millions of all ages. The ways in which they move their arms, hands and fingers, head and eyes and the ways they sway, stoop, and bend are sheer genius. Even when they don't utter a word, their messages are always understood.

Kinesics is the study and application of body movement. Your kinesic behavior can significantly reinforce your verbal message. Such movement adds variety to your overall delivery, as opposed to standing rigidly in one spot. To get more personal with your listeners, move closer to them. To make emphatic points, take a step for each point. Movement can also help you relax by releasing excess energy.

Our Gestures

Gestures play a large role in our daily communication and are usually most effective when performed naturally. There's no question that effective gestures enhance and supplement verbal messages. However, if you constantly use the same hand or arm when making a point, or if your gesturing becomes mechanical, then this activity can quickly become repetitious and boring. Strive for variety and spontaneity.

If you wish to make several points, when making point number one, show one finger; for point number two, show two; and so on. A hitchhiker pointing his thumb, an umpire calling a player out at

---

8. Efram Broughton, "Effects of Expectancies for Social Approval on Visual Behavior," *Journal of Personality and Social Psychology,* 86 (1972): 29–33.

You can communicate explicitly without words.

home plate, and an officer directing traffic at a busy intersection are examples of communicating explicitly without words, as is the sign language of the deaf.

When giving directions, many people find it easier to accompany spoken words with hand movements—straight, to the right or left, up or down. We've probably all been shown, by the extension of the arms, "the size of the fish that got away." A scholar of nonverbal communication has aptly stated, ". . . we respond to gestures with an extreme alertness and, one might also say, in accordance with an elaborate and secret code that is written nowhere, known by none, and understood by all."[9]

Our Touch

Perhaps the most personal mode of communicating without words is our touch. It can signal both positive (a handshake) and negative

9. Edward Sapir, *Human Message Systems* (New York: Harper & Row, 1976), 82.

(a slap in the face) attitudes, depending on the individual being touched and his culture patterns. Touching is a crucial aspect of most human relationships. It can communicate approval and encouragement, tenderness and passion, disapproval and punishment.

Touching starts at birth when babies are introduced to the "outside world" and continues when parents take charge with feeding, holding, cuddling, rocking, stroking, burping, bathing, and changing. Studies show the staggering importance of touch: orphaned babies placed in institutions have died because they were never cuddled or held.

Touching symbolizes different things to different people, depending on the specific situation, environment, time of day, and anticipated intent. Some individuals enjoy, and even crave, touching and being touched. Touching can be an expression of friendliness and affection and could signal sexual desires. Other individuals may regard being touched as disrespectful and even offensive.

Our culture teaches us that it's improper for an individual of lower status to touch one of higher status unless encouraged to do so. For example, it may be acceptable for a professor to put his arm around a student, but not for a student to embrace a professor, or a manager may touch someone from the mailroom but not vice versa.

Our culture frowns on a male hugging, embracing, or kissing another male. If you saw two women dancing or holding hands, you probably wouldn't think too much about it, but if you saw two men dancing or holding hands, you might think it strange. This would generally be interpreted as an act of femininity or homosexuality. However, the exception to this code is often displayed in sports, when a player scores a winning touchdown, goal, or basket and is spontaneously hugged by his fellow players to show their joy.

Although our culture has established certain taboos regarding male-to-male touching, there are times, for example at a funeral, when no action could equal a warm embrace for manifesting affection, love, or sympathy.

How we touch, what part of the body we touch, and the duration of the touch are all important factors in interpreting a message. Notice people shaking hands, hugging, kissing, or pinching. Can you "read" them and their intentions? Touching, according to the messages communicated, can range from the very impersonal to the very personal.[10]

---

10. R. Heslin, "Steps Toward a Taxonomy of Touching," paper presented to the Midwestern Psychological Association, Chicago, May 1974.

Our Vocalics

Vocalics is "how we say it" as opposed to what we say. Some elements of vocalics are voice quality, pitch, inflection, emphasis, rate of delivery, and pauses. For example, let's assume that your professor had a female colleague from New England tape record the following message: "All of you are lucky to be in this speech course." After listening to this tape, the class would probably agree that the speaker had a message; it was conveyed in English and everyone in the class understood it. But *beyond* this, the class would probably be able to say other things about the voice on the tape machine. They would be able to identify the voice as a white American female, probably from the Northeast, because of her regional accent. They probably would agree that her voice sounded professional. Her diction was articulate and pleasant, she pronounced her words correctly, and she had no problem breathing. The class could probably tell if she were young, middle-aged, or older.

They might have received other messages as well, such as that her voice was soothing and sexy. She sounded alive and happy, and she would probably be fun to be with. Whatever it was that enabled the class to infer these messages—other than the actual spoken words—is paralanguage, or vocalics.

The quality of our voice—its pitch, rate of delivery, **inflection,** emphasis, and even **pauses** play an important role in transmitting nonverbal messages. Take the sentence "Yes, I love you." Say it aloud four times, but put emphasis first on the word "yes," then on the word "I," then on the word "love," and finally on the word "you."

Yes, I love you.

Yes, I love you.

Yes, *I* love you.

Yes, I *love* you.

Yes, I love *you*.

You should have no difficulty interpreting the various messages received from the same sentence. *How* we say things is often more important than *what* we say.

"Yes, I love you, dammit!"

OTHER CODES

There are other **codes,** or elements, equally significant in nonverbal communication, such as time, space, artifacts (objects), and environment.

Time

Most of us are very time conscious, and time plays a vital role in the messages we convey. Many people consider time more valuable than money, and, indeed, most of our lives are influenced by a time schedule.

How important is time? To many people, time represents status and power. For example: a boss can keep a worker waiting, and can also be late for a meeting, without consequence. A doctor can keep

"I wonder if she forgot me."

a patient waiting. A college president can keep a dean waiting, who in turn can keep a division chairperson waiting, who can keep a department chairperson waiting, who can keep a professor waiting, who in turn can keep a student waiting. The more influential your position, the more command you have over your time and over other people's time.

Time should play an important role in the classroom. Be sure to be present on the assigned day of your talk and always be on time for your class. Never enter the classroom while a person is speaking. Stay within the time limit of your talk and always remain attentive to the speaker, even though class time may be running out. Don't start to collect your books or to reach for your jacket while a colleague is still speaking. This is only common courtesy, which you should expect to receive under similar circumstances.

Being late or even last to arrive may be interpreted as a symbol of status, depending on a person's importance or popularity. It's common knowledge that, on occasion, airline flights have been delayed for the arrival of a VIP. At a candidate's fundraiser the candidate is usually the last to arrive. At a nightclub or concert the star is usually the last to perform. When Nancy Reagan represented the president at the royal wedding in London in July 1981, she irritated her hosts by arriving late at various functions.

You've heard the expression that "people don't usually appreciate what they have until they no longer have it." It's true. Persons in hospitals and prisons appreciate time because they are forced to do things when other people want them to. This can, and often does, lead to frustration, anger, and hostility.

Remember . . . you can "use time." You can "waste time." Or, you can "kill time."

Space

Anthropologist Edward T. Hall coined the word **proxemics** to describe the study of space as a communicative mode. "Every living thing has a physical boundary that separates it from its external environment."[11] He clearly explains in his book, *The Silent Language*, that each of us has a personal area of space surrounding us clearly established by an invisible boundary. This personal area, which he refers to as a "bubble," establishes distances at which we feel the most comfortable when interacting with people, and any attempt by another person to enter this area constitutes an intrusion. Notice how uneasy people become in crowded situations such as in an elevator, in a bus, or at the theater, when a stranger sits uncomfortably close. If you would like to experiment, the next time you're talking to a person, slowly inch a little closer, then a little closer—and observe that person's physical reaction. The chances are that the individual will slowly retreat. Hall's categories of interaction distance are listed in Table 3.1.

We take our space very seriously. We see signs declaring "No Trespassing," "Keep Out," or "Private Property." These signs indicate private ownership, and an intruder enters at his own risk. You should never invade another's space, or territory.

Throughout history, millions of people have been killed in wars over infringement on someone else's space. Territorial waters and air space are usually respected mutually by all governments.

Territorial behavior is often evidenced in our daily lives. In a

---

11. Edward T. Hall, *The Silent Language* (New York: Anchor Books, 1973), 163.

"Are you there, Miss Froehmer?"

WE CANNOT NOT COMMUNICATE

As we mentioned earlier, certain nonverbal cues can be faked and may contain different messages from what's actually being transmitted. It is easy to misinterpret parts of nonverbal language. Remember, nonverbal cues are not absolute. We must consider them in the total context of the situation in which they are produced.

Some revealing observations on nonverbal communication are contained in a published interview with a prominent Boston trial lawyer. He talks about the extreme importance of nonverbal communication in relation to selecting a jury. What does he look for and why? He prefers women jurors "because they're more attentive and sensitive" and jurors who smile because "[a] happy jury is a good jury."[12]

---

12. *Quincy Patriot Ledger*, Quincy, MA, 31 May 1983, 1.

During jury selection he observes how people walk to the jury box and how they are dressed. Is the walk positive and aggressive or slow and passive? Is the head held high or at half-mast? Are the shoulders slumped or is the posture erect? The attorney is looking for nonverbal clues to the potential juror's attitude and outlook on life. Knowing if a person is the nervous or calm type can be quite significant. From the individual's apparel and personal grooming, he may try to judge his occupation, origin, living habits, and economic and social status.

This trial lawyer knows more than just the law. He is keenly observant and proficient in understanding and interpreting people's nonverbal messages. They can be crucial not only in dictating how the lawyer will present his case to the jurors, but also in trying to anticipate how the jurors will react and make decisions.

Table 3.2 summarizes the ways we can communicate our attitudes nonverbally.

Things to Discuss in Class

1. Listen to a voice on the radio and jot down as much information as possible based on the speaker's vocalics. Discuss your findings in class.

2. While traveling to or from work or class, pay attention to the nonverbal messages around you. Then make a list of the messages you perceive. Discuss them in class.

3. The next time you're talking with a friend, slowly move closer and closer. Tell the class of your friend's reaction.

4. Select someone in your neighborhood with whom you've never spoken. Tell the class as much as you can about that individual based on that person's nonverbal codes.

5. Explain to the class what nonverbal messages you think you transmit to others. The class may wish to respond with interpretations of your messages.

6. Discuss the verbal and nonverbal cues that your professor employs in teaching this class.

7. If your class has access to a videocassette recorder (VCR), you may wish to record some of the following exercises as a learning experience

Table 3.2
Attitudes Communicated Nonverbally

Openness
Open hands
Unbuttoned coat

Defensiveness
Arms crossed on chest
Legs crossed
Fistlike gestures
Pointed index finger

Evaluation
Hand-to-face gestures
Head tilted
Stroking chin
Peering over glasses
Pipe smoker gestures
Putting hand to bridge of nose

Suspicion
Arms crossed
Sideways glance
Touching, rubbing nose/eyes
Buttoning coat
Drawing away

Insecurity
Pinching flesh
Chewing pen, pencil
Rubbing thumb over thumb
Biting fingernails
Hands in pockets

Cooperation
Upper body in sprinter's position

Open hands
Sitting on edge of chair
Hand-to-face gestures
Tilted head
Unbuttoning coat

Confidence
Hands in "steeple" position
Hands behind back
Back stiffened
Hands in coat pockets
Hands on coat lapels

Nervousness
Clearing throat
Whew sound
Whistling
Fidgeting in chair
Hand covering mouth while
  speaking
Not looking at other person
Jingling money in pockets
Tugging at ear
Perspiration
Wringing hands

Frustration
Short breaths
Tsk sound
Tightly clenched hands
Wringing hands
Fistlike gestures
Pointing index finger
Rubbing hand through hair
Rubbing back of neck

Source: Gerard Nierenburg and Henry Calero, *How to Read a Person Like a Book* (New York: Pocket Books, 1973).

in nonverbal communication. Play back the videotape to see how many members of the class received the nonverbal messages that you feel you actually transmitted. The exercises should not run more than a few minutes.

a. Through facial expressions and with your eyes, try to convey different moods, for example, anger, fear, happiness, sadness, and surprise.

b. Pretend that you're at a marketplace in a foreign country. The vendor, who doesn't understand English, shows you something. You admire it and try it on but feel it's too expensive. You want it. Nonverbally, communicate this to the vendor and bargain for a lower price.

c. Again, you're in a foreign country where a language barrier exists. You're at a restaurant, and, when the waiter arrives, you attempt to order a full-course breakfast nonverbally.

d. You're in a pet shop. Without words, convey to the class where you are and what you see. You look at various pets and then pick up the one you intend to purchase.

e. In silent language, demonstrate a line of work performed by a member of your family. First, you must identify the individual and then that person's occupation.

f. Using body language only, describe a vacation spot you would like to visit and the mode of transportation to get there.

g. Visually describe your favorite hobby.

h. If you have a full- or part-time job, describe it without saying a word.

i. Communicate, nonverbally, your major and your short- and long-term educational goals.

What Do You Remember from This Chapter?

1. Approximately what percentage of the meaning derived from a message is nonverbal?

2. Define nonverbal communication and give several examples.

3. Explain the statement "We cannot NOT communicate."

4. What can posture tell us about a person?

5. List five gestures which convey explicit meanings.

6. Explain vocalics and give five examples.

7. Give an example of time being interpreted as a symbol of status.

8. What is proxemics?

9. List the four categories of interaction distance.

10. What is kinesics and its relevance to nonverbal communication?

11. List five phrases or sayings which demonstrate the importance of non-verbal communication.

12. Which nonverbal code can be easily misread? Explain.

13. List five types of messages that a person's eyes can transmit.

14. How important a role does the environment play in nonverbal communication? Explain.

15. List three synonyms for nonverbal communication.

Vitalize Your Vocabulary

A solid knowledge of synonyms (words that have the same basic meaning but may differ in tone and appropriateness) will impart vigor and variety to your speech. An excellent and proven source of synonyms and antonyms (words that mean the opposite) is *Roget's Thesaurus of Words and Phrases.* It doesn't, however, explain differences in meaning; for those shades of meaning you should consult a modern, authoritative dictionary.

Consider the basic meanings of the adjectives *slim* and *slender;* synonyms are *trim* and *svelte.* These four adjectives are complimentary. On the other hand, synonyms like *bony, gaunt,* and *skinny* are anything but complimentary and may even be insulting. The word *thin* falls somewhere between the first four adjectives and the last three. This example proves the vital importance of understanding different shades of meanings.

Each group of words in Table 3.3 is a set of synonyms; however, each group in Column 2 represents antonyms for those in Column 1.

Table 3.3
Synonyms and Antonyms

Column 1	**Column 2** (Antonyms of Words in Column 1)
big, huge, large, immense, vast, kingsize, enormous, tremendous, colossal, mammoth, jumbo, gigantic, gargantuan, ample, abundant	small, little, tiny, petite, peewee, puny, miniature, diminutive, pocket-sized, minute, microscopic
brave, courageous, fearless, bold, valiant, heroic, game, valorous, gallant, lion-hearted, spunky, plucky, dauntless, gutsy, audacious, adventurous, nervy, intrepid	afraid, cowardly, fearful, timid, yellow, faint-hearted, lily-livered, weak-kneed, chicken-hearted, dastardly, pusillanimous
pleased, delighted, charmed, elated, intrigued, gratified, tickled pink, satisfied, sold on, carried away	complain, gripe, bitch, grouse, whine, beef, weep, bellyache, wail, crab, squawk, lament, mutter, fuss, moan and groan, grumble
genuine, authentic, valid, real, true, actual, bona fide, legitimate	fake, phony, artificial, counterfeit, mock, spurious, adulterated, make-believe, bogus, substitute, ersatz, pseudo-
pliable, flexible, tractable, yielding, bending, receptive, malleable, pliant, responsive, relenting	stubborn, obstinate, inflexible, rigid, immovable, bull-headed, adamant, unbending, unyielding, uncompromising, intransigent, resolute
slim, slender, lean, slight, frail, delicate, spare, underweight, gaunt, bony, skinny, scrawny	fat, stout, corpulent, obese, fleshy, beefy, plump, paunchy, full, rotund, tubby, roly-poly, pudgy, chubby, heavy-set, portly, well-fed, thick-bodied, rich, swollen

Column 1	**Column 2** (Antonyms of Words in Column 1)
loudness, noise, racket, din, clamor, clatter, uproar, tumult, hubbub, boisterousness, outcry, disturbance	silence, stillness, quietness, lull, hush, peace, noiselessness
beautiful, handsome, attractive, comely, pulchritudinous, personable, pretty, gorgeous, ravishing, stunning	ugly, hideous, horrible, repulsive, homely, revolting, gruesome, loathsome, ghastly, unattractive
active, lively, energetic, vigorous, dynamic, animated, spirited, vivacious, peppy, brisk, sprightly	inactive, sedentary, idle, indolent, torpid, slothful, lackadaisical, shiftless, languid, listless, lethargic, sluggish, droopy, slow, comatose

4

Nobody has ever listened himself out of a job.[1]

You Can Overhear, but You Can't Overlisten

After reading and understanding this chapter, you should know:

- The difference between hearing and listening.

- The importance of listening well.

- Some major reasons that we listen.

- Some ways to become a more efficient listener.

- The different types of listening.

- The vital correlation between vocabulary development and efficient listening.

Chapter Digest

The act of listening comprises a significant portion of our daily activities. It is the other half of the communication process, since, without listeners, we cannot communicate orally. Yet, few of us pay attention to improving our ability to listen.

Hearing is a passive biological function, whereas listening is, or should

---

1. Calvin Coolidge, thirtieth President of the United States, 1923–29.

be, an active intellectual function that involves your mind, eyes, ears. and memory. As a listener, you influence speakers by your reactions. If you show interest through your facial expression or body language, you will see speakers perk up. If you show boredom or confusion through inattention or lack of eye contact, you will see that speakers tend to change their approach to avoid risking failure.

There are several reasons for listening: to become informed, to understand, to evaluate, and to enjoy. Any intellectual activity that can affect your life to such an extent deserves to be done well. Suggestions for sharpening your listening skills are offered, but they will benefit you only if you make a commitment to help yourself.

When you were a child, how often did your parents criticize you for not **listening?** As a parent, how frequently do you direct your children to listen? At one time or another all of us are guilty of not really listening to what's being said. Our inattention can lead to embarrassment, argument, and at times, even more serious consequences.

All too often in interpersonal communication (between two or more people), we absorb only what we want to, at home, school, work, or play. Many times we choose not to pay attention to certain people because they are boring. We have that arbitrary ability to "tune out" certain people, and let's face it, sometimes it can be beneficial.

COMMUNICATION ACTIVITIES

A study conducted by researchers at a leading university found that adults spend about 70 percent of their waking hours engaged in communication activities. It concluded that the average adult devotes 9 percent of this time to writing, 16 percent to reading, 30 percent to speaking, and 45 percent to listening.[2] Another study found that we listen half again as much as we speak; we speak almost twice as much as we read; and we read almost twice as much as we write.

We wake up in the morning to the sounds of an alarm clock, a radio, or someone's voice. There may be conversation at breakfast, at work, at school, on public conveyances, or in a car pool. We might

---

2. *Communication in the High School Curriculum* (Springfield, IL, 1961), 3.

That arbitrary ability to "tune out" certain people . . .

attend a business meeting, a lecture, or a luncheon. We might hear someone speak in person or on the radio, TV, or telephone. We might attend a concert, a movie, or a social or civic function. Think of all the times in one day, for example, that we listen. How much of that listening experience will we be able to recall? Are we actually *listening* and *understanding,* or are we just *hearing* things? There's a world of difference.

Despite these statistics, listening, the communication activity we engage in most of our waking hours (a third of our lives), is the one that our educational system ignores the most. In most colleges today, courses in basic writing are mandatory for all freshmen. Because of increasing alarm over our low national reading scores, reading courses are offered, and at some colleges they're required. Courses in public speaking and oral communication are offered on most college campuses and, in some instances, taking at least one is a requirement for a degree. But how many institutions require a student to take a course in listening?

In your precollege education, your school's curricula probably emphasized writing skills over reading, reading over speaking, and speaking over listening. Perhaps because we spend so much time listening we feel that we can do it efficiently. What a false conclusion this is!

The fact is that the business and educational communities complain that workers and students don't know how to listen. To address the seriousness of this problem in the business world, a Fortune 500 international corporation took two steps:[3]

1. It set up special listening programs worldwide for all its employees who want to attend.

2. It invested hundreds of thousands of dollars in a two-page color advertising campaign in several national magazines, which ran for months. The theme was "We understand how important it is to listen."

The importance of this activity is effectively expressed in the following excerpt from their ad:

> The fact is, listening, like marriage, is a partnership, a shared responsibility between the person speaking and the person listening. And if the listener doesn't show genuine interest and sensitivity to what's being said, the speaker will stop talking. And the communication will fail.[4]

LISTENING AS AN INTELLECTUAL ACTIVITY

You can listen more effectively and improve your comprehension markedly if you work at it. Listening is just as important to interpersonal communication as is speaking; in fact, "listening is the other half of talking. If people stop listening, it is useless to talk—a point not always appreciated by talkers. . . ."[5]

While hearing is a biological activity, listening is an intellectual one because it requires more than just ears. In fact, it has been said

---

3. Sperry Corporation, *Newsweek*, 20 October 1980, 89.
4. Ibid.
5. Stuart Chase, "Are You Listening?" *Reader's Digest*, December 1962.

Listening is an intellectual activity.

that you hear with your ears, but you listen with your brain. Effective listening is a holistic activity that should include the following active efforts of your mind, eyes, ears, and memory:

- **Your mind.** You should summon your logical reasoning capacity to grasp the intended meaning of the speaker's message. Learn the differences between fact, opinion, and inference.

- **Your eyes.** You should observe the speaker—her posture, gestures, facial expressions, mannerisms, and movements. All of these combine to communicate vital messages.

- **Your ears.** Listen carefully to her voice. Is it pleasant, harsh, reassuring, authoritative, or weak? How about her inflection, rate of speaking, pauses, loudness, and animation? Are they "in sync" with her message? In other words, is her nonverbal message enhanced or contradicted by her oral one?

- **Your memory.** Try to recall as much as you can about the topic at hand. Are you hearing new or different information? Did the speaker omit anything? If so, what and why? By recalling as much as possible about the speaker's message, you should have a solid basis on which to compare or contrast the message with your own knowledge of the subject.

As a listener you not only share responsibility with the speaker, but you also have the ability to aid her during her talk. Your facial and body reactions are quickly communicated to her. If you're looking at her, show interest: lean forward occasionally and appear to catch her every word; even jot down a few notes or a question you may wish to bring up later. These positive responses tell the speaker that her message is getting across to you. If you slouch in your chair, whisper to your neighbor, read a book, or look just plain bored, the speaker will be well aware that she has problems.

REASONS FOR LISTENING

Following are some of the major reasons that we listen:

- To enjoy.
- To become informed.
- To understand.
- To express sympathy.
- To evaluate.

To enjoy.   This is light listening, for example: engaging in a pleasant conversation, listening to music, or watching a movie or TV show for relaxation. Listening to enjoy should not involve any strain but should be casual and relaxed. The change of pace should be enjoyable and pleasant.

To become informed.   Here you seek new information. You listen to the radio for the weather report or school-closing announcement; you attend a class lecture or a business, social, or civic meeting. You should establish in your mind the motive for listening, and, therefore, you should direct complete interest, attention, and concentration to the speaker. If your professor announces that there'll be a quiz following her short lecture, you're motivated to listen. "Know how to listen and you can learn even from those who speak badly," said Plutarch, Greek essayist and biographer, about 2000 years ago.

To understand.   How often have you formed an opinion of a speaker and her subject before she has even opened her mouth or concluded her talk?

Many people find listening to understand most difficult because it requires restraint, fair-mindedness, and objective thinking. As a consequence, many of the world's problems have resulted from selfishness, disregard of other people's opinions, and failure to attempt honestly to understand another's viewpoint. Listening to understand doesn't mean that you must agree or disagree but that you must approach the subject with an unbiased, open mind. You must also listen totally to the message, striving to understand what is being expressed and why. Allow yourself to grasp the entire message before you react.

To express sympathy.   If you're that rare person with a "sympathetic ear," then probably every day you listen to someone "sound off"— a relative, friend, classmate, co-worker, stranger, or perhaps even your boss. To share or just listen to someone's pent-up feelings' breaking loose can have a therapeutic effect on the talker and will distinguish you as a person who cares. This type of listening can be personally rewarding because practically everyone, sooner or later, needs an attentive ear. For example:

- Your good friend feels that her boss is exploiting her abilities and is skimping on her salary.
- A classmate is distraught because all sections of a course she wanted were closed.
- A family member didn't get the promotion he felt he deserved.
- On the way to work someone slammed into your boss' brand new car and he wants to vent his emotions.
- Your neighbor just found out that his three children need dental braces.

To evaluate.   Of all of the types of listening, evaluative listening is the most difficult and the most important because it requires the most effort. There are a number of questions to bear in mind when listening to evaluate:

- What is the main purpose of the talk?
- Is the talk informative, entertaining, persuasive, inspirational, or meant to activate?

Everyone needs a sympathetic ear.

- Is the speaker making logical and valid points?
- Are the arguments convincing? Are they based on fact or on opinion?
- Is the speaker an authority on the subject or does she just have an axe to grind?
- To what needs of the audience is the speaker appealing?
- Can you clearly understand the speaker's message?
- Do the nonverbal elements of her talk coincide or conflict with her verbal message?

These are only some of the countless questions you should consider when listening to evaluate. You now have some idea of the complexity and depth of evaluative listening.

Do you usually take statements uttered by a well-known figure as the last word, or do you make an effort to seek out the other side before formulating an opinion? If you're in a position to disagree with or question people, do you? Remember that you may disagree without being disagreeable. Whether the issues are international, national, local, business, educational, political, or social—evaluative listening is especially crucial.

Probably the most cataclysmic lack of evaluative listening can be pinned on the giants of the auto industry—General Motors, Chrysler, and Ford.[6] In the 1950s, Dr. W. Edwards Deming, an authority on quality control, tried to convince them to make a much stronger commitment to high-quality production and to enlist workers' expertise in solving production problems. The Big Three spurned his advice.

Then Dr. Deming was invited to Japan to explain his philosophy to industrial leaders there. They wanted to rebuild their industrial capacity, which was shattered in World War II, and to wipe out their reputation for producing junk. They listened to Dr. Deming, applied his ideas to their manufacturing plants, and you know what happened. Toyota, Nissan, and Subaru "pulverized" the Big Three and took over a huge share of the American auto business.

It pays to listen to someone who knows the score—and then to evaluate correctly. As Oliver Wendell Holmes once proclaimed, "It is the province of knowledge to speak and it is the privilege of wisdom to listen."

How to Be a Better Listener

Diogenes, a Greek philosopher who lived 2300 years ago, put it very wisely when he said, "We have two ears and only one tongue in order that we may hear more and speak less."

To be a better listener you must first *want* to be one. You must realize the many benefits of improved listening, and you must be prepared to exert the required effort. When you come to class, you know that you'll hear people talk, so prepare to listen. Develop a positive attitude toward the speakers. Tell yourself that you'll hear some exhilarating topics and that, in all probability, you'll learn something new. Motivation can spell the difference between just hearing something and listening and understanding it.

---

6. *Bits & Pieces* (Fairfield, NJ: Economics Press, December 1984), 12–13.

If you're planning to attend a lecture or to listen to a speech outside class, you can get ready for it by learning what you can about the speaker. Who is she? What's her background? Is she an authority on the subject? What's her motive for speaking? By increasing your interest in the speaker and her subject before the event, you can't help but listen more effectively.

The following are some suggestions for honing your ability to listen:

- Develop your vocabulary.
- Concentrate.
- Keep an open and objective mind.
- "Read" the speaker.
- Put yourself in the speaker's place.
- Take notes.
- Compensate for a speaker's flawed delivery.
- Get ready for the wrap-up.

Develop your vocabulary.   Once you commit yourself to improving your listening efficiency, the best step you can take is to expand your vocabulary. Vocabulary development is so vital to effective listening that we have included a "Vitalize Your Vocabulary" section in fifteen chapters.

Fully understanding the meanings and inferences of words is crucial to your total comprehension of a speaker's intended message. Being able to put the speaker's language and message in proper perspective is a significant first step in developing your listening efficiency.

Concentrate.   Interpersonal communication should be on a constant beam from the speaker to the listener and back to the speaker. Don't interrupt this beam by daydreaming or succumbing to other kinds of distractions. Try not to think about last night, this morning, or tonight. If your thoughts begin to wander, take charge and direct them back to the speaker and her message. If the speaker is boring, challenge yourself to make the effort.

Another obstacle to total concentration is the fact that we think much faster than we speak. A comfortable speaking rate lies between 130 and 160 words per minute. The brain, however, can deal with approximately 500 words per minute. So you can see that, while we're listening, we have quite a bit of spare time. We must guard against becoming distracted during this spare time.

From the moment the speaker approaches the stand, rivet your eyes on her. Remember that eye contact is as important to the speaker as it is to the listener. Look interested and you will be interested. Watch her facial expressions and gestures while she's speaking. You can receive many clues to her meanings by observing her mannerisms. As discussed in Chapter 3, gestures can be eloquent.

Beware of distractions. Little things can throw you off: books dropping, people talking and coughing, fire sirens wailing. The speaker herself can be distracting. Her dress may be as loud as the fire siren, her gestures may be uncontrolled, or she may be constantly swaying. If these or any other distractions occur, then you must intensify your concentration on the message because nothing inspires a speaker more than an interested audience.

Keep an open and objective mind.   Don't have the attitude "I know what she's going to say and she's all wet." Preconceived opinions limit your ability to benefit from a true communicative experience. Be objective. Hear the speaker out to the end. Then, if you disagree, ask her to clarify certain points. Give the speaker every courtesy that you would want if you were speaking.

This is one of the more difficult techniques to master for effective listening because many people can be opinionated and make hasty judgments. They establish personal views even before the speaker opens her mouth. As mentioned in Chapter 3, a person's grooming, posture, walk, and eye contact or lack of it can nonverbally transmit positive or negative messages.

"Read" the speaker.   If the speaker opens with a title, grasp it. Closely follow her introduction and main points. In her introduction she should state what will be covered. Take note of her subject and anticipate the main points. How do they relate to the other points mentioned? Is she accomplishing what she set out to do? What about the soundness of her ideas? Are they valid? Is she logical? Does she have supporting material, and how does she use it? These are some thoughts to consider while you're listening.

Put yourself in the speaker's place.   You may be able to better understand and absorb a talk if you try to put yourself in the speaker's place. This means you must strive to feel, think, act, and react like the speaker. What motivated her to select this topic? What is her educational and professional background? What are her qualifications to speak on this subject? What action or reaction is she seeking from the audience and why?

If you can successfully place yourself within the speaker's mind, not only will you understand her message better, but you will take a giant step toward becoming a more effective and responsive listener.

Take notes.   Taking notes can enhance your listening ability because it engages you in two activities—listening and writing. The secret to taking notes is to jot down only the main points as complete sentences, phrases, or key words. Whatever format of notetaking works for you is the one you should use. Writing down key points as you hear them helps you grasp and remember them.

Compensate for a speaker's flawed delivery.   Not all speakers have read this book (what a shame!), thereby denying themselves some of our practical principles which might help alleviate bad delivery habits. Poor speech habits can detract from the message that the speaker is trying to convey. She may talk in a monotone or pause often with "uhs," "ers," and "you knows." Playing with notecards, earrings, eye glasses, or a watch may discourage the audience from listening efficiently.

In this case, what you must do—and it isn't easy—is to separate the speaker from the speech. Just remember, many speakers have significant things to say but, unfortunately, erect obstacles that impede listeners. If you can discipline yourself to ignore the speaker's deficiencies, you may be rewarded with some valuable viewpoints and insights.

Get ready for the wrap-up.   Be ready for the conclusion of the talk. It will be the speaker's final chance to imprint her message in the minds of her listeners. At this time she may repeat some important points that you may have missed during the talk. Listen for them and ask yourself the following crucial questions: Did I get her message? Do I agree, or do certain points need clarification? What were her strongest and weakest arguments?

Never be too embarrassed to ask questions. There is no more important process in education than asking questions. (Refer to the section on the question-and-answer period in Chapter 2.)

Things to Discuss in Class

1. Describe a job environment, school environment, or social environment that you consider ideal for listening.

2. Do you agree that attentive listeners help a speaker communicate better? Explain.

3. What distractions hamper your listening in this class? What can you do about them?

4. What have you observed to be the most common listening deficiencies? Prepare to discuss them.

5. Honestly evaluate your own listening habits. Can you improve them? How?

6. After another student has given a short talk, prepare a brief summary of the main ideas presented. You may do this on your own, or your instructor may call on members of the class at random for a response.

7. Find a very quiet spot at home and for several minutes relax, close your eyes, and try to listen to every sound. Attempt to identify the sounds, their sources, and the directions from which they come.

What Do You Remember from This Chapter?

1. Approximately what percentage of your waking hours is involved in listening?

2. Can a listener aid a speaker? If so, how?

3. Name some types of listening.

4. List some hints for better listening.

5. Is there a difference between hearing and listening? Explain.

6. Is vocabulary important to listening efficiency? Explain.

7. How can taking notes enhance your listening efficiency?

Vitalize Your Vocabulary

Words from Japan

At the end of World War ii, Japan, land of the rising sun, was a vanquished and demoralized nation. Since then, Japan, with guidance and financial aid from the United States, has emerged as the number one nation in technological expertise and industrial productivity.[7] Today, Japan is a world-class power, and a linguistic spin-off from that status is that some of its words have entered our language; a few of these words were part of American English even before World War ii.

Here is a sprinkling of Japanese words that you should know, together with their symbols:

banzai 万歳
Literally "10,000 years," "banzai" is a carryover from the Chinese language, where it means something like "long live the king." Now, it means "three cheers" or "hip-hip hooray." It is said when celebrating something (usually three times in succession) and is accompanied by raising both arms.

geisha 芸者
A female entertainer who serves at a private party

hancho (frequently misspelled "honcho") 班長
Boss; literally squad leader

harakiri 腹切
Suicide by disembowelment

hibachi 火鉢
A charcoal grill

judo 柔道
Japanese art of self-defense. The fundamental principle of Judo is to utilize the opponent's strength to one's own advantage.

---

7. *Newsweek*, 9 August 1982, 48.

kamikaze 神風
A suicide pilot. A divine wind, specifically the typhoon that wrecked the Mongol invasion of Japan in the thirteenth century.

karate 唐手
The Loochoo (Ryukyu) art of self-defense, of hitting or jabbing opponents with one's fist or kicking them. It was introduced from China and gradually became a unique art of combat that uses no weapons.

kimono 着物
A traditional Japanese robe

nisei 二世
Americans of Japanese descent.

rickshaw 力車
A man-pulled cart.

sayonara さよなら
Good-bye

tsunami 津波
A tidal wave

5

First learn the meaning of what you say, and then speak.[1]

Make It Clear, Concise, Correct . . . and Alive

After reading and understanding this chapter, you should know:

- The skills that contribute greatly to effective delivery.
- Ways to sharpen these skills.
- The differences between articulation and pronunciation.
- The importance of listening to yourself when you speak.
- Ways to be more expressive in your speech.
- The three major accents, or "dialects."
- The importance of pauses.
- The importance of pacing.

Chapter Digest

This chapter zeroes in on various aspects of delivering a talk: voice, pronunciation, articulation, rate of speaking, pauses, and expression. Emphasis is placed on voice and pronunciation.

---

1. Epictetus, *Discourses* (2nd c.), 3.23, tr. Thomas W. Higginson.

Your voice influences your speech and also your daily interpersonal communication. A pleasant, expressive voice is an asset in school, on the job, and in your social life. Such a voice is capable of inflection, the ability to go up and down comfortably in order to express different feelings, emotions, and ideas.

Almost all voices can be improved. Listening to your own voice on a tape recorder may spur you to act to improve it. Some practical suggestions on pitch, volume, and proper breathing are offered.

Your pronunciation and articulation immediately mark you as either an educated or an uneducated person. Sloppy speech and rigid lips result in sounds being omitted, syllables being slurred, and incorrect sounds being tacked on. Again, ideas are presented to upgrade pronunciation and articulation to the standards recommended by authoritative dictionaries.

Other topics discussed in the chapter are the rate of speaking, the use of pauses, and the importance of expressing inner feelings and emotions.

Every spring, college campuses throughout the nation are visited by representatives from industry and government to recruit potential employees. Recruiters at several large state universities were asked to explain why they had rejected certain students. In almost 70 percent of the cases, the primary reason was that the rejected students did not "talk effectively during the interview."

My speech consulting practice (AJV) affords me a rewarding opportunity to train men and women in groups and individually, at all levels (from entry to top executive) in both the public and private sectors. Over the years I have asked many executives, who have authority to approve an employee's promotion to a supervisory level, what qualities they considered paramount in making their final decision. The overwhelming response was the ability to communicate orally in clear and understandable language.

CLEAR AND UNDERSTANDABLE LANGUAGE

How many times have you called a company, spoken to a salesperson, heard a lecture at school, or talked to someone on the telephone only to recoil in shock over the gibberish which left you exclaiming, "I don't believe this!" You've found it almost impossible to understand the individual. Perhaps he mumbled, ran words together, didn't articulate, had a monotone, took a breath midword or midphrase, or spoke too fast or too slow. It's amazing the number of people who communicate with the public daily and don't realize their speech shortcomings or who fail to improve their oral communication skills.

Through months and years of study, discipline, practice, trial and error, perseverance, and even failure, people can develop their speaking abilities. You should understand that Luciano Pavarotti was not *born* a great singer, Kareem Abdul Jabbar was not *born* a great basketball player, Albert Einstein was not *born* a great physicist, and Sir Laurence Olivier was not *born* a great actor.

The art of speaking to communicate knowledge, ideas, and feelings is no exception. All of the theoretical knowledge of public speaking will not make you outstanding in the art, and it will not improve your ability, unless you're willing to commit yourself totally. It will take work, perhaps even a bit of needling from your family and friends, but if you have the will and motivation to sharpen your speaking effectiveness, nothing can deter you.

In my childhood, I (AJV) wanted to become a radio announcer. I practiced reading, pronunciation, **enunciation,** interpretation, projection, and—the most difficult challenge of all—eliminating my Boston accent. I practiced in the bathroom, in the cellar, even in my brother's car. I took my share of ribbing, but even today I enjoy these reminiscences every time I appear before a microphone or TV camera. *If you want to do something, make up your mind to do it; then go at it with gusto.*

Certain elements contribute to effective and lively delivery: your voice, breathing, pronunciation, articulation, rate of speaking, pauses, pacing, expression, and oral visualization.

Your Voice

There is no more versatile instrument in the world than your voice. Yet, as with any instrument, its effectiveness depends solely on the way you use it.

Listen to Yourself

The immediate reaction of most people when they hear themselves played back on a tape recorder is usually shocked disbelief. You may recall such statements as "That sounds horrible," "Good God, that's not *me!*" or "You mean I sound like *that?*" In almost all instances,

"I *sound like* that?"

the sad fact is that you *do* sound like that. If you're serious about speech development, you should use a good tape recorder to hear yourself as others hear you. It is an invaluable aid.

Speech skill doesn't remain on a plateau; either it improves or it regresses. You must always work to improve it because that's the only way to banish poor speaking habits. Your tape recorder will "tell." The sound of your voice may play as great a role in getting your message across as do the words themselves.

One good way to improve your speech habits is to hear what you're doing wrong as you speak. This will not be easy. When you've reached the stage of recognizing your speech faults, then you'll be able to correct yourself. Listen very seriously whenever your speech professor offers suggestions on how to improve your speech.

Listening to yourself occasionally on a tape recorder is excellent— but you must discipline yourself to listen critically to every word and sound. Now let's briefly discuss some important characteristics of voice quality and delivery.

Here Comes the Pitch

Every voice has a **pitch.** Pitch refers to the highness or lowness of your tone, or sound. A person whose pitch is too high, too low, or monotonous (continuously on the same level) may not only transmit a negative impression when communicating but may risk losing listeners completely.

The pitch is too high. Your voice may sometimes be pitched too high because of nervousness (remember your first talk?), fright, or overanxiousness to respond. If you suffer no physical problems that affect your voice, the more often you speak, the more relaxed your throat muscles will become, resulting in more pleasant vocal sounds. A good exercise to lower a high pitch is to read aloud solemn passages very slowly.

The pitch is too low. You may know some people who speak with a very low, basslike sound. Usually they speak slowly. Reading aloud happy, lively material—children's stories, for example—at a fast pace is a good exercise that may help slightly raise a low pitch.

The voice is monotonous. The person who speaks in a **monotone** is like Johnny-one-note on the piano. After a short while, the sound is boring, dull, and lifeless. The voice lacks inflection, that is, the raising and lowering of pitch.

To avoid or eliminate a monotone, you must find your normal range. This is the vocal area which is most comfortable for you to carry on a normal conversation and from which you may easily raise or lower your pitch. One way to find your normal range is to match your vocal tones with the tones of a piano. Most women can usually start around middle C on the keyboard, and men an octave lower (if you're not familiar with the keyboard, ask someone who is). Your normal pitch range should be the notes in the scale that feel comfortable for you as you sound them, and from which you may comfortably go up and down. An acceptable range for a normal, healthy voice is about one octave, for example C to C, or 13 half-notes inclusive. (If you lack access to a piano, see your professor about assisting you with this exercise, using a piano at your college.)

Once you establish your normal pitch range, it is crucial to maintain it. Listen to how it sounds and feels when you use it so that speaking becomes as natural as breathing. The up-and-down inflection of your pitch adds variety and vividness to your delivery.

WARNING

Your voice box is such a delicate, complex mechanism that abuse of it can lead to irreparable damage. Never force yourself to lower or raise your pitch drastically. Be sure to consult with your professor before attempting to change your pitch.

The rate of speech is monotonous.   A person who speaks each syllable, word, phrase, and sentence at the same rate of speed suffers from what speech authorities call **monorate.** The delivery, just like the monotonous voice, is boring, dull, and lifeless. It lacks variety and vividness.

Volume

Some people have naturally loud or soft voices. If you speak too loudly or too softly, your audience will communicate this message to you nonverbally. For example, when you start to speak, do they all move back in their chairs as if blown there by a gust of wind? Or do they move up to the edge of their seats, turning their ears in your direction?

The size of the room and the audience should determine your **vocal volume.** If you have a soft voice, start by asking the audience, "Can you hear me in back?" Speaking too loudly or too softly is not only annoying, but it leads to a breakdown in speaker-listener communication.

Besides speaking too loudly or too softly, a speaker must be aware of a third aspect of volume—variety. When your loudness or softness doesn't vary, your voice becomes boring.

BREATHING

Proper breathing is vital to speech communication because the outgoing breath provides the power for producing sound. Perhaps you know someone who takes several breaths in midphrase or midsentence. You feel that any minute he will require a tank of oxygen.

Lung capacity varies.

Learn to breathe deeply; practice filling your lungs with as much air as possible as quickly as possible. This healthful exercise will enable you to communicate a message-idea without interruption. Take deep breaths—mainly through your mouth, read something aloud, and stop when you have to breathe. Time yourself to see how long you can read.

Lung capacity varies widely among people. Some professional singers can hold a note comfortably from twenty to thirty seconds, and some seasoned speakers can complete a marathon sentence in one breath. The ability to speak from fifteen to twenty seconds on a single breath is attainable through deep breathing and should allow you to surmount any difficulty in finishing a sentence without gasping for air.

NOTE

Public speakers should learn to breathe from the diaphragm. It is a special kind of breathing that is discussed in advanced speech courses.

PRONUNCIATION

Nothing stands out more negatively in a speaker than mispronunciation. (If you have a question about the correct pronunciation of any word, consult a dictionary.) Pronunciation, articulation, rate of speaking, vocal volume, and proper breathing all contribute to the effectiveness of your communication. Defects in any of these areas can, unfortunately, impair your communication style.

Your environment—family, friends, city or section of the country where you live—has a tremendous influence on your pronunciation and speech habits. Regional accents, or "dialects," abound in our country. The three major accents are:

- General American—spoken by the largest segment of our population—includes the Midwest, the West, and parts of the Southwest. This dialect is most often heard on radio and TV and in movies.

- Northeast—includes the New England and Middle Atlantic states.

- Southern—includes those areas south of the Mason-Dixon Line.

Each of these three major accents, or American dialects, has a beauty and style all its own, and none is superior to the others. They are all acceptable and totally correct. Even within these geographical areas, local and regional dialects exist. Bostonians can easily be identified because they tend to overlook the letter *r* in the middle or at the end of words. For example, they say, "Pahk yah cah in the Hahvahd yahd." They also tend to sound an *r* when one doesn't appear, as in *Cuber* for *Cuba, Americer* for *America, delter* for *delta,* and *tuner* for *tuna.*

An accepted standard dictionary can be a great aid in improving your pronunciation. Even though recognized dictionaries are accepted throughout the country, some of their recommended pronunciations are ignored in certain locales. Generally, it is wise to use the pronunciation typical of the region you're in, even though it may not be "correct," rather than to allow yourself to sound eccentric. Be flexible enough to bend a little to avoid embarrassment.

Another way to improve your pronunciation is to pay close attention to professional speakers, actors, and actresses and then try to emulate them. A tape recorder will verify your progress. Learning to sound words correctly and clearly will require time and effort, but once you achieve this goal it will pay you life-long dividends at work and socially.

Articulation, or Diction

Articulation, diction, and **enunciation** have the same basic meaning. They refer to clarity, intelligibility, and distinctness of your speech—in other words, the way you produce **vowel, diphthong,** and **consonant** sounds: all the parts of words, and nothing else.

Incorrect articulation usually results in leaving off parts of words, adding parts to words, or slurring words together. It is possible, then, to articulate clearly a mispronounced word. Misarticulation is quite different from mispronunciation. Pronunciation pertains to standards of acceptability either of a particular region or of a dictionary; articulation concerns only the distinctness or clarity of the words.

It's important to articulate sounds clearly. Voice each syllable carefully so that the entire word sounds crisp and understandable. Sloppy speech results from not taking the time to pronounce all of the sounds in a word and from running words together. For example:

Whatimes zit?	for	What time is it?
What'sitdoin outside?	for	What's it doing outside?
How'ya doin?	for	How are you doing?
Ahdunno.	for	I don't know.
Whaja say ya name is?	for	What did you say your name is?
Howzitgowen?	for	How is it going?
Whatchadowen?	for	What are you doing?
Whujasay?	for	What did you say?
Whutsamatta?	for	What's the matter?

Here are some examples of slurred words:

Kinda	for	kind of
Becausa	for	because of
Sorta	for	sort of
Wanna	for	want to
Needa	for	need to
Hafta	for	have to
Mindta	for	mind to

Shoulda	for	should have
Woulda	for	would have
Coulda	for	could have
Shouldna	for	should not have

Not opening the mouth enough is a major cause of poor diction, especially among neophyte speakers. Because the mouth is not opened sufficiently to allow all of the sounds to evolve into clearly spoken words, the sounds seem to be struggling somewhere down in the throat. A beneficial exercise is to repeat vowel sounds aloud slowly, holding the sound of each vowel a full breath (AAAAAAAAAA—EEEEEEEEEE—IIIIIIIII—and so on). Practice until you produce a full, forceful sound and can feel the muscles in your lips and mouth working. Don't hesitate to overexaggerate your lip and mouth movements. Do this every time you speak until the feeling becomes second nature.

Nothing in our spoken language is more beautiful than fully stressed vowel sounds. When you sound them within a word, voice them a little longer. This is called an increase in *duration,* or length, of the sound. Notice the different durations of the *aw* sounds in the words "draw" and "fog." An increase in duration of vowel sounds adds color (variety and vividness) to your speech delivery.

Notice how professional singers, actors, and speakers treat these sounds within words of a song or speech—it's sheer artistry. Listen closely to the delivery of such public figures as Jane Fonda, Johnny Carson, the Reverend Billy Graham, or Frank Sinatra.

There are more than five vowel sounds. For example, note the different sounds produced by the letter *a* in the following words: aggravate, fat, hall, and bah; or the letter *e* in: be, been, sex, feet, and term; or the letter *o* in: hot, go, out, order, and oil. Prolongation of these sounds adds color to speech.

You can learn to produce more colorful vowel sounds, which can lead you to a more captivating delivery. However, it will take commitment, time, and effort. Practice the following vowel sounds aloud and listen to them carefully:

A (ay)	betrayed	be-traayed
	delayed	de-laayed
	conveyed	con-vaayed
E (ee)	received	re-ceeved
	believe	be-leeve
	reprieve	re-preeve

I (eye)	divide	di-viide
	revise	re-viise
	coincide	coin-ciide
O (oh)	behold	be-hoold
	resold	re-soold
	foretold	fore-toold
U (you)	preview	pre-vyuu
	review	re-vyuu
	through	thruu

Another cogent reason to stress vowel sounds is that they impart carrying power to your voice. Relax your neck, throat, mouth, and lips; breathe deeply; open your mouth wide; and let these sounds roll out full and strong. As a result, your listeners will hear and understand you better, and appreciate you more.

The following are common pronunciation and articulation problems to be aware of:

Not pronouncing all vowels and consonants

Bar*bra*	for	Barbara
Bat*try*	for	battery
Boun*dry*	for	boundary
Ca*ni*date	for	candidate
Cho*clit*	for	chocolate
Di*mo*nd	for	diamond
Feb*ua*ry	for	February
Go*va*ment	for	government
Gran*it*	for	granted
Jew*lery*	for	jewelry
Li*bry*, Li*bary*	for	library
La*bra*tory	for	laboratory
P*lee*ce	for	police
R*a*member	for	remember

Running the last consonant of a word into the first vowel of the next word

Your rown	for	your own
Her rauto	for	her auto
Your rinterview	for	your interview
As zif	for	as if

For rus	for	for us
This sevening	for	this evening
Near Reast	for	Near East
The yumpire	for	the umpire
Her rage	for	her age
His sage	for	his age
Her rapple	for	her apple
His zonner	for	his honor

Producing incorrect sounds of letters

Dem	for	them
Dis	for	this
Exscape	for	escape
Jist	for	just
Pitchah	for	picture
Wid	for	with
Winduh	for	window
Yestiday	for	yesterday
Tuday	for	today
Tunight	for	tonight
Tumorrah	for	tomorrow

Eliminating word endings (especially *-ing* in verbs)

Walkin	for	walking
Talkin	for	talking
Coughin	for	coughing
Slep	for	slept
Crep	for	crept
Fine	for	find
Ben	for	bent
Sen	for	send
Reveren	for	reverend
Fence	for	fenced

Adding or reversing vowels and consonants

Athaletic	for	athletic
Athalete	for	athlete
Alumnium	for	aluminum
Acrost	for	across

Calvery	for	cavalry
Evuning	for	evening
Interduction	for	introduction
Laundary	for	laundry
Mischievious	for	mischievous
Often	for	often (silent *t*)
Perduce	for	produce
Pervent	for	prevent
Wunst	for	once
Skoowull	for	school
Skejoowull	for	schedule

It's important, however, not to go completely overboard and o-v-e-r e-n-u-n-c-i-a-t-e, which will result in stilted and phony-sounding speech.

RATE OF SPEAKING

For most people, a comfortable **rate of speaking** lies between 130 and 160 words per minute. Speaking too fast can cause poor diction— running words together, slurring words, and dropping word endings— which could result in listeners' complaining, "What did he say?" A machine-gun delivery can easily lose your listeners.

On the other hand, talking too slowly may irritate your listeners even more than talking too fast. When a speaker takes what seems like five minutes to draaaaag out a phrase or sentence, he is setting up his listeners to yawn or their minds to wander. A sluggish speaker can easily convey an impression of shyness, lack of confidence or intelligence, or illness.

From this moment you should be conscious of your delivery rate. Listen to yourself on a tape recorder.

PAUSES

Some reasons for pausing are to: provide emphasis and variety in your delivery, pull your thoughts together, allow time for your audience to absorb an important point, and make transitions before stressing a major point or introducing new material.

Pausing is an art.

Pausing is an art which every professional performer strives to master in order to achieve maximum effectiveness. Listen closely to how performers like Rex Harrison, Tony Randall, and Sarah Vaughan orchestrate pauses in dialogues and songs. Notice how comic pros Johnny Carson, Rodney Dangerfield, Joan Rivers, and Phyllis Diller use pauses to get laughs. Certainly a master of this art is radio and television news commentator Paul Harvey.

Although pauses are the punctuation marks of speech, you must be careful not to pause excessively, since it could lead to a staccato delivery. This can be abrasive to the ear and can short-circuit communication. With practice, determination, and the right number of pauses sprinkled at the right times, you can give your delivery more variety, excitement, and interest.

On the other hand, far too many speakers can't endure a moment of silence. Either from nervousness, habit, or both, they fill pauses with sounds or words like *er, ah, um, OK, right, you know,* or *something.* Very often they're not even aware that they're making these sounds.

If you tend to sputter during pauses, don't despair. Become conscious of it, concentrate on conquering it, and try to keep your mouth closed during pauses. Here again, perseverance pays off.

PACING

If you were on a long drive and kept your speed at exactly 55 miles per hour, chances are you would soon become bored, and later, perhaps, drowsy. A wise driver thus slows down, speeds up for a while, then returns to average speed. The driver repeats this tactic until he reaches his destination.

The professional runner practices the same basic procedure. He may start out with a burst of speed, slow down a bit, pick up speed, continue at a comfortable clip, and then, when approaching the final stretch, exert a surge of energy and speed to carry him to victory.

Both the driver and the runner perform a very important function of delivery—they pace themselves. It would be wrong to say that you should never talk quickly or slowly. It's only when you do either of these constantly that you sabotage communication.

To use **pacing** effectively means to speak at an interesting rate of delivery, with enough variety to hold your listeners' interest. To describe an exciting event, you would speed up your delivery. When quoting statistics or emphasizing several points, you would slow your pace. Speaking at a constant rate, either fast or slow, can only lead to monotony and the loss of your audience's attention.

EXPRESSION

When you speak, you express yourself through facial and body actions as well as by the words you choose and how you say them. Do your words convey exactly what you intend them to? Are you saying them with conviction and feeling, or are you just mouthing them? There is a difference between a person who bids you "good morning" with a warm smile and one who mutters it like a robot.

After you've prepared a speech, go over it carefully, noting the important points you wish to make. Review the title, opening remarks, main body, and transitional phrases. What points do you want to drive home in the conclusion? What is your appeal and to whom?

Understand what you want to say and practice saying it. Pause to attract attention, show your fingers to enumerate steps, raise an eyebrow to ask a question, frown to show disbelief, or lean toward the audience to make a personal point or to let them in on a secret. Don't hesitate to repeat a point several times if necessary.

What you are doing is making your talk come alive, and this will entice your audience to be more interested and motivated by your message. *Strive to convey emotions and feelings in your words and delivery.*

Oral Visualization

A highly effective way to express yourself with animation is to recall first as many experiences as possible. Then select what you need for your talk and visualize it when you're communicating.

When was the last time you were frightened, thrilled, or pleased? Can you recall the incident vividly? Have you ever been hungry, cold, hot, very thirsty, in extreme pain, grief-stricken? Think about that experience until you're practically reliving it. If you're trying to convey some of these emotions and experiences, recall them again and again and visualize them as you communicate with your audience. Feel and live your words.

By mastering **oral visualization,** you'll not only communicate deeper meaning to your audience, but you'll also generate "electricity" from your message to your listeners, who will reflect it back to you through their expressions. You will have completed the full cycle of successful interpersonal communication. "Eloquence lies as much in the tone of voice, in the eyes, and in the speaker's manner, as in his choice of words."[2]

Things to Discuss in Class

As previously mentioned, no instrument is more useful in speech development than the tape recorder. Most speech classes have access to one—so use it, whenever possible, to record some of the following exercises. There's no better learning experience for personal and instructor evaluation than listening to your own voice.

---

2. La Rochefoucauld, *Maxims* (1665).

1. Record about a minute of your voice on tape. The material may be preselected or impromptu. The purpose of this exercise is for you to hear your voice and delivery as others do. As you listen to the play-back, be alert to your pitch, inflection, pronunciation, rate of speaking, breathing, and expression.

2. Remember, when you breathe, you should inhale as much air as pos-sible to avoid taking a breath in the middle of a word, phrase, or sen-tence. You should be able to read each of the following sentences on a single breath.
   a. The future belongs to those who are willing to prepare for it.
   b. They say money isn't everything, but you must admit it sure beats poverty.
   c. Breathing is a basic biological process that continues as long as life is maintained.
   d. More people could enjoy much happier lives, if they could only learn to be more assertive.
   e. "Nature has herself appointed that nothing great is to be accom-plished quickly, and has ordained that difficulty should precede every work of excellence."
      —*Quintilian*

3. Here are some words that are often mispronounced and misarticu-lated; usually one sound is substituted for another. Use a dictionary, if necessary, to write the correct pronunciation beside each word before you record your voice.

anesthetist	indict
chasm	masochist
chiropodist	pantomime
diary	pitcher
et cetera	pronunciation
handkerchief	radiator
hearth	robot

4. Here are some words that are often mispronounced and misarticu-lated; usually one or more sounds are omitted. Follow the same in-structions as in exercise 3.

accessory	figure
arctic	length
asphyxiate	picture
casualty	probably

correct	recognize
environment	regular
February	twenty

5. Here are some words that are often mispronounced and misarticulated; usually one or more sounds are added to the word. Follow the same instructions as in exercise 3.

accompanist	film
across	laundry
athlete	monstrous
athletics	often
chimney	positively
disastrous	statistics
escape	

6. Here are some words that are often mispronounced and misarticulated; usually the accent is placed on the wrong syllable. Follow the same instructions as in exercise 3.

admirable	incomparable
amicable	irreparable
autopsy	magnanimous
barbarous	mischievous
comparable	police
guitar	preferable
impotence	theater

7. Here are some words that are often mispronounced and misarticulated; usually two or more sounds are reversed. Follow the same instructions as in exercise 3.

asterisk	prescription
cavalry	prevent
hundred	professor
introduction	solemnity
irrelevant	voluminous
perspiration	

8. As you read the following sentences aloud, prolong the vowel sounds to produce full, rich tones.
   a. The most beautiful sounds in our language are produced when we open our mouths and prolong the vowel sounds within words.
   b. Be nice to people on your way up the ladder, because you'll meet the same people on the way down.
   c. The friendly, round-faced native traded corn and coffee for a large amount of cinnamon-flavored honey.
   d. Noreene maintained that Gregory Wayne should not be blamed for the injury, which became inflamed.
   e. Running into debt isn't so bad; it's running into your creditors that could produce problems.
   f. Round and round went the wheel and when it came to a stop, it landed on my lucky number—thirteen.
   g. The orange was large, perfectly round, seedless, firm, deliciously juicy, and sweet.

9. Read the following sentences aloud with feeling and expression. Try to visualize the words and thought-ideas as you read.
   a. The battalion of tall, determined waves, slowly, but steadily, approached the unsuspecting, jagged shore like military columns. When they arrived, their fury was unleashed as they exploded against the rocks and ledges.
   b. The raindrops happily tiptoed across the barn's metal roof almost in unison. Then, as if playing a game, they decided to slide off onto the soft, soggy ground.
   c. "We shall fight on the beaches. We shall fight on the landing grounds. We shall fight in the fields and in the streets. We shall fight in the hills. We shall never surrender."
      —*Winston Churchill*
   d. "If a free society cannot help the many who are poor, it cannot save the few who are rich."
      —*John F. Kennedy*
   e. He rose, shivering, chilled, infected, bending beneath this dying man, whom he was dragging on, all dripping with slime. He walked with desperation, without raising his head, almost without breathing.

10. You may find this reading interesting since it contains all of the sounds of the English language.

    It is usually rather easy to reach the Virginia Theatre. Board car number 56 somewhere along Churchill Street and ride to the highway. Transfer there to the Mississippi bus. When you arrive at Judge Avenue, begin walking toward the business zone. You will pass a gift shop displaying little children's playthings that often look so clever you will wish yourself young again: such things as books and toys and, behind the counter, a playroom with an elegant red rug and smooth, shining mirrors. Beyond this shop are the National Bank and the Globe Garage. Turn south at the next corner; the theater is to your left.

What Do You Remember from This Chapter?

1. Name several elements that contribute to effective delivery.

2. How can you find your normal pitch range?

3. What is a good exercise that will help eliminate a monotonous delivery?

4. Why is proper breathing important to oral communication?

5. Explain the following terms: *oral visualization, pacing, duration,* and *articulation.*

6. Comment on the statement "She was a born singer."

7. Is it a good idea to listen to yourself when you speak? If so, why?

8. Name the three major accents found in the United States.

9. When speaking before an audience, how can you tell if you're speaking too loudly or too softly?

Vitalize Your Vocabulary

Court and Law

accessory (n.)   one who knowingly aids a criminal.

acquittal (n.)   the freeing of a person from an accusation of wrongdoing.

affidavit (n.)   a written statement made under oath before an authorized officer.

appellant (n.)   one who appeals to a higher court for a retrial of his case.

arraign (v.)   to summon before a court to answer a charge.

circumstantial evidence (n.)   evidence that is only indirectly related to the facts in a trial or lawsuit.

defendant (n.)   the person against whom a legal action is brought.

exonerate (v.)   to free from an accusation.

extradition (n.)   the surrender of an alleged criminal by one state for trial by another.

felony (n.)   a serious crime, such as burglary, rape, or murder.

indictment (n.)   a formal written statement listing charges against an accused person.

injunction (n.)   a court order prohibiting or requiring a specific course of action.

litigant (n.)   a person engaged in a lawsuit.

misdemeanor (n.)   an offense less serious than a felony.

perjury (n.)   the willful utterance of false testimony while under oath.

plaintiff (n.)   a person who brings a lawsuit against another (defendant).

reprieve (n.)   a temporary postponement of punishment.

subpoena (n.)   a legal order requiring a person to appear in court and to give testimony.

6

Nature has herself appointed that nothing great is to be accomplished quickly, and has ordained that difficulty should precede every work of excellence.[1]

Selecting a Speech Topic and Doing Research

Chapter Objectives

After reading and understanding this chapter, you should know:

- How to go about selecting a topic.

- Several ways to conduct research.

- How to use library facilities.

- How to take research notes.

- How to summarize, paraphrase, and select apt quotations.

- What plagiarism is.

Chapter Digest

If you're able to select your own speech topic, choose one that interests you, one that you can handle, and one that suits your audience. Your next step usually involves paring the topic to a manageable size that you can cover in a short talk. When the topic is focused clearly in your mind, it's time to seek

---

1. Quintilian, eminent Roman teacher of speech (A.D. 30?–96?).

solid information—very often the only basis of effective interpersonal communication in business and professional careers.

There are several ways to find information, and you should feel free to use the ways that will suit your needs best: dredge up your own experiences, opinions, and observations; contact various organizations and agencies, both public and private; consult nonprint media (television, radio, documentary films, and recordings); interview specialists from all walks of life; and utilize libraries.

You'll probably find the bulk of your information in print—newspapers, journals, magazines, and books. It's vital that you read and take notes with a critical eye. Question constantly. The fact that a statement is published does not guarantee its accuracy.

CRITERIA FOR SELECTING A TOPIC

Before you can give a brief, stimulating talk, you need a topic and information on it. Your professor may assign a topic and ask you to research it. At other times she may specify a general area—for example, inflation, unemployment, or white-collar crime—and request you to select a particular facet of it. Some students prefer to have a specific topic selected for them, because it's easier than having to choose one themselves.

The professor may tell you to choose your own topic. If this is the case, your first reaction will probably be, "What will I talk about?" Without question this is the most common response by students. With a little thought and with the suggestions in this chapter, you may find that selecting a topic is not as difficult as you first imagined. In any event, you should weigh the following guidelines in searching for a topic:

- Your interest in it.
- Your ability to handle it.
- Its appropriateness to the audience.

The topic should be interesting to you.   If you're not interested in the topic, chances are that nobody else will be, and your talk will probably fizzle. Interest, enthusiasm, or zeal—call it what you will— is reflected in your voice and by your nonverbal communication (facial expressions, emotions, and gestures; nonverbal communication is discussed further in Chapters 2, 3, 5, 15, and 16). Audiences sense enthusiasm, or the lack of it, in a speaker, and they respond ac-

Audiences sense enthusiasm, or the lack of it.

cordingly. Remember Ralph Waldo Emerson's statement "Nothing great was ever achieved without enthusiasm!"

What you talk about should depend on what interests you. Perhaps you're engaged in one of the following hobbies:

- Repairing and reconditioning antique cars.
- Stamp or coin collecting.
- Candle making and design.
- Rug braiding or needlepoint.
- Photography.
- Music.
- Ham radio.
- Comic book collecting.
- Playing an instrument.
- Reading.
- Painting.
- International doll collecting.

If you're interested in politics and government, you may consider one of the following:

- Don't say, "What's the use of voting?"
- Judges should be elected instead of appointed.
- What we need is a woman as president.
- The vice-president should be elected by the people and not selected by the presidential candidate.
- The president should be elected by popular vote.
- The federal government is too large.
- How does a bill get through the legislature?

How about choosing one of the following topics if you enjoy sports?

- The adventure of scuba diving.
- Getting high by sky diving.
- The case against expansion teams.
- Is jogging healthful or harmful?
- Pro athletes are overpaid.
- Sports complexes should not be subsidized by the taxpayers.
- Our Olympic sports teams should be federally subsidized.

If you have strong feelings on education, how about one of these?

- Politics in education.
- Speech should be a required subject.
- Students should be permitted to evaluate their teachers.
- Attendance in class should be required.
- Earning a college degree should take three years instead of four.
- Students should be able to attend their state colleges free of charge.

Do you still want more topics for talks? Then you and your classmates might venture into a **brainstorming** session, a technique used occasionally in the business world to dredge up solutions to problems (see Chapter 14). In brainstorming, the cardinal rule is complete freedom to suggest any topic without being criticized: No matter how zany or cockeyed an idea seems, *nobody can ridicule it.* Following these wide-open, nonthreatening rules, a cooperative group can often create answers to a problem—in this case, producing more topics for your talks.

All of the suggestions should be recorded on the chalkboard and on your notepad and evaluated at the next class session, when everybody has simmered down. The worthwhile ideas can be used and the poor ones discarded.

If you're deeply interested in a particular topic, chances are your audience will be, too. Your enthusiasm can't help but be transmitted to your listeners, because it's contagious. If you can get totally wrapped up in your subject, the end result could be electrifying.

John Wesley, founder of the Methodist church in the eighteenth century, was once asked how he attracted such large audiences and held them spellbound. "I set myself on fire," he replied, "and they come to watch me burn."

The topic should be within your capability. In other words, can you handle the topic on the basis of your personal experiences, book learning, first-hand knowledge, family background, personal convictions, and acquaintances in specific fields? If some or all of these factors are in your favor, then the odds are that you'll be able to prepare for and speak intelligently on your selected subject.

For example, let's assume that you're planning to select the subject of the operation and safety of a nuclear power plant. Nuclear safety has been a vital concern since the Three Mile Island accident in Pennsylvania in 1979; our concern has been further intensified by the Chernobyl disaster in the Soviet Union in 1986. To handle this kind of topic, you need a strong technical background, several visits to a nuclear plant, and interviews with engineers and administrators. Then, you face the challenge of compiling all of this scientific information and translating it into a level of English that your audience can understand.

Suppose, however, that you want to address the question "Should the use of marijuana be legalized?" You could easily find yourself knee-deep in facts, opinions, half-truths, and myths. Consider the sources of information available to you, for example, acquaintances who smoke pot and swear by it, law enforcement officials who think otherwise, doctors involved in drug treatment, and legislators determined to control the problem. Remember to check out as many

"I'd like to talk for a minute on nuclear power . . ."

sources of information as possible, because almost all controversial issues are complicated and seldom lend themselves to simplistic solutions.

The topic should be suitable to the audience. Knowing the makeup of your listeners will help you shape a more effective person-to-person communication. To know your listeners, you should try to answer several questions about them: What are their age level, ethnic background, occupation, financial status, sex, and educational level; and what are any other elements that may affect your performance?

Consider a speaker at a meeting of the National Organization for Women. If she explains innovative tactics that would help qualified women break into public school administration, higher echelons of civil service, or corporate executive suites—the three areas in which women have traditionally been shut out—she might receive a standing ovation.

In other words, try to assess the problem from the standpoint of the audience. Put yourself in the role of an active listener and ask yourself: What do I expect from this speaker? Will the message be interesting, informative, and understandable? Will I want to hear more? (Audience analysis is discussed in depth in Chapters 8 and 12.)

SELECTING MATERIAL AND NARROWING THE TOPIC

A common tendency among beginning speakers is to select a subject that is so general that it cannot be covered thoroughly in a short presentation. Suppose you find a subject that arouses your curiosity, for example, how to cope with violence in a permissive society. Should you use this subject for a talk? Definitely not, because it's so vast and complex that you couldn't even dent it in a half-hour. You must restrict the subject so that you can discuss it in the allotted time, usually five to ten minutes.

What you need at this point is a thesis statement that focuses your talk into one clear, concise sentence, for instance:

> To reduce the amount of violence in American society, our judicial system must begin to impose much stiffer prison sentences.

Now you have a vital, current statement that you can sink your teeth into in a short speech. Not only that, but this statement will save you much library time because it will help restrict your research to relevant information. From a speaker's viewpoint, a talk without solid, current information isn't worth giving, and from an audience's viewpoint, it isn't worth listening to. Your next step is a quest for knowledge, in other words, research.

DOING RESEARCH

The difference between a speech stocked with the latest accurate information and a speech lacking it can be the difference between acceptance and rejection by the audience. We say "acceptance" because most audiences listen to and respect a knowledgeable speaker. This hard-won knowledge will give you an injection of self-confidence, and, together with your listeners' respect, you're off and running.

The following ideas will help you ferret out information on any topic.

Probe your own knowledge, experience, and observations.   If you stop to think, you'll probably discover opinions, ideas, and knowledge that you didn't know you had. Jot them down. And don't forget to question friends and acquaintances, because some of them may know a good deal about your topic.

Write to organizations.   Government agencies, corporations, labor unions, research consultants, colleges, and publications are often helpful in providing information. If you do write to them, be very specific in your requests. The only drawback to this approach is that you may wait weeks for answers.

Check out TV and radio documentaries and talk shows, tapes, films, film clips, and cassettes.   In recent years these nonprint media have assumed more and more importance as carriers and recorders of vital information.

Suppose that you're curious about the solemn occasion and exact wording of President Franklin D. Roosevelt's Declaration of War against Japan on December 8, 1941. You could, of course, turn to the Congressional Record, biographies of FDR, or history books to find the answer. But another approach will allow you to capture the real-life gravity of that momentous day: ask your audiovisual department to get the recording of the Declaration so that you can listen to it in President Roosevelt's unique voice and speaking style.

Talk to people.   Authorities on various subjects are everywhere, and many of them are willing to share their expertise. Be sure to have a list of questions ready so that you won't waste the expert's time. After she has answered your questions, thank her and leave immediately.

A tape recorder can be used in a face-to-face information quest because it is a time saver, but first request permission from the interviewee to use the recorder. Some people are "allergic" to being taped and tend to clam up.

Don't feel that you must always seek out authorities sitting on top of the organizational pyramid. Some of them tend to be "long" on administrative plans, policies, and procedures but "short" on nitty-gritty savvy. On the other hand, many people in everyday positions essential to the functioning of society can brief you on

Talk to the man under the street.

problems in specialized areas, and they may do so if you ask. You'll be astonished at what you can get simply by asking.

Do you want to know about muggings, rapes, and armed robberies? Talk to police officers, judges, prison officials, and victims. Do you want to learn about financial hardships plaguing welfare families? By all means, talk with sociology professors, but don't forget to talk with welfare mothers, social workers, and members of legislative committees on human services. This many-sided approach to gathering information allows you to "see" an issue as it is in the real world, and not just as it appears in print and nonprint media.

Read. The most dependable and extensive of all information sources, reading opens endless horizons to you. Just about "everything you ever wanted to know about anything but were afraid to ask" can be found in books, magazines, journals, newspapers, government reports, almanacs, encyclopedias, dictionaries, diaries, and so on.

How much information should you garner? Far more than you need. Learn from the best filmmakers. They normally shoot at least

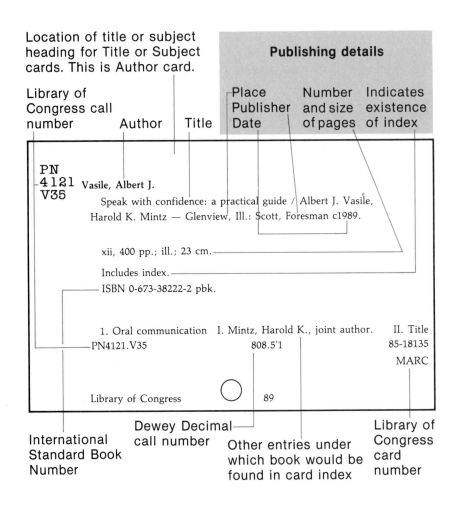

FIGURE 6.1
A card from a library card catalog

five times more film than they'll use; then they select the best footage and splice it into a unified package. By the same token, the best speakers usually gather and master two or three times more material than they'll use. This extra knowledge pays dividends in the confidence and fluency with which they deliver their talks and answer audience questions.

To extract the maximum benefit from the printed word, you must know how to use a library. So, let's touch on the highlights of exploiting your library's resources. Every library has a **card catalog** that lists all of its books. This catalog is broken down by author name, title, and subject, which means that at least three cards pinpoint each book. In addition, each card contains a call number that indicates the book's location in the library. Figure 6.1 shows a typical card from a library catalog. (Many libraries today, instead of having card catalogs, provide you with faster and more efficient methods of searching for material—microfiche and computers.)

When searching through books, you can save time by skimming the table of contents and index for the particular phases of a topic that you plan to discuss.

For periodicals (magazines, journals, and newspapers), visit the periodical section, where you'll find the latest authoritative information on countless specialized fields. This is the tremendous advantage that periodicals offer—information that may be only weeks or days old, in contrast to books that require several months to a year to publish.

To find articles in periodicals relevant to your topic, turn to the indexes, especially *Readers' Guide to Periodical Literature*. This guide lists, by subject, the contents of more than one hundred and twenty-five popular American publications. Without question, it is the best source of general information on current topics and is an excellent aid in getting your research off the ground. The *Guide* is published bimonthly in green paperback and annually in green hard cover. Here's a sample listing of magazines indexed in the *Guide*: *Atlantic, Business Week, Down Beat, Ebony, Esquire, Forbes, Glamour, Harper's, Ladies' Home Journal, Money, Nation's Business, Popular Science, Reader's Digest, Sports Illustrated, Time, U.S. News & World Report, Vital Speeches of the Day,* and *Writer*.

If you're searching for material on business, industry, education, or public affairs, consult some of the following indexes:

Bibliography Index

Business Periodicals Index

Christian Science Monitor Index

Dun & Bradstreet

Education Index

Moody's Investor's Service, Inc.

New York Times Index

Public Affairs Information Service

Ulrich's Periodical Directory

United Nations Documents Index

Wall Street Journal Index

For science and technology, use the following:

Applied Science & Technology Index

Aviation and Space Technology

For statistical data, you might dig into the following:

Government Publications

Information Please Almanac

United Nations Statistical Yearbook

U.S. Statistical Abstracts

World Almanac

To learn about people, consult the following:

Current Biography

Dictionary of American Biography

International Who's Who

Leaders in Education

Who's Who in America

Who's Who in Finance and Industry

Who's Who in Law

When you're searching for appropriate quotations, use the following excellent sources:

Bartlett's Familiar Quotations

Oxford Dictionary of Quotations

Stevenson's Home Book of Quotations

For general information and for an overall view of thousands of subjects, check the following standard encyclopedias:

Collier's Encyclopedia

Encyclopedia Americana

Encyclopaedia Britannica

For authoritative newspapers that have achieved a worldwide reputation, delve into the following: *Atlanta Constitution, London Times, Los Angeles Times, Manchester* (England) *Guardian, New York Times* (has its own index), *St. Louis Post-Dispatch,* and *Washington Post.*

As a speech student and, in fact, all through life, you should make a habit of mining these wordbooks:

Funk & Wagnall's New Standard Dictionary

Random House Dictionary of the English Language

Roget's International Thesaurus

Webster's Dictionary of Synonyms

Webster's Third New International Dictionary

Here are two hints for using libraries wisely: First, browse around your college or public library. Explore the card catalog, periodical section, reference section, and open stacks. After you do that a few times, you'll be amazed at how much faster you'll find the facts, figures, and authoritative opinions that will help you master your topic, communicate your message, and earn your listeners' respect. Second, get acquainted with reference librarians. No matter how sharp you are, research is a time-consuming process that librarians can speed up by guiding you to the right reference aids. However, don't expect them to do your research; that's your task.

Diagnosis

AIDS: fear of foreigners [testing Africans abroad] R. Nordland. il *Newsweek* 109:36 Ap 6 '87

An AIDS plan touches a nerve [expanding testing to include more groups] *US News World Rep* 102:11 F 16 '87

Mandatory testing for AIDS? J. Seligmann. il *Newsweek* 109:22 F 16 '87

Mandatory tests for AIDS? [interviews with B. Primm and M. Silverman] pors *U S News World Rep* 102:62 Mr 9 '87

A new panic over AIDS [testing of blood recipients] L. Martz. il *Newsweek* 109:18–19 Mr 30 '87

Putting AIDS to the test [merits of mass screening] A. Wilentz. il *Time* 129:60 Mr 2 '87

Secondary infection [blood testing for AIDS] *Nation* 244:165 F 14 '87

Strictly speaking, watch your mouth [oral leukoplakia as precursor to AIDS; research by John S. Greenspan] *Sci News* 131:135 F 28 '87

A transfusion of fear [blood recipients tested] A. Wilentz. il *Time* 129:24–5 Mr 30 '87

Legal aspects

AIDS & the law [discussion of October 1986 article, Sodomy and the Supreme Court] D. Robinson. *Commentary* 83:2+ F '87

The AIDS debate: call it a draw [conflict between French and U.S. researchers resolved] *Newsweek* 109:64 Ap 13 '87

Crewmember with AIDS barred at Gatwick [Delta Air Lines steward] *Aviat Week Space Technol* 126:36 F 23 '87

Yalta of AIDS [agreement between French and American researchers] *Time* 129:57 Ap 13 '87

FIGURE 6.2A
A sample listing from *Readers' Guide to Periodical Literature*, May 1987, Vol. 87, No. 5, p. 10

At this point you're primed to dip into reference works in order to locate sources of information. Magazines, journals, newspapers, and books are all fair game in this hunt. Whether you plan to refer to a few sources or to a dozen, you should number and list them on notepaper or cards (5-by-7 is a good size). This list is your preliminary bibliography; the list of sources that you actually use in your talk is your final **bibliography.** Figures 6.2A and 6.2B show sample listings from the *Readers' Guide to Periodical Literature* and the *Business Periodicals Index.*

Before studying your sources, you might save time by evaluating them and weeding out the poorer ones. Some yardsticks for judging the worth of a magazine or newspaper article or a book chapter are:

- Recency of publication. (This is not always a reliable measure.)

- Reputation of the author. (Is she a recognized authority in her field?)

- Reputation of the publisher. (What is the firm's "track record"?)

Testing
Birmingham news requires AIDS tests for new employees. *Ed Publ Fourth Estate* 119:16 N 8 '86

D.C. AIDS law withstands challenge by Sen. Helms [insurers not allowed to test for AIDS] *Bests Rev (Life/Health Insur Ed)* 87:5 N '86

Insurers look to fight ban on AIDS testing [California] A. G. Haggerty. *Natl Underwrit (Prop Casualty Insur Ed)* 90:24 D 19 '86

Insurers look to fight ban on AIDS testing [California] A. G. Haggerty. *Natl Underwrit (Life Health Insur Ed)* 90:8–9 D 6 '86

NAIC adopts AIDS rules. J. Diamond. *Natl Underwrit (Prop Casualty Employee Benefits Ed)* 90:65 D 29 '86

NAIC reaches accord on AIDS tests. J. Diamond. *Natl Underwrit (Life Health Insur Ed)* 90:3 D 20 '86

Oncor to offer test to detect AIDS virus. il *Chem Eng News* 64:6 O 6 '86

Therapy
AIDS-retarding drug provokes controversy [ribavirin] R. Dagani. *Chem Eng News* 65:18–19 Ja 26 '87

AIDS (Disease) and employment
AIDS in the newsroom. M. Fitzgerald. *Ed Publ Fourth Estate* 119:15+ O 18 '86

AIDS: what happens when the good life turns tough. P. Sloan. *Advert Age* 57:3+ O 20 '86

Birmingham news requires AIDS tests for new employees. *Ed Publ Fourth Estate* 119:16 N 8 '86

Employers face lawsuit explosion over AIDS. A. G. Haggerty. *Natl Underwrit (Life Health Insur Ed)* 90:18–19 N 29 '86

FIGURE 6.2B
A sample listing from *Business Periodicals Index*, April 1987, Vol. 29, No. 8, p. 24

For example, an article dealing with international news in the *New York Times* or *Chicago Tribune* carries far more clout than a similar article in a small-town newspaper. Admittedly, one or both of the last two yardsticks may be difficult to apply, but they do help in comparing one work against another and in deciding which would make a better source.

Taking Notes

There are various ways to take notes: Write a summary, write a paraphrase, or copy a direct quotation. If you can capture the essence of an important paragraph in a few sentences, you are summarizing. While researching a topic, you'll probably summarize often. Figure 6.3B shows a summary of the original text that appears in Figure 6.3A.

When you rewrite a sentence or a paragraph in your own style and in about the same number of words as the original, you're

Through four months, Washington was to sit silent in the Convention, even when they went into Committee of the Whole and he came down from the chair. He voted with the Virginians; before the Convention met he had made clear that his sympathies lay with a national government. Yet only on the last day, September seventeenth, did Washington rise to take part in the debates. Silence in public debates was, it seems, natural to him. Jefferson, who served with Washington in the Virginia legislature and with Dr. Franklin in Congress, testified afterward that he "never heard either of them speak ten minutes at a time, nor to any but the main point which was to decide the question. They laid their shoulders to the great points, knowing that the little ones would follow of themselves."

Washington showed himself firm, courteous, inflexible. When he approved a measure, delegates reported that his face showed it. Yet it was hard to tell what the General was thinking and impossible to inquire. In his silence lay his strength. His presence kept the Federal Convention together, kept it going, just as his presence had kept a straggling, ill-conditioned army together throughout the terrible years of war.

FIGURE 6.3A
Original text from *Miracle at Philadelphia*, by Catherine Drinker Bowen

As president of the Constitutional Convention (May to September), Washington made no speeches even when he stepped down from the chair. Only on the last day, Sept. 17, did he enter the debate. Apparently, silence in public debates was his style. As chairman, he was courteous and unbending, and his silence reflected his strength. His presence kept the Convention together, just as it "had kept a straggling, ill-conditioned army together" throughout the Revolution.

FIGURE 6.3B
Summary of original text

paraphrasing. Figure 6.3C shows a paraphrase of the text in Figure 6.3A.

Occasionally you'll run across a key idea phrased so strikingly that you can't summarize it or improve the wording. In that case, copy it exactly, word for word, and enclose it in quotation marks (see Figure 6.3C). Be sure to jot down the author's name and other information needed to document the quotation.

As president and chairman of the Constitutional Convention (May to September), Washington made no speeches even when he came down from the chair. Before the Convention met, he had stated his preference for a national government. Only on the last day, September 17, did he participate in the debate. He felt more at home keeping quiet in public debates. Jefferson, who served with Washington in the Virginia legislature and with Dr. Franklin in Congress, said that he "never heard either of them speak ten minutes at a time, nor to any but the main point which was to decide the question. They laid their shoulders to the great points, knowing that the little ones would follow of themselves."

As chairman, Washington was courteous and unbending. When he liked a measure, his face showed it. But it was difficult to know what he was thinking, and one did not ask because of his dignity and silence. His presence kept the Convention together, just as it "had kept a straggling, ill-conditioned army together" throughout the Revolution.

FIGURE 6.3C
Paraphrase of original text, including two direct quotations

When you take notes, you may think of a question to ask, a doubt to ponder, or a lead to follow up. Record these thoughts immediately before they vanish from memory and initial them so that you won't mix your ideas with those of the original author.

Here's a time-tested tip on using research notecards. Indicate the following on each card: a brief heading, information from one source and on one topic, and the source (for example, magazine name, author, title of article, volume number, date, and page number).

As a researcher, you enjoy a tremendous advantage over historical information seekers like Thomas Jefferson, Charles Darwin, and Winston Churchill. Say, for example, that you run across a few pages full of meaty, relevant information in a book, magazine, or encyclopedia that can't be borrowed. You could easily waste an hour or so copying the pages in longhand. Since almost all libraries have photocopy equipment, use it to save time. Reading important information into a cassette tape recorder can also save time. (Be sure to document the source.)

Take a few notes.

WARNING

When you quote, summarize, or paraphrase an individual or published source without giving due credit, you are guilty of **plagiarism,** *a very serious offense, especially since passage of the copyright law in 1978. Most libraries post that law near copy machines, and it would be prudent to familiarize yourself with the regulations before photocopying information.*

No question about it, conducting research can be a prolonged, difficult, and sometimes discouraging activity, but the overall results will be most rewarding. Remember the words of Quintilian, who said 1600 years ago, "Nature has herself appointed that nothing great is to be accomplished quickly, and has ordained that difficulty should precede every work of excellence."

Things to Discuss in Class

1. List a few subjects that interest you but which, because of your lack of knowledge, would require research if you were planning to talk about them.

2. Would you prefer to select your own topics or to have them selected for you? Why?

3. List a few speech topics that would apply only to specific audiences. Explain your reasons for choosing them.

4. Select a topic that would interest the class and list some possible sources of information on it.

5. Research some significant events that took place on the day you were born.

6. List five topics which you think would make an interesting talk. Carefully look over the list and, if you find any which are too general, narrow the topic so that it can easily be covered in a five- or ten-minute speech.

7. Discuss the types of information you can find in the *Readers' Guide to Periodical Literature*.

8. Select what you feel is an interesting topic, then go to the library and prepare a bibliography on that subject.

What Do You Remember from This Chapter?

1. After you've decided on a topic for a talk, what should the next steps be?

2. List several ways to find information.

3. Name some guidelines to be used in searching for a topic.

4. What role does the audience play in your selection of a topic?

5. Name two sources that provide statistical data.

6. Name two publications that specialize in word usage.

7. What type of information can you find in a library's card catalog file?

8. Explain the difference between a summary and a paraphrase.

9. What is plagiarism?

10. List some sources that would be helpful if you are looking for material on business, industry, public affairs, or education.

11. Name two sources that would supply information on people.

12. Explain the function of a brainstorming session.

Vitalize Your Vocabulary

Business and Finance

assets (n.)   property, equipment, merchandise, and money owned by a business.

balance sheet (n.)   a financial statement showing the condition of a business on a particular date.

bankrupt (adj.)   unable to pay one's debts; insolvent.

discount (n.)   a reduction from the usual price.

depreciation (n.)   a loss of value because of age or wear; in financial records, an allowance made for the loss.

dividend (n.)   a share of profits paid to a stockholder.

endorsement (n.)   a signature enabling a check to be cashed.

entrepreneur (n.)   a person who organizes and operates a business.

fiscal (adj.)   pertaining to financial matters.

inventory (n.)   the supply of goods on hand; stock.

liabilities (n.)   debts or obligations.

liquidation (n.)   paying off debts; closing down a business by paying off debts.

maturity (n.)   the time when a financial note becomes due for full payment.

monopoly (n.)   complete control of producing or selling a product or service.

overhead (n.)   the operating expenses of a business, such as heat, lighting, taxes, insurance, rent; overhead does not include the cost of labor or materials.

partnership (n.)   a relationship in which two or more persons own a business and share the profits and losses.

promissory note (n.)   a written promise to pay a sum of money plus interest by a certain date.

proprietor (n.)   the owner or owner-manager of a business.

prospectus (n.)   a description of a proposed business, sent out to gain financial support.

recession (n.)   a period of reduced economic activity.

repossess (v.)   to take back for failure to pay installments when due.

7

Order and simplification are the first steps toward mastery of a subject. . . .[1]

Putting
It All
Together

Chapter Objectives

After reading and understanding this chapter, you should know:

- The two principal types of outlines.

- How to prepare an outline.

- The four parts of a talk and how to bond them together.

- How to come up with a title for your talk.

- How to prepare an introduction to your talk.

- How to prepare a conclusion to your talk.

- What transitions are and how to use them.

Chapter Digest

At this stage you've done your research and you know your subject. Now you must plan, or outline, your talk. In the long run, a good outline will save you far more time than you will devote to preparing it. The two most common outlines, the topic outline and the sentence outline, are explained and illustrated so you can compare them and decide which one is best for you.

---

1. Thomas Mann, *The Magic Mountain* (1924).

When you construct your talk, you may work on the body first and then the introduction or conclusion. A well-thought-out introduction will usually win audience goodwill and interest. Numerous suggestions for an effective introduction are given, and all of them appear in introductions quoted from actual speeches. In addition, some ideas for forming conclusions are listed, and excellent examples are included.

Since every talk should have a title, actual titles of many speeches are listed, along with pointers on their distinguishing characteristics.

In every talk you give, the introduction, body, and conclusion should be linked smoothly to each other by means of transitions. Examples of transitions, together with the conditions that call for their use, appear in a table.

NOTE

Everything you learn in this course comes together in this chapter. In other words, the way you organize your talk can "make or break" your overall performance. For that reason, this chapter deserves a great deal of your time and effort.

PREPARING AN OUTLINE

You've done your research, you've uncovered more than enough material—always a wise policy—you've turned the material over in your mind, and you understand it inside out. Where do you go from here?

What you need now is a plan to organize all of the information you've gathered. In a sense, you're in the same position as an architect about to design a building, an airline pilot about to fly the Atlantic, or a motorist about to drive from Boston to San Francisco. To accomplish these objectives, the architect needs blueprints, the pilot needs a flight plan, and the motorist needs road maps.

By the same token, you need a plan, or **outline,** of your talk. Before grimacing at the thought of preparing an outline, weigh all of the advantages of doing so:

- It helps you decide what information to use, how to sequence it, and what information to leave out.
- It helps you classify information and separate main ideas from subordinate ones.
- It helps you see the relationships between main ideas and their

supporting materials and helps you determine whether those relationships are logical.

- It saves you time by revealing possible gaps or redundancies in your body of information.

- If your talk is well organized—and an outline will help you achieve that—your audience will get your message. And after all, isn't that the point of this task?

An outline, whether it's for a five-minute talk (quite likely in this course) or a twenty-minute talk, should consist of five parts: a title; a **thesis statement** (the main idea of your talk); an **introduction;** a **body,** or discussion; and a **conclusion.** The body of your outline should usually encompass three to five main points, each supported by data. You should strive to use various types of information, such as statistics, quotations, definitions, anecdotes, contrasts, comparisons, and examples. Keep in mind, however, that everything you include must be relevant to the topic at hand. Here's a useful format:

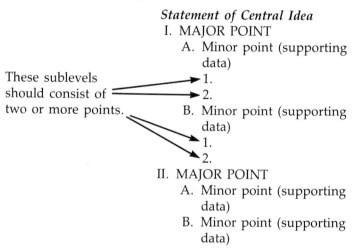

Statement of Central Idea
I. MAJOR POINT
    A. Minor point (supporting data)
These sublevels should consist of two or more points.
        1.
        2.
    B. Minor point (supporting data)
        1.
        2.
II. MAJOR POINT
    A. Minor point (supporting data)
    B. Minor point (supporting data)

In this basic speech course you should not have to delve deeper than the second level of supporting data. If you wish to change this suggested number/letter system to suit yourself, you may do so. You may use any organizing system you wish, as long as it's logical and coordinate in structure. This means that major point I, in importance, equals major point II, equals major point III, and so on. Similarly, minor point A, in importance, equals minor point B, equals

You need a plan.

minor point C. If your outline adheres to the principle of coordination, you're on your way to a well-organized speech.

It's possible that your professor may ask you for an outline before you speak so that he can judge how well you've prepared and can see if you fulfill your objectives. But whether or not an outline is required, you should prepare one because it will help you perform better.

Types of Outlines

The principal outlines commonly used are topic and sentence outlines. In a topic outline, one or a few key words stand for a topic and should start your thoughts flowing. In a sentence outline, a complete sentence stands for a topic. A sentence outline is more difficult to construct because it calls for thinking through and phrasing a complete idea. This kind of outline is usually more helpful because each sentence stands for a topic that requires one or more paragraphs for development. You should choose an outline that suits your style.

Sample Outlines

Let's assume that your long-range career plan (something for you to think about!) includes making enough money to buy a condominium someday, and so, you decide to give a talk on the expenses involved. Here's a topic outline for such a talk:

Thesis statement: The expenses of owning a condo are basically the same as for an individual home, except for points II.E. and F.

- I. Introduction
  - A. Reasons for buying a condominium rather than living with Mom and Dad or renting an apartment
- II. Body—Expenses
  - A. Mortgage principal and interest
  - B. Taxes
  - C. Utilities—telephone, gas, electricity, water, etc.
  - D. Insurance
  - E. Inside maintenance and repairs (not responsible for outside maintenance)
  - F. Monthly maintenance fees and periodic assessments
- III. Conclusion
  - A. Sale of condo at a profit after living in it some years, and purchase of a single-family home

Kindly observe that points I.A. and III.A. are standing alone; that's perfectly acceptable in the introduction and conclusion. However, if you have other things to say that pertain to the introduction and conclusion, you would number them I.B. and III.B.

Here's another sample outline, but this time it's a sentence outline. Let's say that a year ago you went on a health kick that has drastically changed your life-style, especially concerning diet and exercise. You've read up on these topics because you want to be fit and healthy, and now you're eager to tell the class about a diet that pays off in better health and appearance. The following outline is suitable for a five-to-seven-minute talk, and its title is spiced with a touch of slang:

Suggested Title: If you want to be healthy, you gotta eat smart.

Thesis Statement: To get the nutrients you need for good health, you should eat daily from the four food groups.

I. Introduction
   A. Sensible nutrition, based on eating nutrients from the four food groups, is vital to achieving good health and keeping it.
   B. An essential nutrient is any substance that must be supplied in the diet to maintain life, to carry on normal functions, and to promote growth and repair of the body.

II. Body—Four food groups
   A. Milk Group—You need two servings daily from any of the following: 1 cup milk or buttermilk, 1 cup yogurt, $1\frac{1}{2}$ slices cheddar-type cheese, 2 cups cottage cheese, $1\frac{3}{4}$ cups ice cream.
   B. Meat Group—You need two 2-oz. servings daily of cooked lean meat, fish, chicken, or turkey.
   C. Fruit-Vegetable Group—You need four servings daily. A serving is: a medium potato; 1 cup raw fruit or vegetable; a medium fruit.
   D. Grain Group—You need four servings daily. A serving is: 1 slice bread; 1 cup ready-to-eat cereal; $\frac{1}{2}$ cup noodles, cornmeal, rice, or grits; 1 small muffin, roll, or biscuit; 5 saltines.

III. Conclusion
   Because of this diet, I feel much better and look much better, and it can do the same for you.

THE BODY OF YOUR TALK

Since every talk should have four parts: a title, an introduction, a body, and a conclusion, your outline must reflect that arrangement of elements. In preparing your talk, however, a logical order is to outline the body first and then the introduction or conclusion. The reason for this sequence is that you need to know your message before you can introduce it. However, if you prefer to work on your introduction first, body second, and conclusion last, then do it your way.

As mentioned before, the main points and subpoints that support your thesis statement comprise the body, or main discussion, of your presentation. For short talks such as you'll probably give in this basic course, three or four main points should be enough. Each main point, when subordinated, or broken down, is usually supported by two or more subpoints. Proper development of each subpoint will require one or more paragraphs.

Clearly, it's impossible to know in advance how many points and subpoints you'll end up with, or, for that matter, how many paragraphs each point will require for adequate coverage. You'll find the answers when you translate all of the bits and pieces that form your outline into sentences and paragraphs. You can arrange your main points in any one of the following sequences:

- From simple to complex—a much used strategy in teaching.
- From cause to effect.
- From effect to cause.
- From problem to solution.
- According to space.
- According to time.

From simple to complex. If, for example, you're explaining and demonstrating various tennis strokes to your class, you'd logically start with the basic forehand and backhand. You'd then cover more advanced strokes like the serve and the lob. Finally, you'd move into the really difficult strokes like the smash and the volley. If you were to begin with the smash and the volley, you would confuse and discourage most novice players; they'd lose interest. In other words, when discussing something technical or new to an audience, be sure to start with elementary concepts.

From cause to effect. Reasoning from cause to effect involves a situation, event, or condition (an effect) that will happen in the future. For example, in a speech on energy conservation, you might reason that if you insulate your house or apartment (install storm windows and doors, caulk them, lower the thermostat, use an economical shower head, and so on), your heating bill will decrease substantially. All of these causes, but especially insulation, will result in an effect—a lowered heating bill. Here a caution is in order. An effect is usually produced by more than one cause. To win, a football team needs a sharp, hard-driving coach; talented players who are willing to go all the way; some "cooperative" opponents; and a smidgen of luck.

From effect to cause. This kind of reasoning involves finding a cause for an event that has happened. Suppose you witness an auto

accident and notice that one of the two drivers moves unsteadily, slurs his words, and has slightly glazed eyes. You may conclude that the accident was caused by a driver under the influence of alcohol. For another example, suppose that the number of burglaries in your city has doubled in the past two years, and in the same period your police force was cut 40 percent. In a speech, you might assert that the increase in crime (effect) was caused at least partially by the cut in police protection.

These simple cases illustrate kinds of thinking that we do throughout life. Some cases, however, are not so clearcut; because they combine many causes and effects, they will require hard, straight thinking.

From problem to solution. Pollution of air and water is a critical problem in today's industrialized societies. Some of the steps being taken to solve the problem are: improving the internal combustion engine, controlling the exhaust of industrial smokestacks, and restricting the dumping of waste into bodies of water. In your speech, first state a problem, then suggest possible solutions.

According to space. Let's say that you want to discuss the mountain ranges in the United States. A logical approach would be to start with the White Mountains in New Hampshire and move westward to the Sierra Nevada Mountains in California. Or you could go the other way around. But you would surely not go from New Hampshire to California and then back to the Rockies in Colorado.

According to time. Suppose you decide to speak on wars engaged in by the United States. There are two logical approaches: start in the 1960s and work your way back to the American Revolution, or vice versa. In either case, you are handling your subject according to time.

THE INTRODUCTION OF YOUR TALK

Now that you know what the substance of your talk will be, you're in a much better position to frame a strong introduction. Such an introduction is vital to the success of your talk because it can win over your audience immediately. Since the first few sentences are crucial, you should consider memorizing them. Rehearse them until you can speak smoothly and confidently.

Your introduction should serve three major functions:

- To divulge the purpose and reasons for your talk.
- To gain audience goodwill.
- To arouse audience interest.

To achieve those aims, your introduction may include any one or a combination of the following:

1. Reference to the occasion and sponsor.
2. Reference to the audience.
3. Reference to the speaker.
4. Reference to literature.
5. Questions to the audience.
6. Quotation and question.
7. Anecdote.
8. Quotation.

9. Startling statement.

10. Statistics.

All of these suggestions are illustrated in the following introductions from actual speeches.

Reference to the Occasion and Sponsor

Good afternoon. It's a pleasure to be here today. And it's especially appropriate that the YWCA should be sponsoring this seminar on civic responsibility and the corporate woman. Few organizations have put themselves on the line quite the way the "Y" has in its concern to provide equal opportunities for growth and development to everyone.

Looking back through history, whenever there's been an important women's issue, or relevant needs to be addressed, the "Y" has been there. This includes being in the forefront in initiating programs for women returning to the labor market after absences of many years; offering career-oriented workshops for teenagers; and using "Y" buildings which were formerly dormitories as shelters for battered women or as senior citizen centers.[2]

Reference to the Audience

Madam Chairman, Distinguished Guests, Ladies and Gentlemen. Thank you for that kind introduction. It is indeed an honour for me to have been invited to address the Empire Club of Canada. Before I begin my prepared text, I'd like to ask all war veterans in the audience to please stand up at their places, and remain standing.

Now, would everyone who has ever taken a Red Cross First Aid or Water Safety course please stand.

Would those who have ever volunteered for the Red Cross, are Red Cross employees or have ever made a donation to a Red Cross international appeal, a local Red Cross or United Way campaign please join those already standing.

---

2. Mary M. Gates, "The Changing Role of Women in Voluntarism: Individual Growth and Worth," speech delivered to the YWCA, Seattle, Washington, 27 February 1981.

And finally, of those still seated, if you have ever donated blood or received a blood transfusion, would you also please stand?

Ladies and Gentlemen, it gives me great pleasure as Secretary General to dedicate my presentation to the constituents of the Red Cross. Please be seated.[3]

Reference to the Speaker

I did not want to come to Los Angeles to give this lecture for many reasons. I am neither a philosopher nor a political activist. However, because of the heated debate between biomedical scientists and antivivisectionists, I felt an obligation to speak on behalf of the right of the incurably ill to hope for cures or relief from suffering through research using animals. I am crippled—by paraplegia—which today is incurable. Those of us who have an incurable disease or have permanently crippling injuries can only hope for a cure through research. Much of this experimental work will require the use of animals, and accordingly, we must find some compromise that defends both human rights and animal welfare. In the determination of a compromise between the reduction of human suffering and the violation of animals' welfare, which at times includes causing pain or discomfort, I unequivocally choose to reduce human suffering.[4]

Reference to Literature

Thank you for this chance to keynote Kent State's honors week events. We gather this week to recognize academic achievement. Oddly, the theme of these proceedings is the approach of 1984, the year George Orwell made a metaphor for totalitarianism. I say "oddly" because the central feature of Orwell's *1984* was the mass mind—whole populations thinking in state-imposed uniformity. Such uniformity strikes me as the antithesis of the individual intellectual excellence that we gather to honor this week, the excellence that Rene Descartes celebrated in saying, "I think, therefore I am."[5]

---

3. George B. Webber, "The Red Cross—Our Path into the 21st Century," speech delivered to the Empire Club of Canada, Toronto, Ontario, Canada, 19 February 1987.

4. Dennis M. Feeney, "Human Rights and Animal Welfare," *American Psychologist*, (June 1987): 593–94.

5. Alton W. Whitehouse, Jr., "The Misinformation Society: Renewing Our Commitment to the Power of Education," speech delivered at Kent State University Honors Week, Kent, Ohio, 20 April 1981.

Questions to the Audience

Why are we here to discuss the theme "Rethinking the American Economy"? Why are we perplexed? Doesn't our evident desire to "rethink the economy" indicate a form of dissatisfaction? Furthermore, if the economy we have is not satisfactory, how should we change it? What sort of an economy do we want? How would it differ from what we now have?[6]

Quotation and Question

Speaking as "Poor Richard," Benjamin Franklin once asked, "Who is wise?" His answer, as usual, was both definitive and provocative:

Who is wise?

He that learns from everyone.

He that governs his passions.

He that is content.

Nobody.[7]

Anecdote

Before starting my talk, I have a humorous story about diplomacy, which is my subject today. Just after the Russo-Japanese War in 1905–06, Admiral Togo, who had defeated the Imperial Russian fleet at the Tsushima Straits, visited Washington, D.C. The Secretary of State, William Jennings Bryan, did not drink. This posed a problem for the festivities. Bryan, a real diplomat, rose to the occasion. He stood up to toast Admiral Togo and declared: "Admiral, you have won a great victory on water, and therefore I will toast you with water. When you win a similar victory on champagne, I will toast you with champagne."[8]

---

6. Robert H. Edmonds, "Appropriate Economics: The Goals of Zero Inflation and Full Employment," speech delivered at Monterey Peninsula College, Monterey, California, 17 May 1981.

7. Ronald Roskers, "Who is Wise? To Learn About Caring," speech delivered at Commencement at the University of Nebraska, Lincoln, Nebraska, 9 May 1981.

8. Ramon H. Myers, "Options for American Foreign Policy in the 1980s: East Asia," speech delivered before the Inland Southern California World Affairs Council Seminar, Riverside, California, 14 November 1980.

Quotation

In the waning days of his exciting, productive life, Samuel Eliot Morison urged us to face the future resolutely and to adapt boldly to a world in which unsettling change was an ever-present reality. "Have faith," he exhorted. "Hang on! In human affairs there is no harbor, no rest short of the grave. We are forever sailing forth afresh across new and stormy seas, or into outer space."[9]

Startling Statement

Ladies and Gentlemen: The security of corporations is seriously threatened by the growing incidence of white collar crime. It's a major national problem. Right now, at this moment while you're listening to me, some 60 to 65 percent of the companies you represent are being ripped off. And I'm being generous, not sensational.

White collar crime, excluding computer and industrial espionage crimes, currently costs this country nearly $70 billion a year! And that's only a guesstimate. It has become a high priority with local law enforcement agencies in the country, and ranks as one of the three top programs for the FBI. The Assistant Director of the FBI's Criminal Investigative Division recently reported that there are almost 16,000 white collar crimes—including 1,100 cases of public corruption—now pending nationwide.

The new emphasis is proving effective. Last year the FBI recorded more than 3,000 convictions, recovered $60 million, and prevented almost $1 billion in losses. But white collar crimes are increasing almost as fast as the efforts to combat them.[10]

Statistics

Mr. President, Mr. Speaker, fellow delegates, colleagues and friends: I stand before you today not only as your president-elect, but also as a dean and as a professor. As a professor, I am programmed, once started, to speak for fifty-five minutes. However, I have been

---

9. Elliot L. Richardson, "National Security: The Law of the Sea," speech delivered at the launching of the *USS Samuel E. Morison*, Bath, Maine, 14 July 1979.

10. Herschell Britton, "The Serious Threats of White Collar Crime: What Can You Do?," speech delivered to the Executives Club of Chicago, Chicago, Illinois, 14 November 1980.

reminded that the story of the creation of the world is told in Genesis in 400 words, that the world's greatest moral code, the Ten Commandments, contains only 297 words, that Lincoln's immortal Gettysburg Address is but 266 words in length and that the Declaration of Independence required but 1,321 words to set up for the world a new concept of freedom. I think I get the point.[11]

THE CONCLUSION OF YOUR TALK

With your main discussion and introduction ready to go, you should be all set to work out a conclusion. Two cautions are in order: (1) A conclusion should not drag on and on. (2) It should not contain any new material.

Here are some ideas to incorporate in your conclusion:

1. A summary of key ideas.
2. A prediction.
3. A quotation, either emotional or factual.
4. A quotation from literature.
5. A quotation from an authority.
6. An anecdote or question, or both.

All of these suggestions are illustrated in the following conclusions from actual speeches.

A Summary of Key Ideas

In conclusion, I feel sure that these programs of communication are proving of great benefit to both managers and employees. Even if they were expensive, *which they are not*, it would still be worth it. *The cost of economic ignorance would be much, much greater.* After all, better communication reaps the following benefits for a corporation:

—Employees know decisions and the reasons for them
—Less misunderstandings occur

---

11. C. John Tupper, "A New American Revolution: 'Do Your Own Thing vs. Guaranteeism,' " speech delivered before the California Medical Association, Los Angeles, California, 12 March 1979.

—The possibility of cooperation with change is greatly increased
—The damaging effects of rumor are lessened
—The role of management is reinforced

Managers, union leaders and rank-and-file employees readily understand the need for these improvements in their relationships. And, as the Japanese have proved, whether working with their own nationals, or American or Australian workers, employee understanding and involvement works for everybody's benefit. Certainly we are experiencing these benefits in some corporations in Australia.

Enterprise Australia is proud to have contributed toward these advancements in employee communication.[12]

A Prediction

Where does this leave us? I wish I could conclude with a flourish, evoking some grand Tofflerian vision of accelerating future and captivating you with images of exotic technology and effortless movement in the city of tomorrow.

In reality, I believe, we will evolve along a more conventional and prosaic trajectory. Barring some cataclysmic developments on the energy front, the automobile is likely to remain the preferred means of transportation of most Americans well into the next century— although, as we have noted, it will be a vehicle vastly different in design and performance. At the same time, public transportation— or, I should say, collective transportation—will assume a much more significant role in our daily lives. Transit of tomorrow will have more varied forms and utilize a wider range of vehicles, service modes, and operating arrangements, as it tries to serve a broader, more differentiated market.

While public transportation will tend to become more flexible and personalized, the automobile will . . .

Rail transit of the surface variety may . . .

Finally, pedestrians will have regained some of the territory they lost to the automobile during the last fifty years, as cities and suburbs impose more stringent requirements on the use of cars in congested centers and residential neighborhoods.

---

12. J. T. Keavney, "Australia: Turning Away from Socialism," speech delivered to the Board of Trustees of the American Economic Foundation, New York City, New York, 19 January 1981.

And—oh yes—we will still have rush-hour traffic and potholes. They will be there to remind us of the good old days back in the late 1980s, when gasoline was still only one dollar a gallon, when parking in government buildings was still free, and when one could still afford the luxury of driving to work in one's own automobile.[13]

A Quotation, Either Emotional or Factual

In conclusion, we need to be reminded of the famous words of the Protestant minister who recounted the prevailing attitude during the Holocaust:

". . . They came first for the Communists, and I didn't
   speak up because I wasn't a Communist.
Then they came for the Jews,
   and I didn't speak up because I wasn't a Jew.
Then they came for the trade unionists,
   and I didn't speak up because I wasn't a trade unionist.
Then they came for the Catholics,
   and I didn't speak up because I was a Protestant.
Then they came for me.
   and by that time no one was left to speak."

Thank you.[14]

A Quotation from Literature

The late George Bernard Shaw once wrote, "Nothing is worth doing unless the consequences could be serious."

By that or any other measure, this is a job worth doing—for this nation's older citizens, for the business community, and for our nation itself.[15]

---

13. C. Kenneth Ovski, "Urban Transportation: A Profile of the Future," speech delivered at the NASA Colloquium on Profiles of the Future, Washington, DC, 11 September 1979.

14. R. Y. Woodhouse, "Equality Faces a Dangerous Decade: Defend Our Beliefs and Speak Out," speech delivered at the Naval Supply Systems Command Human Resource Management Conference, Seattle, Washington, 18 November 1980.

15. M. H. Beach, "Business and the Graying of America: Opportunities for Older People," speech delivered before the National Council on the Aging Annual Conference, Nashville, Tennessee, 29 March 1981.

You might conclude with a prediction for the future.

A Quotation from an Authority

I want to conclude my talk by quoting in its entirety a brief but, I think, superb exposition of what I've been trying to say. The author is Leo Rosten, and, believe it or not, I once worked with him too. He called his little essay *The Power of Words*, and it goes like this:

"They sing. They hurt. They teach. They sanctify. They were man's first immeasurable feat of magic. They liberated us from ignorance and our barbarous past. For without these marvelous scribbles which build letters into words, words into sentences, sentences into systems and sciences and creeds, man would be forever confined to the self-isolated prison of the scuttlefish or the chimpanzee. 'A picture is worth 10,000 words,' goes the timeworn Chinese maxim. 'But,' one writer tartly said, 'it takes words to say that.' We live by words: Love, Truth, God. We fight for words: Freedom, Country, Fame. We die for words: Liberty, Glory, Honor. They bestow the priceless gift of articulateness on our minds and hearts—from 'Mama' to 'infinity.' And the men who truly shape our destiny, the giants who teach us, inspire us, lead us to deeds of immortality, are those who use words with clarity, grandeur and passion. Socrates, Jesus, Luther, Lincoln, Churchill.''

The power of words . . .[16]

An Anecdote or Question, or Both

And I'll close with a true story to illustrate how we *are* set apart and what our values really are. During the days of the Soviet triumph with their first Sputnik, a grade school class in Russia was discussing that remarkable feat—eclipsing the whole world in scientific genius. The teacher asked the class if they were thrilled with the prospect of a Russian satellite probing space and perhaps some day landing a Russian on the moon.

The class smiled with pride and agreed it would be a great achievement to go to the moon. But one thoughtful student broke the silence and spoke a different kind of response.

"Yes, it would be wonderful to go to the moon,'' he said. "But I would like to know—when may we go to Vienna?''[17]

THE TITLE OF YOUR TALK

Just as every book has a title and every newspaper story a headline, so every talk should have a title. Your title is an ad, a billboard for your speech. And audiences generally appreciate knowing immediately what they are about to hear rather than waiting to find out your message. If you try to imagine a movie without a title, you can appreciate the importance of a title for your talk.

Usually, the most propitious time to consider a title is after you've developed the main ideas of your speech. It's possible, however,

---

16. Melvin J. Grayson, "The Last Best Hope: Words,'' speech delivered to the Society of Consumer Affairs Professionals in Business, New York, New York, 3 April 1981.

17. Harvey C. Jacobs, "Finding Your Way Through the Woods: It's a Lifelong Challenge,'' speech delivered at the Defense Information School, Fort Benjamin Harrison, Indianapolis, Indiana, 24 January 1981.

that during the process of building the introduction, body, and conclusion of your talk, a striking title may suddenly appear, seemingly out of nowhere. If it does, you're lucky. If it doesn't, try to create one that meets these criteria:

1. It should be provocative enough to pique your listeners' interest.
2. It should be short and simple, say from three to ten words.
3. It should indicate the purpose and content of your talk.

The following are titles from talks printed in the journal *Vital Speeches* as well as from talks given by various students. These titles are listed with their chief traits.

Trait	Title
Questions	"Who's Got the Energy?" "Where Is This Black Progress?" "What Can American Industry Learn from the Japanese?"
A new twist on a book title	"Braving a New World"
A new twist on an ad slogan	"Pave Now, Pay Later" "Come to Where the Favor Is. Come to High Tech Country."
Fairy tale opener	"Once Upon a Time"
A sentence	"A Humanist Views the World Hunger Problem." "Despite Everything We Have Reason for Confidence."
Startling statements	"Here Comes World War III" "Raising Corn and Beans and Hell" "Higher Education Is a Fraud"
Alliteration	"Women and Work" "Change and Challenge" "Communication and Credibility"
Brevity	"Welcome Home" (Pres. Reagan to former Iranian prisoners) "What Now?"
An unusual statement	"Can't Nobody Here Use This Language?" "Almost Nobody Writes Silence Anymore" "How the Truth Becomes a Lie"

Words that rhyme	"Town and Gown" "Taxation Without Representation" "TV's Jiggle and Wiggle"
Words from a foreign language	"Whatever Happened to Ceteris Paribus?"
A play on words	"Today's Dollar Doesn't Make Much Cents" "How Secure Is Our Social Security?" "If You Don't Think *Die*ting Is Serious Business—What Do Its First Three Letters Spell?"

TRANSITIONS, OR CONNECTING LINKS

Just as a brick wall needs cement to keep it intact, a speech needs something to hold it together. That "something" is **transitions**—statements, questions, or phrases that connect the introduction to the body and the body to the conclusion. Transitions also show the relationships between ideas.

You use transitions in daily communication, but when you speak to a group, you may tend to forget them. Don't. They help your listeners follow your train of thought and, thus, make your communication task easier. The following is a list of some transitional phrases and the conditions that call for their use:

To indicate	Use these transitions
Place	Adjacent to, on the opposite side, diagonally across, diametrically opposite
Time	After a few hours, meanwhile, in the meantime, afterward, immediately, earlier, later, then
Purpose	For this reason, to this end, with this goal
Concession	Of course, to be sure, naturally
Comparison and contrast	On the other hand, nevertheless, on the contrary, in contrast, in the same way, conversely, however, in like manner, similarly, whereas
Summary or repetition	In other words, to review briefly, in short, on the whole, to sum up, as previously noted, here again, in summary, in brief, if I may repeat
Explanation	For example, in particular, more specifically

Addition	Furthermore, in the second place, besides, more-over, again, in addition, equally important, finally, also
Cause or result	On that account, therefore, as a result, thereupon, for this reason, consequently, accordingly, under these conditions, hence
Conditions	Although, because, even though, since, if, unless, under these circumstances, nevertheless, otherwise, this being so

When you complete your introduction, the right connecting links can help you move smoothly into the body of your talk. The same principle applies when you cross over from the body to the conclusion. Remember, also, that asking a question or two can lead you and your listeners comfortably into the next phase of your speech.

To sum up, then, transitions afford you the means to "telegraph" to your audience that:

1. The introduction is over and you're swinging into the body.
2. The body is over and you're moving into the conclusion.
3. The conclusion is almost over and you're ready to answer questions or to sit down.

Now that we have covered outlines, the four parts of a talk, and transitions, we're ready to discuss the makeup of your listeners and your choice of the right words to communicate effectively with them, which we will do in Chapter 8.

Things to Discuss in Class

1. Give the class an example of a sentence outline and a topic outline. Explain why you prefer one over the other.

2. Find several speech titles you consider outstanding. Explain why you think so.

3. Write an outline for a short talk on any subject you could give in class. Don't forget the title.

4. Consult the journal *Vital Speeches* for an outstanding introduction and/or conclusion. Bring either one to class for discussion.

5. In your library, investigate several sources, such as *Vital Speeches*,

and bring to class some examples of the various ways that speakers arranged their main points during their talks.

6. Bring to class a short speech and prepare to point out its various transitional elements.

7. Select several general topics that you feel would make an interesting talk, and suggest at least six titles for each of the topics.

What Do You Remember from This Chapter?

1. Why should you outline your talk?

2. Describe the two principal types of outlines.

3. List a few characteristics of a good title.

4. What are the chief purposes of an introduction?

5. Explain the main parts of a speech.

6. Mention a few ways to prove your main points.

7. What elements should be present in a conclusion?

8. What are transitions and why should you use them?

9. What two cautions should you keep in mind regarding the conclusion of your talk?

10. Explain the difference between a main point and a subpoint.

Vitalize Your Vocabulary

Because thousands of English words are derived from Latin words, there's no question that the study of Latin would strengthen your English vocabulary, but you don't have to study that ancient language in order to benefit from it. To increase your word power, we suggest that you learn the meanings of dozens of Latin prefixes and hundreds of roots. By doing this, you'll improve your command of the English language in four ways: in speaking, writing, reading, and listening.

To get you moving, below are a few Latin prefixes, along with their meanings, and some sample English words:

Prefixes	Meanings	Sample words
Ambi	Both	Ambidextrous, ambiguous
Anti	Against, opposite	Antifreeze, antibiotic
Circum	Around, on all sides	Circumference, circumlocution
Equi	Equal	Equidistant, equilibrium
Intra, intro	Within	Intramural, intrastate, introvert
Sub	Under, beneath	Subcontract, subhuman, submarine
Super, supra	Above, over	Superhighway, supersonic, supernatural

Now let's do the same with some Latin roots:

Roots	Meanings	Sample words
Aqu	Water	Aquarium, aquatic, aqueduct
Aud, audit	Hear	Audio, audience, auditorium
Ben, bene	Good, well	Benefactor, benefit
Cid, cis	Cut, kill	Homicide, incision, suicide
Cred	Belief, trust	Credible, credit, creed
Flu, fluct	Flow	Fluctuate, influence
Leg	Law	Legal, legislate, legitimate
Medi	Middle	Medieval, mediocre, medium
Nov	New	Innovate, novelty, renovate
Tors, tort	Twist	Contortion, distort, torque
Viv	Life, lively	Vivacious, vivid

If some of these sample words are not clear to you, then poke your nose into that dust-covered dictionary.

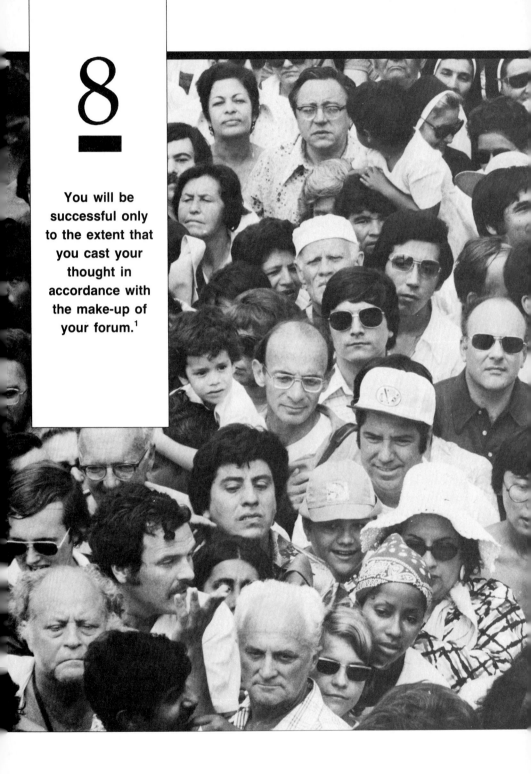

8

You will be successful only to the extent that you cast your thought in accordance with the make-up of your forum.[1]

Know Your Listeners and Speak Their Language

After reading and understanding this chapter, you should know:

- The importance of audience analysis.
- Some ways to research your audience.
- Some differences between oral and written communication.
- The differences between concrete and abstract words.
- The meanings of loaded words, clichés, slang, and vocalized pauses.
- How to use words that motivate people.

Chapter Digest

The words and sentences that flesh out your thoughts, feelings, and opinions critically influence your total impact on your audience. For that reason, audience analysis should rate top priority in preparing for any oral interpersonal situation. Several ideas are given to help you with that analysis.

---

1. Cicero, *Paradoxa Stoicorum* (46 B.C.).

Your career can be helped or hindered by the way you use words in speech. Some examples of the power of words are sprinkled throughout the chapter. Many different kinds of words are discussed: specific and abstract words, short and pretentious words, loaded words, clichés, and slang.

Next, oral communication and written communication are compared. They share traits, such as clarity, accuracy, and appropriateness, but you should always be aware of differences between the two methods.

As for sentences, some suggestions are advanced regarding their length, structure, and human warmth. Again, real-life examples spice up the text.

The chapter closes with several steps for developing your use of language to its full potential.

AUDIENCE ANALYSIS

Before you speak to any audience, you should learn as much about its members as possible. Only in that way can you best adapt the level of your language and the content of your talk to your listeners.

Where are you likely to speak? Certainly, in this class you'll give several talks, and since you know most, if not all, of the students, you should face no major problems in adapting your approach to them. Another speaking possibility exists in your workplace. For example, your department manager may ask you to explain and demonstrate a procedure to some fellow employees. Or she may select you to address your department on behalf of the local blood donor drive. In both speech situations—in class and on the job—you're familiar with your audience; you speak their language; you have things in common with them.

A third speaking possibility exists in any organization (social, cultural, athletic, and so on) that you belong to. You may be asked to speak at the next meeting or at the annual banquet. Here again, you know the people involved, their background, their education level, and their attitudes, and that's a tremendous advantage for you.

Since we're upbeat and positive in this course, we'll assume that you've given successful talks under all three circumstances, and with this course under your belt, you can do it again. Since good speakers are hard to find and word about them travels fast, suppose that one day you get an invitation to speak to an organization in which you don't know a soul. What do you do now? If you feel able to handle the topic you're asked to speak on, accept this rare challenge. Here's

Know your audience and speak their language.

where audience analysis comes into play. Be sure to ask the person who invited you for information on the members, information that encompasses a broad spectrum, such as in the following areas.

Age.   Are the members recent college graduates, senior citizens, or business executives in midcareer? Just remember, age exerts a powerful impact on people's attitudes, values, and motivations. Yes, they all speak English, but with differences based on occupation, education, and so on. Yes, they're Americans, but with different needs and interests. For example, back in the 1930s your grandparents may have been ecstatic over President Franklin D. Roosevelt and his New Deal: as senior citizens in the 1980s, they might have switched to Reagan republicanism, just as former President Reagan himself switched parties. Back in the 1930s they probably romanced to music of the big bands, and they still like it, but chances are that you prefer another type of music. Age does make a difference.

Sex.   If you're invited to speak to a women's or men's organization, you know the answer to this question at once. Quite often, however, audiences are mixed fairly evenly, although at times one sex may predominate. Let's say that you're to speak to a group of women.

In today's world, as opposed to fifteen or twenty years ago, women do just about everything that men do. They occupy high positions in business, government, education, and politics. They attend the same colleges as men do, including the service academies, and they participate in just about all sports. Yet, there are differences between men and women that you, as speaker, should make allowances for in your preparation. You would not, for example, use the same language at a meeting of Women in Management as you would with a contingent of Marines just back from a grueling three-month training mission in a sweltering insect-infested jungle. Nor would you use the same kind of anecdotes to make points.

Interest in topic. Are the members of the organization interested in the topic or are they required to attend regardless of their interest? If the latter is true, what types of material will most likely pique their curiosity?

Attitude toward topic. Do they have prejudices that will interfere with their listening or understanding? Are they sympathetic? If so, you should prepare material that will capitalize on that positive attitude.

Knowledge of topic. The level of understanding possessed by the audience will largely determine the intellectual level of your talk. If the listeners know little, you should start with basics. If they know the basics, you should try to carry them at least a few steps beyond their current status.

Education. As you prepare your talk, keep two depressing facts in mind:

- The average adult in America has but slightly more than a high-school education.
- Four out of every ten adults have not graduated from high school.[2]

Generally, a talk on tax shelter investments to assembly-line auto workers should be geared at a lower level than the same talk given to computer analysts. Both groups probably know little about such

---

2. Leon Fletcher, *How to Speak Like a Pro* (New York: Ballantine Books, 1983), 27.

investments, but the computer analysts, assuming they are better educated, are likely to grasp complex issues faster.

Cultural interests.   Do members of your prospective audience spend evenings watching TV movies and drinking beer at a local tavern, or do they read the Harvard Classics and attend concerts of Beethoven and Mozart? Do they play bingo and 21, or do they pursue the intriguing intricacies of contract bridge and chess? Answers to these questions can help you choose the most appropriate material and language for your audience. Your choices can be crucial in determining the success or failure of your presentation.

Occupation.   If, for instance, many members of your audience work in a particular field, say electronics, you'd be wise to include some references to that specialty. More often, however, audiences tend to represent a variety of occupations, and that fact rings a warning bell to you to make allowance for many differences among people. White-collar workers usually differ in attitude and interests from blue-collar workers. Business employees and business owners have different values on many issues. Civil servants may well react differently from military personnel. A line of reasoning may succeed with one occupational group and fail with another. All of these differences represent a challenge to you.

Economic status.   People's feelings and attitudes toward government policies, political parties, labor unions, and current happenings are deeply colored by their economic status. High-income people are usually interested in stock market activities and tax legislation. Low-income people, on the other hand, are more concerned about having enough to live on and a roof over their heads. You would talk to people at these two economic levels in different ways.

Religious affiliation.   If you're not familiar with the religious beliefs held by members of the audience, you may say something that could offend some of them. Do most of them belong to the same religion, or do they belong to all three of the major religions in the United States? Don't forget that Protestants, Catholics, and Jews may have different attitudes toward such issues as divorce, abortion, and the Middle East.

Ethnicity.   There are many ethnic groups in the United States, the largest ones being: black Americans, about 11 percent of the population;

Irish-Americans, about 6.5 percent; Spanish-Americans (Cubans, Mexicans, Puerto Ricans), about 5 percent; Italian-Americans, about 3.5 percent; Jewish-Americans, about 2.9 percent; and Slavic-Americans, about 2.5 percent.[3]

If you're invited to speak to audience members from a particular ethnic group, you should try to get acquainted with its history, values, motivations, and achievements. Your audience will appreciate your efforts.

As we suggested at the outset of this discussion on audience analysis, you should be able to get most of the needed information from the person who invited you or from officers of the organization concerned.

LANGUAGE AND YOUR FUTURE

You can have a powerful delivery, an expressive voice, an attractive appearance, and thorough knowledge of your subject, but if your words are poorly chosen, your speech will fail to communicate.

With the right words, you can communicate your thoughts, your feelings, and your emotions. With the right words you can teach people, give them understanding, entertain them, persuade them to change attitudes, and even persuade them to do your bidding. But before you can do any of that, you should learn as much as possible about words.

Words are double-edged tools of communication that can both help you and hurt you. They can make you happy or miserable; they can inspire you or depress you; they can propel you toward a full, useful life; or they can hinder your progress. Whoever said, "Sticks and stones may break my bones, but words will never hurt me" lived in a world of fantasy, not in the real world of men and women, of love and hate, of success and failure, of hope and despair, of honesty and crookedness.

In the 1976 Democratic presidential primaries, Governor Jimmy Carter said, "I see nothing wrong with ethnic purity being maintained" (in the suburbs). The expression "ethnic purity" outraged millions

---

3. Bert E. Bradley, *Fundamentals of Speech Communication*, 4/e (Dubuque, IA: Wm. C. Brown Publishers, 1984), 96.

"Sorry, we don't need no grammar books."

of black and liberal voters, and it shook up his smoothly functioning campaign. Carter later apologized for that blunder.

Eight years earlier, a similar incident occurred in the Republican presidential primaries. This time, however, it ended in a shambles for George Romney, governor of Michigan and a powerful candidate. Powerful, that is, until he said that the White House had "brainwashed" him regarding Vietnam. That one word torpedoed Romney's campaign for the nomination, because anyone who could be brainwashed is not shrewd enough or strong enough to be President of the United States.

The way you use words will leave an indelible impression on people's minds. From your words, people will form opinions of your education, intelligence, and character, as well as your economic and social status. You may be highly intelligent, but if you trample on the English language, most bright, educated listeners will write you off as someone who's not going anywhere, someone who's a loser.

Mangling the language will place you in a predicament similar to that faced by Commodore Cornelius Vanderbilt, a nineteenth-century American shipping and railroad tycoon. Because he had little formal education, he was embarrassed when he had to deal with "all them British lords. I know I am smarter than they are," he said, "but they sound smarter." Tape-record yourself sometime, and evaluate how your language sounds.

Before discussing words and their ways, let's first compare the oral with the written word because some words are better suited for speaking and others are better suited for writing.

SIMILARITIES AND DIFFERENCES BETWEEN ORAL AND WRITTEN COMMUNICATION

There are many differences between communicating in written and spoken words—one to one or one to many. Because speaking is face to face and personal, it is much more direct than writing. Hand and body gestures, facial expressions, and vocal variety help greatly to support face-to-face communication. It is also reinforced by instant feedback from listeners in the form of smiles, frowns, applause, catcalls, clenched fists, and so on. An alert speaker who is sensitive to feedback can "shift gears" and adapt to changing circumstances.

Writing, however, depends solely on words and punctuation to deliver the message. There are no gestures and no voice, and if there is any feedback, it takes time to reach the writer.

Good talking is wordy, repetitive, and far less structured than efficient writing. (Perhaps that's why so many more people find talking well much easier than writing well.) A good speech, reproduced word for word on paper, usually does not read well because it rambles and repeats words and thoughts. It is not nearly as disciplined and organized as good writing.

Effective talking is aimed at people's minds and hearts through their ears, and ears prefer short, direct, conversational sentences. Long, involved sentences are acceptable in writing for two reasons: (1) The eye can absorb many more words in an instant than the ear can hear. (2) If a reader stumbles on a marathon sentence, she can read it again. Not so with spoken words—once uttered they're gone, especially in a speech. If a listener misses a sentence, both she and the speaker have lost part of the message; there is no going back, except perhaps during the question-and-answer period. In a conversation, of course, the listener can ask the speaker to repeat. Table 8.1 summarizes and offers insight into the differences between speaking and writing.

Now let's focus on three standards that apply equally to talking and writing—clarity, accuracy, and appropriateness.

Clarity

If the audience doesn't understand the message instantly, then the speaker has, to some extent, failed. Thus, every possible measure must be taken to ensure that all your words and thoughts are perfectly clear to the audience.

Throughout your talk, words are your prime means for helping your audience understand your message. And to harness the profound power of words, you should develop a lifelong habit of using a dictionary and a thesaurus. If you do not exploit these resources, you will fail to achieve your full potential as a speaker and conversationalist.

Another device that will help you achieve clarity in your talk is a summary. If your talk consists of three well-researched major points, list those points in your introduction so your audience will know at once what ground you will cover. Discuss them in depth, summarize them at the end of your talk, and emphasize any conclusions that they lead to; an example of such an ending is given in Chapter 7.

Another aid to clarity is the use of transitions—words that indicate the connections between ideas—which show whether you are continuing in the same vein or are about to shift to another topic. (Transitions are covered in more detail in Chapter 7 and many are tabulated there.)

A common speaking fault is failing to define technical terms, or jargon. For example, one student gave what could have been an interesting talk on his profitable hobby. He is a disc jockey and conducts record hops for colleges and various organizations. During his presentation he frequently used esoteric terminology like pots, cans, fade, segue, equalizer, dBs, mixer, and control board. As a result, very few students understood what he was talking about.

Most hobbies, professions, trades, and sports have their own language, vernacular, shop talk, or jargon. Whether your subject is plumbing, carpentry, auto mechanics, sports, journalism, cooking,

Table 8.1
Linguistic Differences Between Speaking and Writing

Speaking	Writing
Wordy, repetitive	Concise, seldom repetitive
Tends to wander around topic	Better organized, sticks to topic, more relevant
Sentence length—roughly 5 to 20 words	Sentences usually longer
Sentence structure—usually simple S-V-O (subject-verb-object) sequence	More compound, complex, compound-complex sentences
Style—often informal; may be spiced with slang, contractions, sentence fragments	More formal style—very little slang, if any; few contractions and sentence fragments, if any
Depends heavily on personal pronouns—*we, us you they, them, I, me*	Depends less on personal pronouns
Is reinforced with facial and vocal expressions and hand, arm, body gestures	Depends on words and punctuation to get message across; format or layout may help
Feedback—usually instantaneous	Feedback may take days, weeks, or longer
Transitions—verbal are same as in writing; pauses and change in body position can signify a new topic coming up	Verbal transitions—same as speaking
Can be marred with vocalized pauses—*er, ah, like, ya know*	No equivalent distractions
Planned strategic pauses can produce a powerful effect	No verbal equivalent
Words—uses more concrete words and shorter words	Tends to be more abstract and polysyllabic
Tends to repeat and restate more	

ceramics, or law, you must realize that the audience may not be familiar with your subject. You should, therefore, be prepared to explain uncommon terms and to ask if they understand your language.

Confucius, the Chinese philosopher, said it all 2400 years ago: "In language clearness is everything."

Accuracy

As a conscientious speaker, you must see to it that your information is as current and as accurate as research can make it. The surest way for you to damage your credibility is to spew forth misinformation or outdated information.

How many times have you seen a story, a name, an important fact, or a charge against someone retracted in newspapers? Unfortunately, the damage was done when the misinformation first appeared in print. Such unwarranted embarrassment and mental anguish could have been avoided if someone had taken the time to recheck the information. If your talk is on a current or crucial topic, do your homework and arm yourself with quotations and sources to fortify your facts.

Appropriateness

In addition to being precise, your language should also be suitable to the subject, audience, and occasion. For example, a speaker who's addressing a Parent-Teacher Association should avoid the statistical and psychological jargon of advanced educational researchers. By the same token, she should not indulge in teenage slang. Any speaker worth her salt will analyze her audience first and adapt her language accordingly. (See Chapter 12 and the introduction to this chapter.)

COMMAND OF THE LANGUAGE

We are concerned here with two goals—to capture and condense some insights and practices of the best oral communicators. From them we can learn a great deal about using words to get results. What follows is not the Ten Commandments on using language, but, rather, guidelines or suggestions on how to generate maximum power in your command of the language.

Concrete, Specific Words Versus Abstract Words

For informative as well as persuasive speaking, there's no question that **concrete,** specific words carry a message most effectively. Concrete words pertain to tangible things—objects that we can see. The meanings of such words should be easily understood and leave little room for personal interpretation. Obviously, the more concrete words you use, the better your chances will be that the listener will comprehend your intended message exactly.

If **parallel construction** can be built into a sentence of such words, the emotional impact can be intensified. Here are two statements composed of concrete, specific, vivid words strengthened and immortalized with parallel construction. In 1933 President Franklin D. Roosevelt said to the Depression-battered American people:

> I see one-third of a nation ill-housed, ill-clad, ill-nourished.

Early in World War II, Prime Minister Winston Churchill declared to the English people, staggering under military setbacks and facing conquest by Hitler's Germany:

> . . . we shall fight on the beaches, we shall fight on the landing grounds, we shall fight in the fields and on the streets, we shall fight in the hills; we shall never surrender.

Note the striking force of the parallel construction in that sentence. Note that the words are short and specific and that they permit instant understanding. Not even one abstract, nebulous word emasculates those sentences.

Here are some examples of concrete, specific words:

Flood	Traffic jam	Rubbish
Airplane	Parking ticket	Desk
Gun	Money	Trees
Tax bill	Rain	Nuclear plant
Mansion	Baby	Daycare center

Democracy—whose?

You cannot, of course, avoid **abstract words** in public speaking. Sometimes they're necessary and serve a worthwhile purpose, but remember that they're subject to various interpretations and arguments depending on people's backgrounds, religions, education, nationality, and so on. For example, when you speak of our democracy, you mean a particular kind of government. When citizens of the German Democratic Republic (East Germany) speak of democracy, they mean another kind of government. Yet, we and they are both using the same word—*democracy.*

Abstract words pertain to the intangible things, such as ideas and concepts which cannot be seen. Here are some examples:

Freedom	Fascism	Morality
Liberty	Justice	Character
Democracy	Patriotism	Humility
Religion	Honesty	Integrity
Philosophy	Ideology	Science

Short, Simple Words Versus Long, Pretentious Words

Again, for the purpose of informing your listeners, the simple, one- or two-syllable words are usually better suited. A classic example of using such words is Lincoln's Gettysburg Address. He delivered it not to inform people but to inspire them. Of its 266 words, 195 consist of one syllable.

Yet, some audiences expect longer, more elegant words. The more you know about your audience, the better you can judge what kinds of words to use. Table 8.2 provides a sample listing of what some people refer to as pompous and pretentious words, together with their simple, direct equivalents.

A glaring example of pompous, inappropriate language was given by the former U.S. ambassador to Great Britain, Walter H. Annenberg, when he was presented to Queen Elizabeth. She asked him a simple

Table 8.2
Comparison of Words with Similar Basic Meanings

Showy, polysyllabic words	Short, direct equivalents
Ablution	Washing
Ameliorate	Improve
Assimilate	Absorb, digest
Cognizant of	Aware of
Conflagration	Fire
Consolidate	Unite, combine
Contiguous with	Touching
Delineate	Describe
Designation	Name
Effectuate	Carry out
Enumerate	Count, list
Facilitate	Make easy, simplify
Expedite	Speed up
Incombustible	Fireproof
Initiate, institute	Begin, start
Innocuous	Harmless
Modification	Change
Optimum	Best
Progenitor	Forerunner
Subsequent to	Later, next
Termination	End

question about his housing arrangements and he replied: "We are in the ambassadorial residence subject, of course, to some of the discomfiture as a result of the need for elements of refurbishing and rehabilitation." He might have said, "We're redecorating now so the house is a bit messy."[4]

Equally verbose and pedantic is the following letter from a Houston, Texas, high-school principal to a student's father:

> Our school's cross-graded, multi-ethnic, individualized learning program is designed to enhance the concept of an open-ended learning program with emphasis on a continuum of multi-ethnic, academically enriched learning using the identified intellectually gifted child as the agent or director of his own learning.
>
> Major emphasis is on cross-graded, multi-ethnic learning with the main objective being to learn respect for the uniqueness of a person.

The parent wrote the principal:

> I have a college degree, speak two foreign languages and four Indian dialects, have been to a number of county fairs and three goat ropings, but I haven't the faintest idea as to what the hell you are talking about. Do you?[5]

Loaded Words

Some words that concern race, religion, and politics can provoke heated and sometimes overpowering reactions. Loaded words can either infuriate or humiliate people, and they can induce people to commit irrational acts. Loaded words are like a loaded gun; they can cause devastating damage. Here are examples of words that spell potential *danger* to you and to others:

Race or religion

Whitey	Uncle Tom
Honky	Wasp
Racist	Hebe
Nigger	Kike
Oreo	Fish-eater

---

4. Barbara Walters, *How to Talk with Practically Anybody About Practically Anything* (Garden City, NY: Doubleday, 1970), 136.

5. *Boston Sunday Herald American*, 6 February 1977, 23.

"Conflagration!"

Nationality

Gringo	Hun
Spic	Polack
Harp	Slant-eyes
Wop	Chink
Dago	Jap
Frog	

Political philosophy

Radical	Nazi
Anarchist	Fascist
Revolutionary	Communist
Imperialist	Right wing
Reactionary	Left wing

Whereas loaded words are extreme in their potential for trouble, there are other words and their synonyms that can either be complimentary or belittling. Here are some examples:

Complimentary	Belittling
Slender	Skinny
Inexpensive	Cheap
Imported	Foreign
Prudent	Stingy
Pre-owned	Used
Cocktail lounge	Bar
Discriminating	Finicky
Deliberate	Indecisive
Courageous	Reckless
Overweight	Fat

In some situations your choice of words can either make or break you. Think before you speak.

Clichés

Clichés are expressions that have been used so often that they have become meaningless. Since they reflect a sparse vocabulary and a pallid imagination, avoid them "at all costs." Below are a few examples:

Tough as nails	Goes without saying
Leave no stone unturned	By leaps and bounds
Last but not least	Lean over backward
In the final analysis	Equal to the occasion
Sweet as honey	Slept like a log

Slang

The use of slang depends largely on the occasion of your talk and on the relationship between you and the audience. At a formal or even semiformal affair, slang would violate good taste even if you know most of the guests. In any case, it's important to resist the temptation to overuse slang; too much of it will degrade any talk.

PUTTING WORDS INTO SENTENCES

In this text, the subject of sentences received some attention in the comparison of oral and written styles. What else need be said about spoken sentences? By all means, they should be of different lengths, mostly short, say from five to twenty words. These figures are merely estimates that stress the vital importance of short, conversational sentences.

Varied structure is another vital aspect. Try to avoid composing all of your sentences in the same form. More than half of your sentences can follow the conventional *subject-verb-object* pattern, but if *all* of them are structured like that, you may lull your listeners to sleep.

In his immortal Gettysburg Address, Abraham Lincoln pointed up a third valuable lesson, that of the personal, human approach. Even though the occasion was most solemn, the dedication of a national cemetery, he touched his listeners with noble ideas clothed in personal pronouns and nouns in every sentence: ". . . our fathers . . . we . . . us . . . they . . . the brave men, living and dead, who struggled here . . . of the people, by the people, for the people . . ." These words breathe life and humanity into communication; use them.

Your thoughts and the way you phrase them are often influenced by context—by surrounding circumstances—and by events preceding your talk. A relevant example is the attention-getting introduction often used by Jimmy Carter in the 1976 Democratic presidential primary campaign. In 1976, Watergate, one of the worst political scandals in U.S. history, dominated American newscasts and newspapers, and the principal perpetrators of that shame were mainly lawyers based in Washington, D.C. Here are the opening remarks of many of Carter's campaign speeches:

> Hi, I'm Jimmy Carter and I'm running for President. I am not a lawyer. And I am not from Washington, D.C.

Also, in his vote-winning speeches Carter said something that struck a responsive chord among Americans wearied and angered by deceit in high office:

> I will not lie to you.

He communicated—and the voters sent him to the White House. Short, personal sentences can be very convincing.

One more outstanding introduction comes to mind: the one used occasionally by President Harry S. Truman in the nip-and-tuck presidential campaign of 1948. The pollsters tabbed him as a loser to Republican nominee Thomas E. Dewey, governor of New York. Here is Truman's no-nonsense, no-doubletalk introduction:

> My name is Truman, I'm President of the United States, and I'm trying to keep my job.

He communicated—and the voters sent him back to the White House.

A third example of a blockbusting statement was President Reagan's answer regarding the very sensitive issue of age. During the second TV debate with Walter Mondale, in reply to a question referring to his ability to keep up with the demanding schedule of his office (an obvious attempt to introduce the age question), President Reagan confidently declared:

> And I want you to know that I will not make age an issue of this campaign. I am not going to exploit for political purposes my opponent's youth and inexperience.[6]

He communicated—and the voters sent him back to the White House.

Things to Discuss in Class

1. Tell the class about a recent experience in which you felt that the speaker either talked over the heads of or talked down to the audience.

2. Give a few examples of the power of words and how they've affected people's lives.

3. Relate to the class an experience in which a speaker received negative treatment from the audience due to insufficient audience analysis prior to the presentation.

4. Identify several speakers (professionals on TV or radio, professors, and so on) whom you greatly admire because of their ability to successfully communicate with an audience and explain why you admire them.

---

6. *Newsweek*, November/December 1984, special issue, 109.

5. Try to think of several people in public life who are excellent communicators and some who are not. Prepare to discuss them in class.

6. Try to think of a speaker who is successful as a communicator because he or she uses a large number of concrete words. Prepare to discuss them in class and list several examples.

What Do You Remember from This Chapter?

1. Explain the importance of researching and analyzing an audience.

2. Explain several differences between oral and written communication.

3. What types of words carry the message most effectively in informative speaking?

4. What is a danger in using abstract words in communication?

5. Explain three ways to research an audience effectively.

6. List several ingredients critical to achieving clarity in your talk.

7. Give five examples each of abstract and concrete words.

8. What historic speech contains 266 words, 195 of which consist of one syllable?

Vitalize Your Vocabulary

Education

accreditation (n.)   recognition held by a school certifying that it meets prescribed standards.

alma mater (n.)   the school that one attended, usually a college.

alumnus, alumna (n.)   a man or woman who has graduated from a specific school, college, or university.

baccalaureate (n.)   a bachelor's degree awarded after completion of four years of college.

curriculum (n.)   the courses of study offered at a school.

doctorate (n.)   the highest degree awarded by a graduate school.

elective (n.)   an optional course, in contrast to a required one.

emeritus (adj.)   retired but holding an honorary title.

extracurricular (adj.)   school activities outside regular course work.

intramural (adj.)   carried on between groups in a school and involving no outsiders.

liberal arts (n.)   the course of instruction at a college comprising the arts, natural sciences, social sciences, and humanities.

matriculate (v.)   to enroll as a student at a college.

orientation (n.)   a program to acquaint new students with school procedures.

Ph.D. (n.)   Doctor of Philosophy.

registrar (n.)   a college official responsible for registering students and keeping their records.

syllabus (n.)   a description of the main points in a course or lecture.

valedictorian (n.)   the highest ranking student in the graduating class and the one who delivers the farewell address at commencement.

9

All the great speakers were bad speakers at first.[1]

Delivering Your Speech

After reading and understanding this chapter, you should know:

- The various methods of delivering a talk.

- The advantages and disadvantages of each method.

- The differences between an extemporaneous and an impromptu talk.

- How to deliver a talk that you have prepared.

- The importance of speaking with enthusiasm.

- The importance of practicing your talk.

- How to cope with nerves before you speak and while you're speaking.

Chapter Digest

There are four methods of delivering a speech: speaking extemporaneously, reading from a manuscript, speaking from memory, and speaking impromptu. For most people, an extemporaneous talk is the most effective. It requires you to know your subject in depth and allows you to use notecards. You can

---

1. Ralph Waldo Emerson, "Power," *The Conduct of Life* (1860).

also look at your listeners and speak in the language most appropriate to them and to you.

Those who have significant statements to make to the public or to a special audience often read from a manuscript. Beginning speakers who need 110 percent security also tend to read. The disadvantages of reading are that, usually, the talk sounds "read," eye contact is lost, and the speaker may become addicted to reading all the time. If, however, you must read your talk, try to follow the suggestions given in this chapter.

Speaking from memory invites trouble. What do you do if you forget a word? In addition, this method of delivery can sound cold and mechanical. Memorizing, however, can help you in your introduction and conclusion. Memorizing is also recommended for very short talks, such as introducing a speaker or presenting or accepting an award. (See Chapter 13.)

However, there is another way of speaking. If you are called on to say a few words—without prior notice—you are speaking impromptu. The best advice on speaking impromptu is to have some remarks prepared if there is any likelihood you might be called on without warning.

SPEAKING EXTEMPORANEOUSLY

In our opinion, the most successful speakers in business, politics, religion, and education speak extemporaneously. They perform the following tasks after analyzing the audience.

- Select a topic and limit it to the time available.
- State the purpose of the talk.
- Decide on three or four main points and a few subpoints under each.
- Gather supporting material.
- Prepare an introduction and conclusion; sometimes these are memorized.
- Practice the speech aloud three or four times, with or without notecards, and preferably to a few critical listeners.

By doing these tasks, successful speakers smooth their **delivery** and bolster their self-confidence. If you follow this method of preparing your talk, you should be so immersed in your topic that you need refer only occasionally to your notecards or outline.

An **extemporaneous talk** enables you to speak in your own style, even to the extent of choosing some words on the spur of the moment.

Thus, your presentation will not sound memorized, or "canned." Since notecards reinforce your memory and give you confidence, you'll be able to maintain that all-important eye contact and, at the same time, convey sincerity and spontaneity. You can even move away from the lectern because you're not chained to a written manuscript. With these advantages, you can talk in your own conversational style and, thus, establish a rapport with most audiences.

As you can see, extemporaneous delivery offers you a great deal of latitude. If you wish to quote someone, you can read the quotation verbatim or recite it from memory. If you give the talk more than once, chances are that you will not use the same wording each time. The talk will be conversational and spontaneous—the reward for advance preparation.

On the other hand, there are pitfalls to be aware of: looking at notecards too often or playing with them too much can distract an audience, and a weak, limited vocabulary will not result in a spontaneous, vivid, and attention-getting speech.

All things considered, extemporaneous speaking is the most effective method of delivery and the one that you should try to master.

Using Notecards in Extemporaneous Speaking

After you've studied your topic and know it well, it's time to prepare notecards if you need them. Suitable notes consist of key words and phrases that will remind you of your main points and subpoints. Keep your notes as concise as possible and print them, on one side only, in large capitals so you can skim them in a flash and resume eye contact with your listeners.

For a five-minute talk, your notes should fit on a 3-by-5-inch notecard. If you have quotations and statistics, put them on other cards. Whenever you use more than two cards, be sure to number them just in case you drop or misplace them. (We discussed using notes at the end of Chapter 2.)

Speaking with Enthusiasm

One of the most significant elements of oral delivery is speaker **enthusiasm.** If you're genuinely excited and stimulated by your topic, then the chances are excellent that you can conduct this "electricity" to your audience.

The talk will be conversational and spontaneous.

Having enthusiasm for your topic means speaking with sincerity about your topic and empathy for your listeners. It means talking with excitement—elevating your voice here, then lowering it there. It means talking quickly on occasion, and slowly at other times. It means emphasizing action and descriptive words and phrases. It means pausing just before making an important point or two and visualizing what you're expressing. And it certainly means looking directly at members of your audience. Strive to make your listeners active participants in the speaking event.

The ability to communicate orally with enthusiasm may not come naturally to many speakers, both beginners and professionals; however, that ability can and should be developed. Just remember, it takes commitment and practice.

OTHER METHODS OF DELIVERY

The other three methods of delivering a speech—reading from a manuscript, speaking from memory, and speaking impromptu—do not approach the extemporaneous method in overall effectiveness; however, they are useful in certain speaking situations. We now turn to a discussion of these three methods.

Reading from a Manuscript

We strongly urge beginning speakers to refrain from reading their entire talks. There are, however, circumstances in which very limited reading may be helpful, such as when you're presenting statistics or a quotation.

When accuracy is extremely important, speakers will often read from a manuscript. For example, officials who must make policy statements don't want to risk omitting points or being misunderstood or misquoted. Reading from a manuscript also allows them to use precise, polished language and helps them comply with time limits. For example:

- The President of the United States addressing the Congress and the nation on the massive budget cuts he is proposing as part of his economic program.
- An industry spokesman explaining to stockholders why he is recommending a merger.
- A school committee spokeswoman announcing the reasons for the massive layoffs of teachers and administrative personnel.

These speakers are fully justified in reading their statements; they can't afford a wrong word. For you, as a nonprofessional, however, reading your entire speech word for word could create one or more of the following problems:

- Your speech may sound read and, therefore, lack spontaneity and enthusiasm.
- You may become so engrossed in your manuscript that you forfeit rapport with your audience by not looking at them.
- You may be so "glued" to the manuscript that you can't move about and gesture.

- You may communicate only isolated words instead of whole ideas.
- You may become so dependent on reading your talks that you will not develop skill in other methods of delivery.

If, however, you feel compelled to read your speech verbatim, then consider the following tips:

1. Don't use words you don't normally use because you'll run the risk of mispronouncing them or hesitating when you approach them.

2. Be sure that your sentences are short and understandable. A listener has only one chance to hear what you're saying (unless, of course, you repeat very important points). Keep this in mind when you write your speech. Remember that you're writing for the ear—which likes short, conversational sentences—and not for the eye.

3. Type your speech all caps, either double-spaced or triple-spaced. Number each page and type only on one side of the paper. For ease of reading and quickly finding your place again after looking at the audience, use the large ORATOR style type which is available for electric typewriters with interchangeable elements. When you finish a page, turn it or slide it aside quietly.

4. Practice reading your speech aloud over and over until you know it so well that you can look at your audience more than at your manuscript and so that your speech will sound conversational. This will take a great deal of practice, but it'll be worth the effort.

Rehearsing is imperative. Once I (AJV) listened to a speaker who read his entire speech and had not practiced sufficiently. The last line at the bottom of one page was repeated as the first line of the next, and he read both! Can you imagine the audience's reaction?

Speaking from Memory

The riskiest method of delivering a talk is to memorize it and to speak completely from memory. This method often lacks warmth, feeling, and enthusiasm because the memorized words usually pour

Suppose you forget a word.

forth very mechanically. The chilling risk is that forgetting a word or key phrase could throw you into a state of confusion.

Very few people can deliver memorized speeches effectively. Those who can are very likely professionals who have been speaking this way for years because they have trained their memory.

Many years ago, as a college student in a speech class, I (AJV) was assigned a short memorized talk. I chose to speak on memory development, since I was interested in improving this ability. I started by explaining how important memory can be in everyday living, how it is a God-given talent but one that can be developed with perseverance and application. I stated, "Basically there are three important factors involved in the development of memory. One is association." On the blackboard I wrote the words "One—Association." "Two," I continued, "is repetition." Again, approaching the blackboard, I wrote "Two—Repetition." Then, facing the class, I announced, "And three!" . . . dead air, silence. I drew a blank. The silent seconds seemed like horrendous hours and, for the life of me, I couldn't remember the third point.

The class thought my performance was humorous, as I stood motionless with a look of desperation. After getting myself together, I embarked on an impromptu talk on the fallacy of attempting memorized speeches.

Memorizing can help you with introductions and conclusions, the two most crucial parts of a talk. Memorizing your opening and concluding remarks allows you to begin and end confidently and enables you to look at your audience directly instead of glancing at notes. By the same token, it may be wise to memorize a short talk (a minute or so), for example, introducing a speaker or presenting or accepting an award (discussed in Chapter 13).

If you happen to be gifted with a highly retentive memory, speaking entirely from memory does offer a few other advantages: you're free to move around the platform and use gestures; you can more accurately meet time limits; and you can phrase your opinions, ideas, and facts in precise, polished language.

NOTE

Very few people can deliver a memorized talk spontaneously and enthusiastically.

Speaking Impromptu

An **impromptu talk** is one for which you've had no previous notice, so you're denied the advantage of preparation. Yet, if you analyze your daily conversation, you'll find that most of it, by far, is impromptu: in class, over coffee, at home, on the phone, with a date—or somebody else's date, on the job, and during interviews. In all of these cases, except interviews, you may be conversing with one or a half-dozen people. You talk, they listen; they talk, you listen.

Because of your experience or degree of involvement in a group or organization, you should have a pretty good idea whether you may be called on "to say a few words" at a formal meeting. Before going to a meeting, banquet, or any gathering, ask yourself, "If I were called on to speak, what would I say?"

An impromptu situation doesn't require a fifteen-minute talk. Driving home one sharp point in a few minutes of a carefully prepared "off-the-cuff" talk can make you look like a pro. If there's any possibility, no matter how remote, that you may be asked to say a few words, prepare some comments. It's better to be prepared and not called on than to be called on and not be prepared.

Although you may be ready to say a few words, you must focus your thoughts on a specific topic. Here are some ideas that may help:

- Refer to what previous speakers have said and add your own opinion.
- Comment on some of the topical views expressed by people at your table. They could be a fertile source of ideas.
- Compare the past and present, with possibly a word on the future.
- Compare certain advantages and disadvantages.
- State the problem and a possible solution. (Perhaps you may wish to recommend that a special committee be named to investigate the matter further and then file a report at the next meeting.)
- State the importance of the problem and its effect on your daily lives.
- Consider the topic from the viewpoint of childhood, adulthood, or old age.
- Consider the topic from political, economic, or social aspects.
- Consider the topic geographically—by city, state, country, or the world.

One or more of these approaches should work for you, because your obligation is to speak only two or three minutes. But you have to think fast; make no mistake about that. And under no circumstances should you start by apologizing for your lack of preparation.

If you're completely unprepared to speak about a particular topic and don't wish to address the group, bow out as gracefully as possible (again, prepare a short statement ahead of time).

We have discussed four methods of delivery—speaking extemporaneously, reading from a manuscript, speaking from memory, and speaking impromptu. Since the most effective speech delivery may contain a combination of all of these, experiment with them to establish the most comfortable style for you.

An "off-the-cuff" talk can make you look like a pro.

"PRACTICE IS NINE-TENTHS"

You've just studied the major methods of delivering a talk, but one crucial step still remains before you face your audience—rehearsal.

Facing an audience is not theory. It's your moment of truth, and there's no better way to prepare for that moment than to practice aloud beforehand. Many beginning speakers skip this exercise and then regret it. Ralph Waldo Emerson, the "Sage of Concord," struck the bull's-eye when he said, "Practice is nine-tenths."[2] He knew the truth of that aphorism because he made outstanding speeches in public for fifty years.

Unique proof of Emerson's words was the acceptance speech delivered by President Gerald Ford at the Republican National Convention in August 1976. It was "the best speech of my life," he said

---

2. Ralph Waldo Emerson, "Power," *The Conduct of Life* (1860).

You can conduct "electricity" to your audience.

later. It electrified the delegates and gave them hope of victory. It changed Ford's lifelong image of a bumbling, stolid, lackluster speaker to a powerful, dynamic, fighting-mad speaker who could inspire an audience.

How did he do it?

First of all, the speech was planned for many weeks. President Ford spent more time rewording and polishing it than any speech he had ever given in his thirty-seven-year political career. For two weeks, with the aid of a speech coach, he practiced delivering it. In addition, he went through two complete videotaped rehearsals, always concentrating on delivery. As a result of all this work, he was able to maintain almost constant eye contact with his audience and to use powerful, spontaneous gestures at the right moments. The main ingredients that made the speech a smashing success were Ford's efforts—the importance he placed on it and his emotions of the moment. No wonder he was interrupted with cheers more than sixty-five times.

Great speakers are made, not born. If Gerald Ford could do it at age sixty-two, you can do it at twenty-two, thirty-two, or whatever.

If you can't find a volunteer. . . .

Preparation and practice are the keys to successful speaking. The purpose of practice is to ensure, as much as possible, that your talk in front of the audience will flow smoothly. Try to practice your talk in front of at least one person who will listen and offer a suggestion or two. If you can't find a volunteer, use a tape recorder (a videotape recorder is even better because you see and hear yourself as an audience does), and then listen to the playback. It's a sobering and educational experience. Another idea is to speak in front of a mirror; you'll benefit from this once you get over feeling self-conscious about doing it.

You have three choices for practice—a live audience, a tape recorder (audio or video), or a mirror. In fact, why not use all three? Whichever method you choose, PRACTICE before you face your audience.

And don't forget to devote attention to seemingly minor details. In 1962 President John F. Kennedy made a historic speech in Berlin (see Appendix B). The following four words in that address helped win over the Germans: *"Ich bin ein Berliner"* ("I am a Berliner"). JFK practiced at least ten minutes to master the German accent in its two-second delivery. And a half-million Berliners exploded with tumultuous approval during the speech.

COPING WITH NERVES

Whichever method of speaking you select, one condition is predictable—you'll suffer the jitters: butterflies in the stomach, trembling knees, parched mouth, sweaty palms, and thumping heartbeat. But don't be alarmed, because these are normal reactions that grip most speakers, even seasoned ones. Chances are high that your audience will not notice your discomfort.

Many students have confided that while they were speaking they were so nervous at times that they didn't think they could finish their talks. But, in most cases they never looked one quarter as nervous as they felt. Many speech instructors from all over the country have conveyed similar experiences, and fellow students generally agree that their classmates don't look as nervous as they claim to be.

Many communication scholars believe that stage fright, or speech tension, is the result of anxiety rather than fear.[3] Fear is a spontaneous reaction to a present negative event, whereas anxiety involves the anticipation of a future event. How many times can you recall being upset over something you had to do or that you expected to take place, only to find the actual situation was nowhere near as negative as you had anticipated? For example:

- Perhaps when you were in junior high school, one Friday afternoon your teacher told you that the principal wanted to see you first thing on Monday morning. Can you recall that ruined weekend, during which you conjured up all of the worst scenarios possible, only to find out that the principal wanted to ask you if one of your parents could accompany the class on a field trip?

- Just before going to lunch you receive a telephone message from your boss' secretary stating that your boss would like to

---

3. J. A. Daly and J. C. McCrosky, *Avoiding Communication: Shyness, Reticence, and Communication Apprehension* (Beverly Hills, CA: Sage, 1984), 188.

see you at 2:30 P.M. to discuss an important matter. Instead of enjoying lunch (if you even have one), you spend the time upsetting yourself to the point of indigestion, only to discover that your boss merely wanted to discuss the vacation schedule.

- You're one of three finalists for a job you want very much. The salary is generous, the hours are compatible with your school schedule, and the location is close to home. You have been told that a final decision would be made in a few days and you would be notified by phone. Would you experience any anxious moments waiting for the call?

Hopefully, by now you have found that the anxiety you suffered while waiting to give your first talk was far worse than actually giving it.

Suggestions for Relieving Your Tension Before Speaking

1. Be sure that you're deeply interested in your topic.
2. Prepare thoroughly so that you know your topic very well. Most professional speakers master much more information than they need.
3. Think positively. As you prepare and practice your talk, keep telling yourself that you will do a good job and that the audience will be very interested in what you have to say.
4. As soon as your name is called, take several very deep breaths while you're still sitting and take several more while walking to the front of the class. It helps to get a healthy supply of oxygen into your system.

Suggestions for Relieving Your Tension While Speaking

1. Just before you begin to talk, place your notes on the speaker's stand; look around at the entire class; take another deep breath; and, with a smile, greet your audience.
2. Use vigorous, but not constant, gestures with your hands, arms, shoulders, head, and body. Such physical actions will channel your nervous energy constructively, attract attention, and fortify your oral message.

Take several steps to the left.

3. As you look around the class, don't just scan the audience with only your eyes. Move your entire head to the left, then to the right, and back to center. Fully moving your head in this manner should considerably ease neck tension.

4. Don't rivet yourself behind the lectern. Take several steps to the left and remain there for ten or fifteen seconds before returning to the center position. Then, after a while, repeat this movement in the opposite direction. Deliberate movement is an excellent aid in lessening tension.

5. Focus on your message and audience. Try to become message-conscious, not self-conscious, and your nervousness should diminish, allowing you to communicate more effectively.

6. If you suddenly feel tension building or muscles tightening while you're at the lectern, try gripping the sides of the lectern and squeeze, then slowly release the grip and squeeze again. Repeating this exercise several times can be quite effective and hardly noticeable to the audience.

7. *Act* confident and you'll begin to *feel* confident.

NOTE

Many students find it helpful to admit their nervousness at the beginning of their talk. There's nothing wrong with doing so. Such an admission to your classmates can gain you sympathy and understanding because soon it will be their turn to speak.

DEVELOPING STYLE AND CONFIDENCE AS A SPEAKER

If you have believed, as many people do, that great speakers are born and not made, we hope that reading this chapter has changed your mind. For one final example of a speaker being made, let's flash back to Boston in 1947. Sometime in that year I (HKM) was in a small audience of World War II veterans listening to a speech on foreign policy by freshman Congressman John F. Kennedy. He was witty and knowledgeable, but his voice lacked depth and variety, his language contained *er*'s and *ah*'s, his Boston accent was strong, and his hands were stuck in his pockets much of the time.

JFK was aware of his limitations. He knew that great speakers are made, not born. He knew that President Franklin D. Roosevelt and Prime Minister Winston Churchill struggled for years before they reached their full potential as speakers. He knew what he had to do and he did it.

Kennedy gave speeches often, read good literature to strengthen his vocabulary, and received coaching from a Boston University speech professor. In addition, he rehearsed his speeches, used a tape recorder to improve his voice and diminish his Boston accent, observed competent speakers, and wrote newspaper articles on social and political problems. He spoke before live audiences, on radio, and on television. As a result of his strenuous efforts, by 1960 he was ready for the crucial television debates with Vice-President Richard Nixon. Many historians agree that Kennedy's performance won the presidential election for him.

Granted, JFK had many things going for him—wealth, education, family contacts, a brilliant mind, a sense of humor, good looks, personal drive—but if you do half of what he did, you will greatly improve as a communicator.

To summarize, the following are ways to speed the development of your personal speaking style:

1. Speak at every opportunity.
2. Observe capable speakers and learn from them.
3. Read good literature.
4. Use a dictionary and thesaurus to strengthen your vocabulary.
5. Practice writing (including your talks).
6. Rehearse your talks with a tape recorder and a critical listener.
7. Know your subject and feel deeply about it so you can speak with enthusiasm.

Things to Discuss in Class

1. Which methods of delivery do you think are used by political campaigners? Discuss this.

2. As a listener, which method of delivery do you prefer? Why?

3. Cite two or three examples of speakers you've recently heard, and discuss their methods of delivery. In your opinion, which delivery was the most effective? Why?

4. Select a short passage and read it aloud in your normal delivery. Then, try reading the same passage aloud with enthusiasm, using inflection, feeling, and excitement in your delivery. Notice the vast improvement. Use of a tape recorder would be invaluable.

5. Recall for the class several instances in your life in which anticipating an event was far worse than the actual event.

6. If you've ever seen a speaker deliver a presentation without benefit of a lectern, tell the class how the speaker used his hands and notes.

7. To develop your ability to speak with enthusiasm and to improve your interpretation of the spoken word, read poetry and children's stories aloud and record them.

What Do You Remember from This Chapter?

1. List four methods of delivering a talk.

2. Explain the advantages and disadvantages of each method of delivery.

3. Is it permissible to use more than one method of delivery in the same talk?

4. Explain the difference between extemporaneous and impromptu talks.

5. Is it possible to prepare for an impromptu talk? Explain.

6. Why is practicing a talk important?

7. Is it a good idea to memorize the introduction and conclusion of a talk? Explain.

8. What role, if any, does enthusiasm play in speech delivery?

9. List three suggestions for relieving tension prior to speaking.

Vitalize Your Vocabulary

Government and Politics

bipartisan (adj.)   representing members of two parties.

bureaucracy (n.)   the whole body of nonelected government officials, often accused of red tape and insensitivity to human needs.

caucus (n.)   a closed meeting of a political party to decide policies.

conservative (adj.)   tending to oppose change and to favor traditional ideas and values; (n.) a person who holds such views.

constituent (n.)   a voter in a politician's district.

electorate (n.)   the people qualified to vote in an election.

grass roots (n.)   the local level, as opposed to the centers of political power.

gubernatorial (adj.)   pertaining to the governor.

impeach (v.)   to legally charge a public official with misconduct in office.

incumbent (n.)   the current holder of an office.

left wing (adj. and n.)   see *liberal.*

legislate (v.)   to enact laws.

liberal (adj.)   favoring civil liberties and the use of governmental power to promote social reforms; (n.) a person who holds such views.

lobby (n.)   usually a group of people trying to influence lawmakers in favor of the group's special interest.

platform (n.)   a formal statement of a political party's goals and principles.

radical (adj.)   extreme, as in an approach to social, economic, and political problems; can be either left wing or right wing; (n.) one who holds such views.

referendum (n.)   the practice of submitting a measure to the voters rather than to the legislature.

registration (n.)   the official enrollment of citizens eligible to vote; if not registered, they cannot vote.

right wing (adj. and n.)   see *conservative.*

10

In one of the most famous and fateful incidents in the Bible, the Lord summoned Moses to the top of Mount Sinai. There He appeared to Moses in the form of a fiery cloud, and there—to the appropriate accompaniment of thunder and lightning—He presented Moses with the Ten Commandments. That, so far as I know, is the earliest recorded use of audiovisual techniques for mass education.[1]

First Aid on Using Audiovisual Aids

Chapter Objectives

After reading and understanding this chapter, you should:

- Understand the power of audiovisual aids to persuade an audience.

- Understand the value of using audiovisual aids to enhance and complement your talk.

- Become familiar with the various types of audiovisual equipment and know what to be aware of when using them.

- Be able to select a topic and present a demonstration talk on it.

Chapter Digest

Specialists in modern educational psychology agree on at least one principle: the more senses involved in learning, the greater the learning. That is a convincing reason to use audiovisual aids whenever you think they will enhance your presentation.

    The chapter contains a review of two historic events which graphically

---

1. Harold Howe II, former U.S. Commissioner of Education, addressing the National Audio-Visual Association.

display the power and impact of audiovisual media. This event was a horrendous tragedy involving the in-flight explosion of a United States space shuttle.

Audiovisual aids described in this chapter include charts and graphs, flip charts, photographs, chalkboards, slides, overhead transparencies, audiotapes and videotapes, records, models, and maps. Several pointers on how to use and operate projectors and similar equipment are presented.

Also discussed is the demonstration talk: what it is, how to prepare for it, and how to present it.

On September 1, 1983, a South Korean civilian airliner en route from New York to Seoul, Korea, was intentionally struck by a Russian missile. The plane crashed into the Sea of Japan, killing two hundred and sixty-nine people; sixty-one of them were Americans. The world was angered over the destruction of an unarmed plane that had strayed off course into Soviet airspace. But far more than that, the world was outraged over the senseless murder of innocent people.

Four days after the tragedy, President Reagan, in a televised address to the nation and world, condemned this action as:

> An act of barbarism born of a society which wantonly disregards individual rights and value of human life. Make no mistake about it, this attack was not just against ourselves or the Republic of Korea. This was the Soviet Union against the world.[2]

Soviet-American relations sank to an all-time low. After five days of silence, the Soviets finally admitted responsibility for the attack. They claimed their jet fighter had only "fulfilled the order of the command post to stop the flight." They further declared that the civilian airliner had appeared to be a spy plane sent by the United States to snoop on secret Russian installations. Soviet interceptor jets had trailed the 747 for two and a half hours, and apparently had made no attempt to use the international distress frequency to alert the airliner to its danger. The Soviets insisted that their pilots had been unaware that the South Korean plane was civilian and stressed that the jet had been flying at night without any lights.

THE IMPACT OF AUDIOVISUAL AIDS

To rebut Russia's version of the tragedy, particularly the claim that the plane was flying without lights, the United States Information

---

2. *U.S. News & World Report*, 19 September 1983, 24.

Agency (USIA) appealed to the United Nations. Allowed to set up television monitors on the floor of the U.N. Security Council, USIA personnel broadcast tape-recorded conversations of the three Russian pilots. Their words, which supported the American position, were not only heard but were translated into English and shown on the TV monitors. (See Figure 10.1.)

Further support for the American version was supplied by Japanese tapes of radio contacts between the Soviet pilot and his ground control. Figure 10.2 is an excerpt of a conversation that was heard and seen by members of the Security Council, the nation, and the world.

The power of pictures to persuade is incontrovertible. Indelibly imprinted in the memories of millions of people throughout the world are vivid photographs of such tragedies as:

- The death camps and crematoriums of Nazi Germany, in which millions of Jews and others were exterminated during World War II.

- The devastating earthquakes in Mexico City is 1985 in which thousands of people were killed and tens of thousands were left homeless.

- The assassination of President John F. Kennedy in Dallas in 1963.

And what television viewer can ever forget that Tuesday morning, January 28, 1986, at Cape Canaveral? The space shuttle Challenger was scheduled to blast off with an unusual crew member on board—Christa McAuliffe, a high-school teacher selected from a national field of eager candidates to undergo vigorous NASA training to become the first teacher-astronaut to fly into space.

This event was highly publicized because of former President Reagan's decision that the first civilian in space should be a teacher. Millions of people, here and abroad, planned to watch the launch with increasing interest.

Although a Rockwell Company engineer in California, watching by closed-circuit TV, telephoned the Cape to urge a delay of the launch because of visible ice hugging the rockets, the Kennedy Space Center director, having been advised that there was little risk, permitted the countdown to continue. At 11:38 A.M., the twenty-fifth space shuttle mission, carrying seven astronauts, blasted off. Seventy-three seconds later, ten miles high, and at a speed of almost 2000 miles per hour, Challenger exploded and became engulfed in a raging orange cloud of flames. The Challenger crew entered history as victims

Figure 10.1
Members of the U.N. Security Council listen to the tape and view a
translation of the Soviet pilot's words on the downing of the South
Korean airliner.

of the worst space disaster the world has ever seen. People everywhere,
including many school children, witnessed this incredibly chilling
event televised live; many viewers were not only shocked but required
emotional counseling. The effect of the TV image of the disaster is
a striking example of how the power of pictures can have a jolting
impact on an audience.

ADDING SIGHT AND SOUND TO YOUR PRESENTATIONS

After speaking with numerous business executives and managers, I
(AJV) learned how amazed they are at the huge number of sales
presentations that miss the mark. Yet, with a little more effort and

America says:
The pilot of the Soviet attack plane reported the following to its ground
control, according to transcript released by the United States:

3:18:34 A.M.	(Korean time): The ANL (air-navigation lights) are burning. The strobe light is flashing.
3:19:02 A.M.	I am closing in on the target.
3:26:20 A.M.	I have executed the launch.
3:26:22 A.M.	The target is destroyed.
3:26:27 A.M.	I am breaking off attack.

Russia says:
The following is excerpted from a Soviet government statement released
from the official Russian news agency Tass:

> The Soviet pilots, in stopping the actions of the intruder plane,
> could not know that it was a civilian aircraft. It was flying without
> navigational lights, at the height of night, in conditions of bad
> visibility and was not answering the signals. The assertions . . . are
> not in keeping with reality.

Figure 10.2
Two versions of the downing of KAL Flight 007. (From *U.S. News &
World Report*, 19 September 1983, 27, and *The Boston Globe*, 7 September
1983, 1.)

imagination in the use of audiovisual aids, such presentations can
convince associates at a business conference, win over potential clients
to the speaker's viewpoint, or close a crucial sale.

Fortunately, more and more companies are realizing the importance
of making presentations with audiovisual aids and are establishing
in-house media departments. Some of the larger insurance, utility,
and industrial companies have media production studios that rival
commercial radio and TV stations. Although you may not have access
to such a first-class team of media production professionals, with
some preparation, imagination, and knowledge of visual aids, you
can offer a successful audiovisual presentation or demonstration talk.

Because of the increasing impact of TV viewing habits in the
home, visual aids are, to a disturbing extent, replacing reading habits.
This fact is substantiated by the dismally low reading scores in the
public schools. In fact, most high-school graduates have seen 15,000
hours of TV and, as a result, expect speakers to use visual aids.
Another astonishing fact is that many adults rely so much on their

TV sets for news and informational programs that the degree of illiteracy in this country is growing at an alarming rate.

The addition of a few graphs (see Figure 10.3), charts, pictures, models, slides, movies, videotapes, audiocassettes, or records, together with a dash of creativity, can transform an average presentation, whether in the classroom or at a sales meeting or business conference, into an exciting and highly motivating event.

The use of audiovisual aids is supported by an established principle of psychology: people learn far more through two senses—hearing and seeing, for example—than through one (hearing or seeing) alone. A recent study by psychologists shows that 85 percent of what we learn comes through our eyes and only 11 percent through our ears.[3] If some of your aids—for example, models or small objects—can be handled by your audience, then the sense of touch reinforces hearing and seeing. The more senses involved, the greater the learning. (This principle is also discussed in Chapter 11.)

Another powerful reason for using visual aids is that they arouse and maintain audience interest and reinforce the message. There's no question that the effort you put into preparing visual aids pays off handsomely. If you plan and practice the use of audiovisual aids, you'll not only be able to put on a performance that will be a credit to you, you will also reinforce your self-confidence. If you're required to give a presentation that involves using visual aids, you'll probably find it challenging and rewarding because it is informative and, in some cases, entertaining, even though it might not start out that way. It will afford you a rich opportunity to further develop your self-confidence, for it will place you in the role of expert lecturer.

Make sure that the physical surroundings are adequate for your audiovisual aids. If a table is needed to hold your models, be sure one is there. Be sure that an electrical outlet for your projector or recorder is within reach or that you have an extension cord.

Always rehearse your presentation a few times, using the same equipment you plan to use in your talk. The key to a flawless performance is practice, practice, practice. It's the only way to veto "Murphy's law": If anything can go wrong, it will. Nothing is more embarrassing in the middle of a presentation than fumbling with a piece of equipment because you haven't practiced using it.

Try to avoid displaying visual aids before you refer to them in

---

3. Robert L. Montgomery, *A Master Guide to Public Speaking* (New York: Harper & Row, 1979), 36.

Number of Major TV Producers in the United States
(by country of parent company)

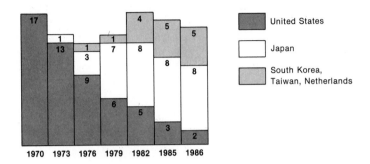

Recording Industry Sales

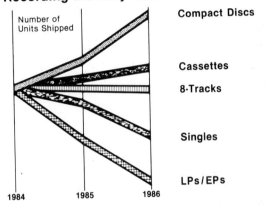

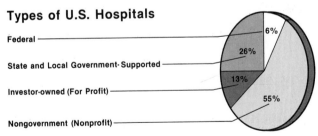

Figure 10.3
Graphs like these make very effective visual aids. (Bar graph figures from U.S. International Trade Commission; line graph information from Recording Industry Association of America, Inc.; pie graph data from American Hospital Association)

If anything can go wrong, it will.

your presentation. If you're going to use charts, graphs, photos, and so on, set them up beforehand but keep them covered or out of view so that your listeners will not get a sneak preview and be distracted.

Using an Easel

Easels are useful for displaying a variety of visual aids, including large cards or poster boards bearing charts and graphs or other information, flip charts, and photographs.

To display large cards.   Charts, graphs, simple statistical tables, and the like may be prepared in advance using pieces of poster board about three feet by four feet. Place all of your cards on the easel, and as you finish with each card, remove it and place it on the floor.

When preparing these cards or boards, be sure to number them in case they get out of sequence. Also, use two or more colors for a more eye-catching presentation. You can also use different colors for headings, subheadings, and overall emphasis. To prevent the possibility of blocking people's view, use a three-foot pointer. In that way you can remain at arm's length from the cards and still reach the material comfortably with the pointer.

To hold a flip chart. A flip chart is a pad of paper approximately 27 inches by 33 inches, normally containing about 50 sheets. This form of visual aid allows you to flip each page up and over the easel when you're finished with it. You may prepare it in advance of your presentation or write on it during your talk. In either case, be sure to use a marker that won't bleed through to the pages underneath. Large dots and blotches on pages are not only distracting but look amateurish.

Be sure you don't talk to the pad of paper while writing on it. Keep your attention focused on the audience. Again, the information you're putting on the pages can be made more interesting and emphatic by using more than one color.

To display photographs. Photographs are an excellent medium, especially before a small group. Size is a critical element; make sure that the photographs are large enough to be seen by everyone. For a larger group, it may be necessary to have enlargements made (this can be quite expensive).

A famous example of the persuasive power of photographs took place during the Cuban missile crisis in October 1962, before the United Nations Security Council. The U.S. ambassador, Adlai Stevenson, confronted the Soviet ambassador, showing him and the world enlargements of aerial photographs that proved that the Soviet Union was building offensive missile bases in Cuba. In light of this overwhelming evidence, world opinion forced the Soviet Union to dismantle the missiles and bases, thus averting a possible nuclear holocaust.

Using a Chalkboard

A chalkboard is a simple visual aid that is readily available in most classrooms. Before you write on it, be sure that it's completely erased. If possible, write before you give your presentation and cover your

If there's a "bleed-through" problem, use two sheets at a time.

material so that the audience is not distracted by it. When you're ready to discuss what you've written, use a pointer and stand sideways so that you can look at your listeners.

If you must write while you're giving your presentation, don't speak while you're writing on the board; talk either before or after. Try to avoid long periods of silence, because silence causes interest to lag. Remember to write clearly and large enough for all to see— and try to write on a straight line. Be sure to hold the chalk at a sharp angle (30 to 40 degrees) to the board; otherwise, the moving chalk will cause nerve-wracking squeals.

Using a Projector

Many schools have audiovisual departments that are well stocked with various types of projectors and other equipment and that usually are staffed by professionals. In a short time, staff members can teach

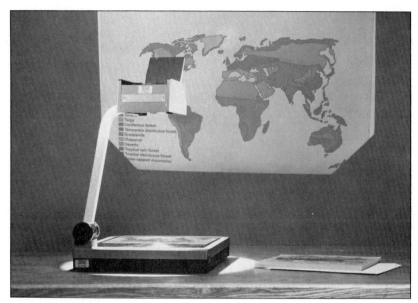

An overhead projector transfers information from an overhead transparency to a screen or a blank wall.

you to operate the equipment. Knowing your audiovisual staff and the equipment can be very helpful to you.

Slide projectors. If you're using slides, be sure that they're arranged beforehand and locked in trays or in a carousel. If you don't, you'll waste time holding slides up to the light to try to figure out how to place them in correct sequence. Remember that color slides are more compelling than black-and-white ones. Also, slides combine well with audio aids.

Opaque projectors. An opaque projector can project the image of a book or magazine page, of the pages of a report, or of a diagram (usually no larger than $10\frac{1}{2} \times 10\frac{1}{2}$ inches). Although this machine tends to overheat and the fan may blow your material around a bit, it does permit you to display material in the detail and color of the original source.

Overhead projectors. An overhead projector requires overhead transparencies, thin sheets of clear plastic on which information has been printed or on which you may write information before or during

Be sure the slides are locked in.

your speech. For optimum projection results, be sure to use the proper writing implements when preparing your own transparencies. You may find that transparencies on a multitude of subjects are available in your school's audiovisual library.

NOTE

Most overhead and opaque projectors have extremely short focal length lenses which necessitate their being placed close to the screen and, therefore, in front of the audience. Since you'll be standing behind or beside the machine, be sure that the image is projected high enough so that everyone can view it easily. Although slide "carousel" and movie projectors produce some noise while in operation, they usually have zoom lenses and can be easily placed at the rear of the audience, where they are less distracting. Remember to set up your equipment beforehand to ensure proper focus and sound level.

Movie projectors.   There are various types of movie projectors—8 or 16 millimeter (mm), sound or silent. When you use sound, be sure to check the volume before the audience arrives. Having the volume too low is as annoying as having it too high. If you use silent film, remember that operation of the equipment produces a hum and that you must speak loudly enough to overcome the hum. Have the film already threaded so that all you have to do is flick a switch to start the film.

Videocassette recorders (VCRs).   One of the fastest-selling and most popular types of home recorders is the VCR. This unit not only allows you to videotape programs directly from your television set, but it also offers you the flexibility of playing back those recorded programs as well as rented VCR tapes and movies. VCRs are often used for educational purposes as well as in private industry.

> *NOTE*
>
> *When using a VCR, be sure that everyone in the class can see the monitor clearly. If the audience is large, consider setting up several monitors throughout the room so that everyone can see what you're showing.*

Using Tape Recorders and Record Players

Audiotapes, records, and compact discs can add another dimension to your presentation. For example, you might use tapes with a silent film or slides or use records to illustrate a talk on music appreciation.

Using Objects

Displaying objects (for example, tools or pieces of equipment) is excellent when you're explaining how something operates. If you can't bring in lifesize objects (for example, an auto engine or 747 aircraft), bring in scale models, but be sure that they are large enough to be seen. Always stand behind or beside the object, never in front of it or between it and the audience. If you're using more than one object, display and discuss them one at a time so that all of the attention will be focused on the item under discussion.

Passing objects around the class can be tricky. If all of the listeners receive the same objects at the same time, they'll be better able to follow you than if you pass around several different objects at different times. Audiences can become more engrossed in looking at objects in their hands than in what you're saying. After your talk, you might

Load your slides into the projector before beginning your talk.

consider displaying the objects on a table so that your audience can inspect them closely.

Using Handouts

Handouts—maps, charts, tables, photographs, and diagrams—are very effective because everyone in the class gets one, and your listeners can follow your talk more closely. If you're planning to pass around several handouts, don't do so all at once because the audience may become more engrossed in them than in what you're saying. Hand them out individually at the appropriate time during your talk and be sure to allow the class enough time to become familiar with the contents before you resume speaking.

Using more than one type of visual aid is not only acceptable but can greatly complement your overall presentation. However, if you select too many types, you run the risk that they will overpower the message that you wish to communicate.

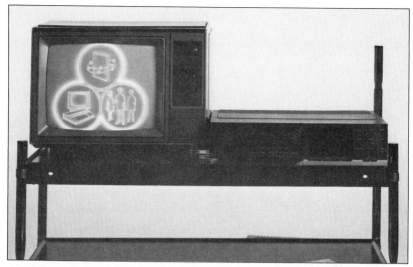

A VCR can be a very useful aid. Be sure to position the monitor so that everyone can see it.

THE DEMONSTRATION TALK

One type of talk that particularly lends itself to the use of audiovisual aids is the demonstration (demo) talk. The practical value of using audiovisual aids, particularly in a demonstration speech, is beautifully expressed in an ancient proverb, a masterpiece in three short lines:

What I hear, I forget.

What I see, I remember.

What I do, I know.

The objectives of the demo talk are:

1. To show the class how to do or how to make something. For example:

   • How to create a flower arrangement.

- How to make a wreath from pine cones.
- How to decorate a cake.
- How to identify counterfeit money.
- How to perform cardiopulmonary resuscitation (CPR).

2. To explain to the class how something operates. For example:

- How a standard transmission functions.
- How a word processor works.
- How a solar panel gathers energy.
- How a nuclear power plant operates.
- How a microwave oven works.

Without question the demonstration talk ranks number one among students. In most cases it truly adds up to a genuine learning experience. A demonstration talk should generally take between 10 and 20 minutes. A shorter time will not give you worthwhile experience in using audiovisual aids, and your audience may just be getting warmed up to your subject when—poof, it's all over.

Involving Members of the Audience

Whenever you can get a member or members of your class to participate in your demonstration talk, your effort will involve your audience more deeply. For example, if you're to demonstrate how to manicure fingernails, use a volunteer as a model. If your topic is sketching, instead of drawing from a picture or photo, use a student from the class as your model. One student showed the Heimlich maneuver of aiding a choking victim. Following the lecture portion of her presentation, she demonstrated the method on a class volunteer. She then had the entire class pair off, and every member performed this life-saving technique on another. The class selected this talk as its favorite. So remember, if possible, involve members of the audience.

If you're planning to use a volunteer as a part of your demonstration talk, arrange this in advance for several reasons. First, you want to be sure you have a volunteer when the time arrives. Second, you need to know that a volunteer will cooperate. And third, you'll prevent the potential embarrassment of someone trying to upstage

you. Most professionals who need a volunteer for their presentation "plant" one in the audience.

Selecting a Topic to Demonstrate

You're probably scratching your head now and wondering, along with many others in the class, what you can demonstrate. This is a common reaction, but from years of experience we've found that those who encounter difficulty in selecting a topic usually end up with a highly satisfactory one. If you're having a problem, tell your professor; a five-minute chat with her may turn up an answer for you.

You can approach this talk from one of two directions. You can either select a topic that you know or one that you know little about but would be interested in researching. If you choose the latter, you'll become involved in a solid learning experience.

A topic you know.   The natural choice is a topic you know something about. You should take inventory of your knowledge, experiences, and skills to decide which topic you will present. Did any of your jobs, full-time or part-time, require special skills? Did you receive special training in the service? What about your hobbies? Have you collected slides or made movies? Do you sky dive, scuba dive, sail, or play tennis or soccer? Do you like to cook or bake? You'll probably be astonished at some of the things you've done that would make a worthwhile presentation. Don't sell yourself short.

The following are some topics that resulted in successful presentations by students whose initial reaction was "There's nothing I can do."

- A student who had worked in an ice-cream parlor demonstrated how to make several types of sundaes.
- A football enthusiast gave an excellent presentation and explanation of the various signals used by referees. He even wore an official black-and-white-striped shirt.
- A young woman intrigued the class with her talk and demonstration of various positions in yoga.
- A young woman, in a presentation on self-defense, effortlessly flipped several men students on a mat.
- A police officer student demonstrated the art of fingerprinting by using classmates for subjects.

A topic you know little about.   If you're ambitious about learning, you may select a topic that you're not too familiar with, conduct research on it, probably receive instruction, and then give the presentation. This approach requires considerable preparation, but it will be rewarding. You'll find a list of ideas and topics below and another list in Appendix C.

Suggested Topics for Demonstration Talks

1. Forecasting the weather.
2. Types and uses of sporting equipment.

3. Photography.

4. Collecting (coins, stamps).

5. Playing a musical instrument.

6. Firefighter and police equipment.

7. How to play games (chess, backgammon).

8. Assembling terrariums.

9. Making balloon animals.

10. How to identify counterfeit money.

11. Some basic exercises in Yoga.

12. How to pack a parachute.

13. What to look for when reading a wine label.

14. How to make an antipasto.

15. How to communicate by sign language.

16. Basic self-defense for women.

17. Some basic carpentry tools and how to use them.

18. How to gift-wrap a package and make bows.

19. How to pack a suitcase.

20. How to coordinate a wardrobe (male or female).

21. Applying makeup.

22. Card tricks.

23. Handcrafts (knitting, macramé, découpage, crocheting).

24. Cooking.

25. Types of artificial respiration.

26. Art (sketching, collage).

27. How to read the stock market page.

28. Taking your own blood pressure.

29. Scuba diving.

30. Giving first aid to a choking victim (Heimlich maneuver).

31. Making a lamp out of a bottle.

Evaluation Guide for a Demonstration Talk

	Yes	No
Introduction		
Did speaker greet audience?	____	____
Did speaker give reasons for selecting the topic?	____	____
Did speaker explain what was to be accomplished during the talk?	____	____
Body		
Was the talk presented in a logical sequence?	____	____
If technical terms were used, did speaker define them?	____	____
Did speaker know how to operate the audiovisual equipment?	____	____
Was equipment or audiovisual aids on hand ready to be used?	____	____
Were handouts used effectively?	____	____
Did too many audiovisual aids lead to confusion?	____	____
Were aids large and clear enough to be seen and understood by entire class?	____	____
Were aids in any way distracting to the presentation?	____	____
Conclusion		
Did speaker have an effective conclusion?	____	____
Did speaker gather visual aids *during* conclusion?	____	____
Did speaker answer questions from audience during talk or after it?	____	____

Things to Discuss in Class

1. Visit your audiovisual department and become familiar with its equipment.

2. Tell about a recent talk in which audiovisual aids were used—for example, a talk given by a TV or door-to-door salesperson or a class lecture.

3. List some professions or occupations in which audiovisual aids play an important role.

4. Select a topic you'd like to talk about and explain which audiovisual aids you'd use and how you'd use them.

5. List a few topics for which it would be necessary to use audiovisual aids. Explain.

6. Bring several types of graphs to class and explain the differences among them.

What Do You Remember from This Chapter?

1. How can the use of audiovisual aids help get your message across to the audience?

2. Is it permissible to use more than one aid in a presentation? Explain.

3. Explain the impact of pictures.

4. Of what must you be careful when you use handouts?

5. What should you keep in mind when you write on a chalkboard?

6. What's a good technique for preparing large cards to be placed on an easel?

7. What is good advice to remember when using a movie projector?

8. If you show objects or scale models, where should you stand in relation to the audience?

9. What's a good thing to remember if you're planning to use a volunteer during your demonstration talk?

10. Explain the persuasive power of tapes.

11. Explain the ancient proverb:
    What I hear, I forget.
    What I see, I remember.
    What I do, I know.

12. Explain the difference between an overhead and an opaque projector.

13. What would be the best location in a room for a projector? Explain.

14. Of what must you be careful when preparing a flip chart?

15. Is it a good idea to have a member of the class participate in your presentation? Explain.

Vitalize Your Vocabulary

Mass Communications and Telecommunications

Amplitude Modulation (AM) (n.)   the method used for transmission of radio waves at frequencies from 535 kHz to 1605 kHz on the standard broadcast band.

Bill of Rights (n.)   the first ten amendments to the United States Constitution, the first of which guarantees freedom of speech and the press.

CATV (n.)   Community antenna television, or cable TV.

compact disc (CD) (n.)   a disc from which sound is picked up by a laser beam rather than by a needle.

cathode ray tube CRT (n.)   the picture tube of a TV receiver or display tube of a computer monitor.

demographics (n.)   statistical data about a population, such as age, sex, education and income.

dish (n.)   an antenna shaped like a dish used for sending or receiving signals to communication satellites.

docudrama (n.)   a dramatic presentation combining fiction with historical facts.

earth station (n.)   the antenna and other equipment needed to receive or transmit television signals from communication satellites.

electronic mail (n.)   messages sent electronically via communication satellites; these can be recorded and played back by electronic equipment in the home or office.

Federal Communication Commission (FCC) (n.)   the government agency that regulates radio and television broadcasting in the United States.

fiber optics (n.)   the science of transmitting information through hair-thin strands of glass by means of light originating from lasers.

Frequency Modulation (FM) (n.)   the method used for transmission of radio waves at frequencies from 88.1 MHz to 107.9 MHz.

laser (n.)   a piece of equipment that emits an extremely narrow beam of pure, high-energy light.

optical fibers (n.)   very narrow strands of glass used to transmit light beams which come from lasers; widely used in the telecommunications industry to carry information.

network (n.)   the originator of programs from one location which are broadcast simultaneously on two or more affiliated stations; programs are transmitted to the stations by telephone lines, microwave relays, or satellites.

scrambler (n.)   a device used in cable and satellite transmission which electronically alters the signal to prevent unauthorized reception.

VCR (n.)   videocassette recorder.

11

Whatever the calling students may later pursue, their effectiveness will depend mightily on ability to express views clearly.[1]

Inform Them

After reading and understanding this chapter, you should know:

- The purposes of and kinds of informative talks.

- Four principles that help people learn better.

- How to use statistics effectively.

- How to prepare the introduction, body, and conclusion of an informative talk.

Chapter Digest

In this age of widespread college education, of national computer networks, and of endless research into the unknown, information has evolved into a crucial national resource. By the same token, information has become an invaluable asset to individuals who can absorb it and share it through talking

---

1. Kingman Brewster, Jr., former president of Yale University, "The Report of the President," 1 September 1976, 11.

with their peers. In other words, speaking to convey knowledge and understanding can help you advance your career.

Adapting the knowledge level of your talk to the knowledge level of your audience is of supreme importance. Three kinds of audiences are described from this viewpoint and, in order to help you meet their needs, various types of informative talks are explained.

Certain principles of learning that help you are discussed briefly. If you apply them, your informative talks will get better results, but applying these principles is not enough. First you need to acquire knowledge, information, and understanding in order to flesh out your talk. And that means doing your homework.

Many down-to-earth suggestions are given for preparing the introduction, body, and conclusion of your informative talk. After you finish your presentation, a question-and-answer period is an excellent way to tie up loose ends.

The chapter ends with a speech that informs us about the hazards of exercise; an outline precedes the speech.

Because the words *information* and *knowledge* appear throughout this chapter, let's define our terms:

information (n.)   facts, data, news; knowledge communicated by others or obtained from study, instruction, or investigation.

knowledge (n.)   comprehension, learning, information, an organized body of facts, or ideas inferred from those facts.

Americans have always set a high value on knowledge. We believe that democracy functions best when its citizens are armed with sound knowledge on which to base intelligent decisions. Because of this belief, the United States has developed the most extensive system of public education that the world has ever known. Because of this belief, the United States has more colleges and universities than do England, France, East and West Germany, and the Soviet Union combined. Because of this belief, the United States has more newspapers, magazines, book publishers, radio stations, television channels, computer networks, and public libraries than those same five countries put together.

Such media, both here and abroad, have created a revolution in the handling of information and an explosion of knowledge in countless specialized areas. As a result, information is now regarded as "a new basic resource that supplements the familiar natural resources of matter and energy."[2] Matter and energy change with use, while knowledge does not. On the contrary, the more that knowledge is used and shared among people, the more valuable it becomes: for example, the knowledge needed to produce and use penicillin and other miracle drugs has saved many lives.

PURPOSES OF INFORMATIVE TALKS

Despite the multiplying numbers of computers (personal, business, and scientific) and databases, we still exchange astounding quantities of information orally. Much of our talking—on the job, in politics, at home, or in social contacts—is focused on one major objective: to present information so that it will be understood, remembered, and possibly utilized.

Briefly, you want to open new horizons for your listeners, to give them new perspectives and understanding. In light of this goal, most audiences fall into three categories that may overlap: not informed, generally informed, and well informed.

With listeners who are not informed, you should deal in elementary matters and explain any jargon or specialized concepts. Here's where relevant comparisons and statistics (discussed later in this chapter) can help your audience understand your presentation. Just be careful not to talk down to them and not to cover too much ground at one time.

With a generally informed audience, you should use fundamental knowledge sprinkled with advanced material. The perplexing question is this: how much of each is appropriate? (For ideas on researching your audience, see Chapter 8.) Since some of your listeners may resent basic information as an onslaught against their egos, you may explain that you're simply laying a foundation on which to build deeper understanding. Another diplomatic "out" for you is that you're reviewing fundamentals for a few people whose memories may need refreshing.

With well-informed listeners, you're free to skip fundamentals and plunge into advanced information in depth. Listeners armed with knowledge are usually easy to handle, but a warning belongs

---

2. *Encyclopaedia Britannica*, 15th ed., s.v. "information processing."

Be careful not to talk down to your audience.

here—know your subject, or a few sadistic members of the audience may revel in "showing you up."

When it comes to listening and observing to gain understanding, several kinds of audiences are involved—for example:

- Classes in school.
- Decision-making individuals or groups on the job.
- Voters assessing candidates at an open forum.
- Consumers listening to purchasing experts for tips on stretching the dollar or conserving energy.
- People listening to radio and television newscasts, documentaries, and so on.

Someday, at school, on the job, in your community, you may find yourself giving an informative talk to one of these audiences and attempting to describe a person or place; to report an event, a problem, or a situation; or to explain a concept, device, process, or theory.

An evaluation guide for **informative talks** appears near the end of this chapter. Since the guide reminds you to include important items in your informative talk, you should consult the guide before you speak.

KINDS OF INFORMATIVE TALKS

Among the major categories of speeches—to entertain, to inspire, to persuade, to actuate, and to inform—by far the speech most often presented is the speech to inform. What does this mean to you? Simply that the way you handle your storehouse of information and share it with others can have a significant impact on the direction of your career.

Let's clarify the use of speech categories. Because a speech is labeled "informative" doesn't mean that it's boxed in a neat compartment called "information." An informative speech may contain elements of persuasion, entertainment, or both, and those extras will, very likely, make it a more effective speech. The point is that, although speeches belong primarily to one category, they often include elements of other categories, as well as the use of audiovisual aids.

The general objective of the informative speech is to convey understanding and knowledge, because humans have an instinctive need to understand themselves and their surroundings. From that general objective we can focus on various types of speeches to inform: reports, instructions, demonstrations, and lectures.

Reports. A chief function of committees in business, education, politics, Armed Forces—you name it—is to give reports on projects and problems. A neighborhood committee, for example, may investigate the need for traffic lights at a dangerous intersection, report its findings, and make a recommendation for or against traffic lights. At the other end of the spectrum, the President of the United States reports, once a year, on the State of the Union. Oral reporting goes on in all walks of life.

Instructions. Today you may tell an out-of-state tourist how to find the new shopping mall at the other end of town. Tomorrow your professor may explain how to do a research paper. He may even supplement his oral instructions with handouts containing specific steps to follow. Very often, written instructions help clarify the oral how-to-do-it phase.

Demonstrations. When you show someone how to use a camera, how to perform a card trick, or how to operate a computer terminal, you are demonstrating. This kind of informative speaking is so important that it rates a chapter all by itself—Chapter 10.

Lectures. In addition to class lectures, this type of informative speaking includes talks at professional seminars, radio and television talks on travel and politics, and book reviews at club meetings. These talks are often given after luncheon or dinner; their prime purpose is to enhance the listeners' knowledge and appreciation of a particular subject.

PRINCIPLES OF LEARNING

Before you embark on your first informative talk, let's review some findings on how people learn. Teachers in the past few thousand years and psychologists in the past hundred or so years have discovered that the following principles, when applied, speed the learning process.

People learn better when you, as a speaker, involve as many of their senses as possible. For example, suppose that you're demonstrating how to make a new kind of spaghetti sauce. You cut and mix the ingredients (seeing), fry them (smelling), explain the procedure (hearing), and then hand out samples to your listeners (tasting). With four of their senses involved in this learning experience, your listeners will remember far more than if you used only words to convey the message.

Of course, this example is an extreme case because you won't always be able to involve four senses in the same talk. Often, however, you'll be able to involve the sense of seeing (with movies, filmstrips, photographs, maps, or models) and the sense of hearing (through the spoken word).

People learn better when salient points of information are repeated a few times or are restated in different words. Here is an example of this principle:

> Doctors and dieticians tell us that breakfast is the *most important meal* of the day. Yet, millions of Americans skip this *crucial meal* daily, to save time, to pare off pounds, or both. After seven to nine hours in bed, these people may be rested sufficiently, but physically and mentally they need the *energy*—"fuel," if you don't mind—that a *well-balanced breakfast* can provide. Without that *energy*, their bodies and minds cannot operate at top efficiency through the morning.

Involve as many of their senses as possible.

That is why, for most people, a *good breakfast* is a *key element* in nutrition that can lead to a healthy life.

Notice that the significant idea (italicized) in the preceding paragraph is mentioned seven times.

People learn better when they're motivated to do so.   Your listeners pay close attention to you when you answer the often unspoken question that most people ask: "What's in it for me?" Tell them how to get a better job, reduce their income taxes, be healthier, live longer, or be more attractive to the opposite sex, and you can be sure that they will hang on to every word you utter.

People learn better when new, relevant information is presented in small, well-organized amounts.   If you're explaining the basic causes of World War II to an audience that knows little about the subject, you should organize your material according to political, economic, and military causes. You should discuss each category separately but not deeply, and in your conclusion you should point out how all three types of causes combined to trigger the most devastating war in history.

GETTING INTO YOUR INFORMATIVE TALK

To inspire, persuade, entertain, and activate people, you don't need a great deal of information or knowledge. But the talk to inform, by its very nature, dictates that you do your research and that you know your subject. After all, your primary purpose is to convey information and understanding that your listeners didn't have before.

Because a strong introduction is crucial to any talk, before you plan your opening remarks you should review the ideas listed in Chapter 7. Most of those ideas apply to introductions to all kinds of talks. At the very least, in the introduction to your informative talk, you should:

- State the purpose of your talk.
- List the three or four main points orally and, if possible, write them on a chalkboard. However, if writing takes unduly long, your listeners' attention may wander. You may consider highlighting the main points on a poster, which is excellent visual reinforcement for your oral listing.
- Stress the subject's importance to your listeners; if it will save them time or money or make their lives easier, say so immediately.

Because first impressions are powerful and lasting, you should practice your introduction aloud many times so that you can deliver it fluently and still maintain eye contact. A well-spoken introduction can perform miracles for you in one or two minutes.

MOVING INTO THE MAIN DISCUSSION

You're now ready to launch into a discussion of the main points mentioned in your introduction. As you know from Chapter 6 (doing research) and Chapter 7 (organizing your information), each main point requires subpoints for support: facts, examples, quotations from authorities, incidents, anecdotes, comparisons, statistics, and so on. Ample research should provide you with many of these supports (which, except comparisons, are illustrated in Chapter 7). Now let's look at comparisons, statistics, audiovisual aids, and questions as supporting elements for your informative talk.

Comparisons

If you're explaining concepts that are new to an audience, try to compare them with something familiar to the audience. A few apt comparisons can bring your explanation to life. For example, assume you tell your speech class that the fastest speed attainable by Olympic swimmers is slightly more than four miles an hour. Compared to dolphins, which can swim sporadically at thirty-five miles an hour, the Olympic speed is nothing special, and some students may snicker at four miles an hour. Then, after saying that this speed is a brisk walking pace, ask how many of them can walk a mile in fifteen minutes.

The following are two concise comparisons, one dealing with specific amounts of money and the other with imagery and science; both can be grasped easily:

1. In 1984 the federal government spent $2.6 billion daily. "Piled flat, one atop the other, 2.6 billion $1 bills would stack 176 miles high—745 times as tall as New York's Empire State Building."[3]
2. Sun flares sprayed streams of particles into space, sweeping the solar system *like streams of water from a revolving lawn sprinkler.*

Statistics

The use of statistics supplies concrete information that may perk up your audience's interest and, at the same time, may prove your point. Try to observe the following cautions in using statistics:

- Don't throw reams of figures at your audience; they're too difficult to remember.

---

3. *U.S. News & World Report*, 24 December 1984, 25.

- In addition to giving statistics orally, present the key figures with a visual aid—a chalkboard, flip chart, poster, or slide.
- Repeat the most important figures at least once.
- Round off long figures. Instead of saying "$1,000,359," say "a little over a million dollars." Your audience will appreciate it.
- Use only the most accurate and most recent statistics.

Notice how the following example dramatizes and clarifies the distance of the moon from the earth, about 239,000 miles:

If you could drive your car nonstop to the moon at 55 MPH, you'd get there in 182 days.

Here's a comparison among one million, one billion, and one trillion:

One million seconds is about 12 days.

One billion seconds is about 31 years.

One trillion seconds is about 31 thousand years.

If you counted one-dollar bills at the rate of one dollar per second, it would take you 31 thousand years to count to a trillion dollars. Our national debt has reached 2.8 trillion dollars.

The next example of statistics might be an extremely persuasive argument if you were testifying for gun control before a congressional committee. These statistics headline the dramatic difference between handgun control in seven countries and no handgun control in the United States.

In 1980 handguns killed
77 people in Japan,
 8 in Great Britain,
24 in Switzerland,
 8 in Canada,
23 in Israel,
18 in Sweden,
 4 in Australia, and
11,522 in the United States.[4]

---

4. *U.S. News & World Report*, 24 March 1986, 20.

Audiovisual Aids

Be sure to use audiovisual aids, such as recordings, movies, photographs, charts, and maps (see Chapter 10). Say, for example, that you're discussing old whiskey bottles. The most compelling visual aids would not be descriptions, photographs, or replicas of bottles, but the actual bottles if possible. Reality "grabs" people.

Questions

A foresighted tactic to carry out while researching and preparing for your speech is to anticipate relevant questions that your listeners may want to ask at various stages of your talk. Asking such questions during your talk often stimulates your audience to think along with you and to bring up new ideas. In your introduction, let your audience know that they, too, can ask questions either during your talk or after it.

WINDING UP YOUR INFORMATIVE TALK

At the end of your main discussion, you might pause a few seconds and move a step or so to either side. The pause and movement signal that your talk is about to end. Then you may say something like:

- In conclusion (or before concluding), I would like to emphasize the following points.
- If you leave with only one thought, I hope that it would be . . .
- And now I would like to close with a quotation from . . . (an anecdote about . . . a comparison between . . . , a poem about . . .)

Again, you may stress the importance of the subject and the benefits that the listeners may derive from the knowledge you've shared with them. Remember that a conclusion should be brief and to the point. Don't drag it out or trail off by muttering, "Well, I guess that's about it."

Another idea for your conclusion is to encourage listeners who want to learn more about the subject. You can list, on the chalkboard, relevant titles of magazine articles or books. Better still, prepare this information as a one-page handout that you can distribute on the spot. Most people like handouts because they're free and can be useful as lasting reminders of your key points.

Whereas other categories of talks seldom require a question-and-answer period, the informative talk does, for these practical reasons: (1) If your treatment of a particular topic was foggy or incomplete, you have a second chance to clarify it. (2) If you omitted a facet of the subject that concerns some of the listeners, you can supply the missing information.

Former President Harry S. Truman summed up the value of the question-and-answer session in these words: "I know of no way of communicating more information in shorter time than the question-and-answer method."

Sometimes question-and-answer periods begin with a resounding silence that embarrasses both speaker and listeners. Almost everyone shies away from being the first to ask questions for fear of sounding stupid. Planning can avert this silence. Ask a few questions—thought out beforehand—and answer them yourself if nobody in the audience cares to try.

Or you can do what many professional speakers do—"plant" a question or two with a friend in the audience; it's perfectly legitimate. If nobody speaks up, your friend can "break the ice." Then other listeners will very likely pop questions at you.

If you've done enough research, you'll be able to answer almost all queries, which should give you a feeling of accomplishment for a job well done. If a question stumps you, don't try to bluff around it. Admit that you don't know the answer but that you will try to find it. Most of your listeners will appreciate that you're an honest human being who doesn't pretend to be a know-it-all.

A Sample Informative Speech and its Outline

An outstanding informative speech, entitled "Exercise," was given by Deidre Wallace of Bradley University at the 1985 annual contest of the Interstate Oratorical Association in Peoria, Illinois. The introduction of her speech (paragraphs 1 and 2) arouses your interest by

A conclusion should be brief.

naming famous people, including a fitness authority who died while jogging.

Throughout the speech, a conversational style predominates—by all means, a definite asset. Deidre's in-depth research uncovered a wealth of information and insight. There are quotations and statistics galore from health and fitness authorities, such as Dr. Kenneth Cooper, Air Force consultant; Stanford University School of Medicine; Cornell Medical College; and the *Journal of the American Medical Association.* This solid research places her speech on an unshakable foundation.

The short, relevant conclusion (paragraphs 10 and 11) tells us what we can do to become healthy and fit and to stay that way. It says just enough and then stops—a practice worth emulating. If anything needs improvement, it's the one-word title. Perhaps a few more words would spice it up—for example: "Exercise? Yes, but Don't Kill Yourself!"

The following is a sentence outline of Deidre's speech.

Title: Exercise

Thesis Statement: Regular exercise, if done moderately, promotes good health and usually a longer life but, if done to extremes, can harm us badly.

  I. Introduction

    A. Exercise can benefit us physically and in other ways, but there are some things it cannot do for us.

    B. A common myth is that pain is a necessary part of exercise.

 II. Body

    A. Exercising excessively or improperly can cause pain, exhaustion, injuries, and sometimes even death.

    B. Common stretching exercises—for example, sit-ups, toe-touches, deep-knee bends—have resulted in injuries.

    C. An issue of *Changing Times* magazine stated that emergency-room treatments were needed in 1980 for countless thousands of cyclists, tennis players, and swimmers, and that over 60 percent of all runners complained of at least one injury.

    D. Both *Science News* magazine and the *Journal of the American Medical Association* have said that overdoing it is causing problems for thousands of exercisers.

    E. A key question, still unanswered, concerns the effect of exercise on the heart. Jim Fixx, author of *The Complete Book of Running*, died while jogging.

    F. In the past decade or so, a national fitness craze has obsessed millions.

III. Conclusion

    A. We should question the qualifications of Jane Fonda, Richard Simmons, etc., to tell us what exercises to perform. Before starting an exercise program, we should have a physical checkup done by a doctor.

    B. "Exercise can be an enjoyable activity as long as we remember that the chief goal is to improve our well-being. Once exercise becomes an end in itself, it places our health in jeopardy."

Exercise

Deidre Wallace
Bradley University

  I. Introduction

    A. Exercise—it's the latest thing, and anybody who is anybody is doing it. Whether it be for that perfect body or just to add ten years onto your life, exercise is the cure-all for any physical problem. Well, just ask Jane Fonda or Richard Simmons or Linda Evans or Jim Fixx.

Well, maybe Jim Fixx isn't the right person to ask. Fixx, the author of the book *The Complete Book of Running*, died of a heart attack while jogging.

B. To think that vigorous activity will always lead to that supreme body is a bit naive. Because there is another side to exercise that Jane Fonda won't tell you about, that Richard Simmons won't tell you about, and that Jim Fixx can't. That's the side of pain, exhaustion, injuries, and in some cases even death. You see, we've too often been told that pain is a necessary part of exercise—do it till it hurts. Not true. According to Doctor Howard Hunt, Chairman of the Department of Physical Education at the University of California, exhaustion doesn't mean your body's weak—it means it is overtaxed. Before we can begin to solve this problem, we must realize that exercise can be dangerous for both the beginning athlete and the experienced, we must understand why so many Americans fall prey to these dangers, and finally we can look at some solutions that will get us back on the right track toward healthy exercise.

II. Body

A. Before I go any further I would like to clarify my position on exercising. I'm not suggesting that exercise in moderation is bad or unhealthy, and I'm not suggesting that we should all abstain from any type of physical activity. However, according to the March 1984 issue of *Current Health Magazine*, over a million people each year huff and puff their way through workouts without even knowing that they may be heading for trouble.

B. Many of the problems caused by exercising are just not knowing the proper way of doing it. And it is usually the overly eager beginner who falls into this category. Understand these problems don't have to stem from some strenuous exercise such as weight lifting or marathon running. It can be as simple as stretching. Stretching—a very natural thing to do and basically what these books and programs are all about. The problem is that we no longer limit ourselves to gentle beneficial stretching. In efforts to become oversized gumbies we tend to overstretch to help loosen and relax our muscles. But we're not loosening them; we're tearing them. Dr. Richard Dominquez, Medical Director for the Sports and Rehabilitation Institute in Illinois, says that there are more injuries as a result of stretching than as a result of stiffness. Even the most common stretching exercises have resulted in injuries—sit-ups, toe-touches, and deep-knee bends are just a few. Both sit-ups and toe-touches put enormous strain on the ligaments in the back, and deep-knee bends put enormous pressure on the cartilage in the knees.

C. But probably one of the most dangerous stretching exercises can be found in Jane Fonda's workout program—The Yoga Plow. Now, you may not recognize the name but I'm sure most of us have done this before. The plow is when you lie on your back and flip your feet over your head and touch your toes on the floor behind you. By doing this the circulation is often cut off to the brain and has resulted in strokes. I'm sure you understand why I don't demonstrate.

D. Even the exercises that seem the most harmless have resulted in injuries. A 1980 issue of *Changing Times* states that injuries worthy of emergency-room treatments for that year were suffered by 448,000 cyclists, 61,000 tennis players, and more than 65,000 swimmers. And of course, we can't forget the most popular form of exercise today— running—unfortunately, it creates the most problems. That same issue of *Changing Times* states that over 60% of all runners complain about one injury or another, and after reading the article I can understand why. It states that as a 120-pound person jogs, there is actually a 360-pound shock on each leg in every stride.

E. But, as beginning athletes become more advanced, their problems seem to shift. They no longer stem from unawareness, but rather from obsession. Many aren't satisfied with exercising in moderation but feel the need to take their workouts to extremes. And this overexercising can throw their entire system out of balance. The June 30, 1984, issue of *Science News Magazine* reported that the repeated jarring of the internal organs during running can break down the intestinal lining and has resulted in internal bleeding. And now the *Journal of the American Medical Association* states that many women suffer from nonexistent menstrual cycles and joggers' infertility. In fact, 83% of all postmenstrual trained athletes suffer from nonexistent cycles. Dr. Colm O'Herily tells about the cases of two women who regularly ran twenty miles a week. After a period of time, both women's menstrual cycles ceased. So he prescribed a fertility drug but it didn't help. Finally, he asked his patients to lay off the track work, and after eight weeks and half the dosage, both women had become pregnant.

F. But probably the biggest question since Jim Fixx's death is the effect that exercise has had on our heart. You see, we have this misconceived notion that not only can exercise help strengthen a healthy heart, but it can cure any heart problems we might have. Not true. Stanford University School of Medicine says that "habitual exercise does not guarantee protection against sudden death before or immediately following exercise." And Fixx is the prime example. Hours before his daily run, Fixx complained of exhaustion, tightness in his throat, and chest pains, and yet he ran. In fact, Dr. Kenneth Cooper, founder of the Aerobics Center in Dallas and a consultant to the United States

Do joggers ever look happy?

Air Force, had urged Fixx just eight months prior to his death to come in and have a heart function evaluation through a treadmill stress test. For reasons unknown Fixx refused. He is not alone. Stanford University analyzed the medical histories of eighteen individuals who died while running. Sixteen out of the eighteen people died of heart-related problems. Why? Why do we continue to push ourselves to these extremes? Well, at a recent seminar at Cornell Medical College, psychiatrists agreed that many exercise programs are potentially addictive and this negative addiction is increasing among exercisers.

G. The problem is growing, and we have no one to blame but ourselves. We've become so engrossed in this entire fitness craze that we have lost sight of what is really important—our health. We can often find short-cut schemes to help us shape up quick. And we can find those schemes on any shelf in any bookstore. Just think about it. Are we not being constantly bombarded with ways to shape up or trim

Is your body telling you something?

down? There are workout programs by Jane Fonda, Christy Brinkley, Richard Simmons, Linda Evans, and now the latest, Garfield the Cat. Who in their right mind would trust their health to a cartoon character? But, then again who is Jane Fonda to tell us what type of workout programs we should be doing? These exercise programs are geared toward the masses, not toward the individual and they are not directed toward health but rather toward profit. Physical fitness has become a highly commercialized, glamorized, profitable business. And let's face it, there is not one exercise program that can do everything for everybody. Once we turn off that tape, Jane Fonda is gone and all we have left are ourselves and the problems that we have created. We are lacking in responsibility—responsibility to ourselves not to let our obsessive vanity and these attractive life-styles blind us to our own medical needs.

III. Conclusion

    A. It's time we do something for ourselves, but this time let's do it right. First, we must not overestimate the qualifications of the people who write these books and programs. They're not experts, they're not doctors, and many are not qualified to tell us what type of exercise programs we should be doing. We should take the initiative to find out which exercises are beneficial and which ones to avoid. Furthermore, we must learn to discipline ourselves both physically and psychologically. Like the dieter who has to discipline himself not to eat that extra piece of cake, exercisers must learn to discipline themselves not to run that extra mile. Plus, we must listen to our own body's warning signals and when pain hits, stop.

B. Probably the best way to assure ourselves of a proper fitness treatment is to see a professional. Through a physical checkup, our doctor will be able to tell us what type of exercise programs are suitable for our specific, individual needs. And if complications do arise, the doctor will already know our workout schedule and be able to help us with these problems.

You see, exercise can be an enjoyable activity, as long as we remember that the chief goal is to improve our well-being. Once exercise becomes an end in itself, it places our health in jeopardy. Now maybe someone should put that on a cassette tape.

SUGGESTED TOPICS FOR INFORMATIVE TALKS

1. What is stagflation?
2. What causes a depression?
3. Is the demise of public education approaching?
4. How to manage your checkbook.
5. Why the voters should be able to recall public officials.
6. The effects on children of living with just one parent.
7. Why public school teachers are leaving the profession.
8. Why Japanese cars require fewer repairs than American cars.
9. Some of the best ways to invest your money.
10. The stock market crash of 1987.
11. How the electoral college works.
12. How safe are nuclear power plants?
13. What the ERA is all about.

14. Alternative ways to heat or cool your home.

15. The meaning of "détente."

16. How a bill becomes a law.

17. Sexual harassment—an occupational hazard.

18. Are colleges doing their job in preparing students for work?

19. The AIDS epidemic in the United States.

20. The startling increase in teenage pregnancies.

21. Who said that crime doesn't pay?

22. How to plant a productive garden.

23. How to get better mileage from your car.

24. How to shop and save.

25. Why this course should be mandatory for all students.

26. Why more marriages are failing.

27. Surrogate motherhood.

28. How can we recruit more students to enter the teaching and nursing professions?

29. The sobering rise in female alcoholism.

30. The dramatic increase in teenage suicides.

31. The Soviet military advantage over the United States—fact or fiction?

32. The serious decline of births in the United States.

33. The high cost of acquiring and keeping public office.

34. The case of our vanishing beaches.

35. The popularity of home equity loans.

For more suggested topics, see Appendix C.

Evaluation Guide for Informative Talks

	Yes	No
Introduction		
Did speaker state purpose of talk?	_____	_____
Did speaker explain the importance of subject?	_____	_____
Did speaker ask a challenging question or two to stimulate audience?	_____	_____
Did speaker use relevant quotations from an authority on subject?	_____	_____
Body		
Did speaker use enough facts, examples, anecdotes, comparisons, and statistics to support statements?	_____	_____
Did speaker use audiovisual aids (recordings, movies, charts, maps, photographs)?	_____	_____
Did speaker occasionally ask audience pertinent questions?	_____	_____
Did audience seem to gain understanding from talk?	_____	_____
Conclusion		
Did speaker signal, by pausing, by inserting transitions, or by doing both, that talk was about to end?	_____	_____
Did speaker summarize key ideas?	_____	_____
Did speaker handle questions competently during question-and-answer session?	_____	_____
Did speaker repeat questions some listeners might not have heard?	_____	_____

Things to Discuss in Class

1. Prepare a short informative talk on one of the following:
   a. a concept or device
   b. a process or theory
   c. an event
   d. a problem
   e. a situation

2. Be prepared to discuss some principles that speed the learning process.

3. Prepare a short talk (a minute or two) giving specific directions on how to get somewhere. Be as concise and explicit as possible. Would visual aids be helpful? Explain.

4. Prepare a five-minute talk on one of the following topics. Be ready to explain how visual aids can enhance your presentation.
   a. the organizational structure of a business
   b. the organizational structure of an educational facility
   c. the organizational structure of a political campaign

What Do You Remember from This Chapter?

1. What are the prime purposes of informative talking?

2. List several categories of speeches. Which one is presented most often?

3. List some principles which, when applied, speed the learning process. Give examples of these principles.

4. What are some elements that should be included in the introduction of your informative talk?

5. What cautions should you observe when you use statistics?

6. Is it a good idea to follow an informative talk with a question-and-answer period? Explain.

7. Can an informative speech contain elements of persuasion or entertainment? Explain.

8. When explaining concepts that are new to an audience, what type of comparisons should you make?

Vitalize Your Vocabulary

Present-day English includes thousands of words based on roots from the ancient Greek language. The following is a sampling of roots, along with their meanings and some relevant English words:

Roots	Meanings	English words
Anthrop	human being	anthropology, philanthropy
Arch, archi	rule, govern	anarchy, monarchy
Auto	of oneself	autonomy, autograph
Bio	life	biology, biography
Biblio, bibl	book	bibliography, bibliophile
Chron	time	chronicle, chronology, synchronize
Dyn	power, force	dynamite, dynamo
Geo	earth	geology, geography
Gon	angle, corner	Pentagon, trigonometry
Gram, graph	write, draw, record	autograph, telegraph
Hydr	water	dehydrate, hydrant, hydroplane
Metr, meter	measure	diameter, metronome, geometry
Onym	name, word	anonymous, pseudonym, synonym
Orth	straight, correct	orthodox, orthodontist, orthopedic
Phil	like, love	anglophile, bibliophile (see biblio)
Phon	sound	euphony, phonetics, telephone
Pod	foot	tripod, podium
Poly	many	polygamy, polytechnic
Scop	look at, watch	microscope, periscope
Syn	together, at the same time	synchronize, synthesis
Tele	distant, far	telephone, telescope (see scop)
Theo	god	theocracy, theology
Tom	cut, split	appendectomy, atomize

12

People are generally better persuaded by the reasons which they have themselves discovered than by those which have come into the minds of others.[1]

Persuade Them

After reading and understanding this chapter, you should:

- Appreciate the importance of speaking to persuade.
- Know the purposes of speaking to persuade.
- Be familiar with methods of analyzing an audience.
- Understand various strategies to help you persuade an audience to accept your views.

Chapter Digest

A form of communication crucial to the achievement of your career goals is persuasive speaking. Several examples of persuasive speaking are listed to show how practical and how valuable it can be to you.

Persuasive speaking has three purposes: to convince people to take action

---

1. Pascal, *Pensées* (1670), 10, tr. W. F. Trotter.

that you want them to take, to change radically their attitudes or beliefs, and to buttress or weaken their current attitudes or beliefs.

Before you can persuade an audience to change their stance and do what you want them to do, you must analyze that audience. Several relevant questions are asked; if you can find answers, you'll stand a good chance of winning the audience to your side.

Armed with some understanding of your audience, you're now in a position to plan strategy. Two types of audiences are considered: (1) friendly and (2) neutral or passive.

Authorities on persuasion, starting with Aristotle 2200 years ago, agree on three ways to persuade:

1. Through logical argument by using evidence and reasoning.
2. Through speaker credibility.
3. Through appealing to basic social, biological, and psychological needs and desires.

Each method is highlighted, and specific examples are given.

The chapter ends with a sample inspirational speech that persuades you to keep on trying, no matter what your goal is. An outline accompanies the speech.

THE IMPORTANCE OF PERSUASIVE SPEAKING

Is the ability to persuade important to you and your career? Instead of answering "yes," we'll simply list examples of **persuasive speaking** that occur all around you. Then you can answer the question.

- A job applicant selling himself to a department manager.
- People who speak for public interest organizations (Common Cause, Sierra Club, League of Women Voters) recruiting members or testifying for or against pending legislation.
- A real estate agent selling a house to you.
- Leaders of charity drives appealing to you to open your purse or wallet.
- An attorney pleading to a jury to acquit her client.

- Political candidates asking you to mark the big X on the ballot.
- A parent trying to organize other parents to work for safer playgrounds.
- A corporation president persuading stockholders that her policies will boost the value of their shares.

We're sure that you get the point that persuasive speaking is a highly valuable skill that you can develop. Although there are no magic formulas or rules of thumb to transform you overnight into an accomplished persuader, there are several suggestions in this chapter to help you sharpen your ability. Of course, before you can convince anybody of anything, your body, your voice, your facial expressions, and your gestures should reflect the fact that you yourself are convinced. Audiences sense whether a speaker is convinced of the truth of her arguments or is faking it.

The Stanford University Graduate School of Business, perhaps the foremost school of its kind in the world, conducted research on successful managers and found that they have five major characteristics in common. "Oral persuasiveness" leads the list because "the successful manager is primarily an effective speaker . . . he is interested in persuading others to his point of view."[2]

THE PURPOSES OF PERSUASIVE SPEAKING

All of the examples of persuasive speeches listed in the previous section have one aim in common: to convince people to take a form of action. Therefore, they're called speeches to *actuate* or to *motivate.*

Another purpose of talks to persuade is to reinforce, strengthen, or dilute listeners' existing attitudes. Let's say, for example, that you favor court-ordered busing of school children and you're to speak to a pro-busing group. You would simply repeat a few powerful arguments in order to reassure your listeners and to harden their position.

---

2. *Nation's Business* (June 1976): 6.

A third purpose of persuasive speaking is to change people's attitudes toward a completely different position. Suppose that you are speaking to a neighborhood group that is neutral and open to discussion. In your introduction, try to capture their goodwill immediately (see the section on introductions in Chapter 7). Follow with some strong arguments for your position. You could describe how, in some places, busing achieved its aims of equal educational opportunities and satisfied teachers and parents.

ANALYZING YOUR AUDIENCE

It is crucial that you learn as much as possible about your audience's beliefs and attitudes toward your topic and your position. If your listeners' beliefs and attitudes are fixed, perhaps you should settle for a chance to speak your piece and hope that they'll give you a fair hearing. Realistically, you cannot expect to change their minds with just one speech, no matter how convincing you are. If, however, your listeners are open-minded, you may be able to swing some moderates among them to your banner.

Figure 12.1 shows the range (from strongly opposed to strongly favorable) of audience feelings, attitudes, and beliefs toward any speaker and subject. Sometimes an audience is polarized at one inflexible position, especially on emotional issues that cut deeply into their lives, such as unemployment, busing, gun control, abortion, and the high cost of energy. At other times an audience may be so fragmented that its members span the entire spectrum from strongly opposed to highly favorable.

No question about it—it's important to study your audience beforehand. (Refer to Chapter 8.)

Turning an audience around is a devilishly difficult task, much tougher than selling an automobile or a house. Convincing an audience to make even a slight change in direction requires a carefully planned approach anchored in a shrewd assessment of the audience's position. Before you can make that assessment, however, you should try to answer the following questions and any others that pertain to your particular situation.

1. What are you trying to accomplish? In other words, what is your specific purpose in speaking?

The importance of persuasive speaking . . .

2. How does your audience feel toward your purpose and position?
3. What emotional or psychological appeals will move these people?
4. What logical reasoning will "reach" them?
5. Are they willing to accept new ideas?
6. Why should this audience listen to you?
7. Do you know anyone who has had previous experience with this audience, and can that person help you answer these questions?

After you've analyzed your audience in terms of these questions, you will better understand their attitudes, feelings, and motives. Only then will you be prepared to plan your overall strategy.

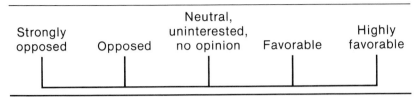

Figure 12.1
The range of beliefs and attitudes

SPEECH STRATEGY

Because this is a basic speech guide, we will delve into strategy just deeply enough to help you cope with some typical situations—for example:

- If the audience agrees with your position, discuss a few major issues so that you will reinforce your audience's position and erase any doubts that may plague them.

- If the audience is interested but undecided, use a few of your strongest arguments, both logical and emotional, to nudge it over the line into your territory. If an audience is "sitting on the fence," sometimes only a gentle prod will spur them to make a decision favorable to your point of view.

- If your audience is not interested in your subject, try to appeal to some aspects of their self-interest (discussed later in this chapter).

- If your audience disagrees with you, don't be aggressive in the introduction. Instead of using a strong, positive statement, phrasing your proposition or solution in the form of a question or two may be a more tactful approach. Let's say that you're to speak to hard-pressed taxpayers (is there any other kind of taxpayer?) in your town about raising taxes to finance a cleanup of the town's polluted lake. You might start by asking, "Do you want your children to have a safe, healthful place to swim, fish, and sail? Or do you want them to hang around street corners, pizza parlors, pool halls, or video game arcades?"

- Under the same circumstances, another approach would be to discuss areas of agreement first—if there are any—and then

Turning an audience around is a devilishly difficult task.

move to areas of disagreement. You might start like this: "We taxpayers all agree on the need for a family recreation area in town. Fortunately, we have a lake and we should use it for family fun. After we clean up the lake, our taxes will return to normal. In other words, this proposed tax increase will last only as long as the cleanup project lasts."

- If your audience understands the problem, spend less time on it and more time on your solution. Let's continue with the lake situation. Since your listeners, the taxpayers, understand the problem, you should devote most of your efforts to describing the benefits that they will enjoy from the restored lake. Be sure to stress that the tax increase is temporary and will stop when the lake is cleaned up.

- Spot your most convincing arguments at the beginning and end of your speech. Arguments in the middle tend to be forgotten. Playwrights know this, which is why the best plays usually open with a bang and close with a crash.

- Try to anticipate questions and objections. Plan your answers beforehand. This tactic applies to all speech situations, not just to persuasive speaking, and it can spare you many a headache. For example, during the Civil War, Henry Ward Beecher, a famous American clergyman, author, and abolitionist, went to England to drum up support for the Northern cause. While addressing a turbulent crowd of rebel sympathizers in Manchester, someone heckled him: "Why didn't you whip the Confederates in sixty days, as you said you would?"

    "Because," answered Beecher, "we had Americans to fight instead of Englishmen."[3]

- The opportunity to participate in a question-and-answer session may win over some hostile listeners. If you've studied your audience, you know who its influential members are. While you're speaking, focus special attention on them, because the other members tend to follow their lead.

METHODS OF PERSUASION

Speech authorities, psychologists, politicians, trial lawyers, and master salespeople know that there are three principal methods of changing people's attitudes or actuating people to do what you want:

1. Persuading through evidence and reasoning. (The formal term for this action is *argument*.)
2. Persuading through speaker credibility.
3. Persuading through appeals to basic social, biological, and psychological needs, wants, and desires.

In most cases of successful persuasion, all three methods are mixed in varying degrees, depending on the speaker's analysis of the audience, on her character, and on her style.

---

3. *The Little, Brown Book of Anecdotes*, ed. Clifton Fadiman (Boston, MA: Little, Brown, 1985), 47.

Try to anticipate objections.

Persuading Through Evidence and Reasoning

Let's consider these methods, starting with argument and its components, evidence and reasoning. Evidence, as you know, consists of facts and expert opinions. A fact is information that can be proved or verified. That there is no human life on the moon is fact. That there is no human life in outer space is not a fact because we don't know.

Opinions may be either your own or those of other people. As with facts, some opinions are convincing and others are not, depending on their sources. Your opinion of the causes and probable cure of inflation will carry weight only if you're an expert economist who has a reputation for sound thinking. Therefore, if you're using opinions in your speech to persuade, identify the sources and their qualifications.

In a presidential TV debate, watched by 90 million people in

October 1980, President Carter committed a gaffe that cost him dearly. During the exchange on whether or not to increase our stock of nuclear arms, he mentioned his daughter Amy's fear of nuclear proliferation. That statement not only turned people off, but it made President Carter the butt of countless cutting comments. The voters couldn't care less about eleven-year-old Amy's opinion on nuclear weapons. The President should have quoted a world-famous nuclear physicist; that opinion would have been credible.

At the close of that same debate, California Governor Ronald Reagan showed how to use people's own opinions to win votes by asking questions that hit Americans where it hurt most—in their pocketbooks: "Is it easier for you to go and buy things in the stores than it was four years ago? Are you better off than you were four years ago?" That masterful use of questions to persuade an audience helped catapult Governor Reagan into the White House.

Such a key question helped another presidential candidate capture the White House. In 1960 Senator John F. Kennedy faced a formidable obstacle—prejudice against Catholics. Never in 180 years had the United States elected a Catholic president, and JFK was determined to alter the course of history. In a landmark speech to a biased audience—the Ministers' Association in Houston, Texas—he made this persuasive point:

> Today I visited the Alamo where, side by side with Davy Crockett and Sam Bowie, died Bailey and Carey and McCarthy. . . . But no one knows whether they were Catholic or not, because there were no religious tests at the Alamo.

"Why, then," JFK asked, "should there be a religious test for the White House?"[4]

Types of reasoning.   If you have facts and authoritative opinions, you're in a position to carry out some reasoning. There are three types of reasoning—deductive, inductive, and causal.

Deductive reasoning means making a specific deduction or drawing a conclusion from a general principle:

> People who speak in a monotone tend to bore their audiences. (general principle)
> Mr. White speaks in a monotone.
> Mr. White tends to bore his audiences. (specific conclusion)

---

4. *Boston Globe*, 20 November 1983, A37.

The following is another example of deductive reasoning:

Under the Bill of Rights, all Americans have freedom of speech.
Armen Khoylian, a refugee from Iran, has become an American citizen.
Armen now has freedom of speech and can say anything, without fear of imprisonment.

Inductive reasoning, the reverse of deductive reasoning, starts with specific *examples* or *cases* and ends with a general *conclusion* based on the examples or cases. For instance, much American food lacks taste and food value; canned produce and packaged bread are notorious in this respect. Compared to European breads, most American bread is flat, tasteless, a spongy mush. In addition, most of our canned fruits and vegetables are "embalmed" with chemical preservatives and additives that may cause serious health problems. Most of these foods are produced, processed, and packaged by giant farm corporations. From these examples, we may draw the general conclusion that these farm corporations are impairing the health of the American people.

This discussion of American food can be condensed in the following syllogism:

Much American food (bread, canned fruits and vegetables) lacks taste and nutritional value. (specific example)
Most of these foods are produced by giant farm corporations.
These corporations are harming our health. (general conclusion)

Here's another example of inductive reasoning:

Some federal laws and regulations promote clean air and water.
Clean air and water are essential to good health.
Therefore, we should support these laws and regulations.

A common weakness in inductive reasoning is illustrated in the following generalization. The Professional Air Traffic Controllers Organization and another union went on strike in violation of their contracts. Therefore, all unions are bad and should be outlawed. That generalization is weak and invalid because it is based on a very limited number of examples. There is no rule about how many examples you need, but the more you can cite, the stronger your case will be.

Causal reasoning, also discussed in Chapter 7, moves from cause to effect (result). For instance, doctors and scientists have proved, through thousands of experiments, that smoking heavily—more than a pack daily—shortens your life by a certain number of years.

Here's another commonsense example of causal reasoning:

> When mortgage rates decline, people are more willing to buy homes.
> Mortgage rates are now declining.
> Sales of homes will soon increase.

The danger in causal reasoning is to oversimplify, to rely too heavily on one cause; in the real world, most effects are brought about by several causes. Regarding heavy smoking, other factors, such as heredity, environment, and life-style, also influence longevity.

To avoid oversimplification in causal reasoning, keep the following two questions in mind:

1. Did the alleged cause, in fact, result in or contribute to the effect?
2. Is the alleged cause the only cause of the effect?

If you use three types of reasoning—deductive, inductive, and causal—you should be able to handle your evidence (facts and opinions) effectively.

Persuading Through Speaker Credibility

During the Watergate crisis in the 1970s, the credibility of the White House plummeted to its lowest ebb in American history. The word "credibility" was bandied about daily—in newspapers, in magazines, on television, on radio, and in conversations everywhere. The scandal had reached such alarming proportions that people no longer believed any statements issued from the White House. Its credibility, an intangible but vital resource, was utterly destroyed.

When an audience believes a speaker and has faith in her, she enjoys credibility. Credibility doesn't just happen; it has to be earned through such personal characteristics as:

- Sincerity and concern for listeners.
- Tact and friendliness.
- Reputation and character.
- Self-confidence and poise.
- Experience and special knowledge of the subject.

He really enjoys credibility.

A crisis reminiscent of Watergate was the 1987 Iran-Contra scandal, in which it was revealed that members of the Reagan administration had made arms deals with Iran and had used the proceeds to finance Contra rebels in Nicaragua. At congressional hearings, the key figure was Marine Lt. Colonel Oliver North, who admitted carrying out the highly questionable deals. It appeared that North was slated to be the scapegoat for his superiors, the hapless victim of his congressional inquisitors.

What actually happened? After four days of testimony, North emerged a folk hero. He became as famous as Lee Iacocca and better known than Secretary of State George Schultz. He drummed up more support for the Contras in four days than President Reagan had done in six years. For a short time, at least, "Olliemania" gripped the nation; T-shirts, bumper stickers, and even pop music sang his praises.

How can we account for this sudden reversal in which the expected victim became the victor? It was, in fact, a triumph of overwhelming credibility. We Americans admire and respect a man of courage. Colonel North appeared in uniform, wearing a chestful of combat medals and decorations. We also admire and respect a man who is dedicated to his wife and family. Colonel North insisted that not only had he been a faithful husband, he had accepted the gift of a home security system only in order to protect his loved ones. We admire and respect a man who shows loyalty to his superiors, especially if one of those superiors is the President. Colonel North made it clear that his loyalty was absolute. And finally, abandoning both military and bureaucratic jargon, Colonel North spoke in simple, folksy English that proclaimed him to be "one of us."

In short, Colonel North fully understood the elements that impart credibility to a speaker and exploited them to his advantage. We're certainly not recommending that you use a manipulative approach when you speak in private or in public—but you would be foolish not to consider the impression you're making and be sure that your credibility is showing.

Persuading Through Appeals to Basic Human Needs, Wants, and Desires

We all have a certain amount and degree of basic needs, wants, and desires. And these important ingredients of life have no age barrier. Many older people wish to be younger and many younger people wish to be older. People seek a higher standard of living, ways to live longer, ways to enjoy greater health, ways to make more money, ways to be more socially acceptable and respected, and ways to be more appealing to the opposite sex.

Audience members are more easily persuaded when you can suggest ways to fulfill their basic needs, wants, and desires, such as those that follow.

Self-preservation. We all need food, clothing, and shelter. We want to escape accidents, fires, violence, and other risks to our well-being and to our family's well-being. These needs are reflected in the escalating sales of fire and smoke detectors. In the same vein, the demand for burglar alarms and other security systems in motor vehicles, as well as in homes and industry, has prompted manufacturers to include them as standard equipment.

In a persuasive appeal to this need, you can assert that your position fulfills your listeners' need for self-preservation. For example, you might try to persuade the audience to buy smoke detectors by pointing out their life-saving feature.

Sexual attraction. We want to be admired and fulfilled by the opposite sex. It's a normal desire that lasts a lifetime. The growing popularity of nude dancing (female and male) and R- and X-rated movies available to cable TV subscribers and owners of videocassette machines reflects this desire.

This sexual need is responsible for the multi-billion-dollar-a-year cosmetic and apparel industry supported by both sexes. These industries are able to persuade potential customers (audience members) that their cosmetics and apparel satisfy customers' desire to be attractive. And how else can you explain the popularity of such services as mate-matching, computer dating, singles clubs and trips, and male and female escort services?

Feeling good and looking good. Again, this is a universal want, and if you can unlock the secrets of good health and grooming, you will always have an audience. Today more and more men go to hair stylists, enjoy facials, and seek the services of plastic surgeons, once patronized mainly by women.

You may also be aware of the dynamic growth of health clubs and weight salons patronized by both sexes and the rising consumption of fresh and natural foods, herbs, and vitamins to improve health and looks. Interest in nutrition has never been higher.

Social acceptance. Most people crave acceptance by their peers at school, at work, and in social activities. Some people continually strive for acceptance and don't "make it"; other people bask in acceptance without appearing to exert much effort. Some individuals would go to any length to become a member of an exclusive club, society, or organization or to have their child attend a "very" private school.

This strong desire for social acceptance is probably the reason that so many people are taking self-help courses and purchasing record numbers of self-development books. Such resources offer ways to become socially acceptable; you can use the same technique in your persuasive speech.

Acquisition of wealth. Just about everyone wants wealth in some form—jewels, stocks, land, real estate, art objects, or just plain old cash. Tell your listeners how to acquire wealth and you'll have them eating out of your hand.

Many best-selling books have targeted the subject of financial security. Titles such as *How to Make a Fortune in Real Estate, How to*

Invest Wisely, The Fortune to Be Made in Penny Stocks, Investing in Gold and Other Precious Metals, and *Create Your Own Treasure with Paintings and Other Artifacts* are not only being gobbled up by a hungry public, but many of the authors are attracting standing-room-only audiences at their public lectures and seminars.

Curiosity.   People need knowledge about many topics—science, business, sports, government, entertainment, other people, and especially themselves. If you can answer their questions, audiences will be mesmerized by your every word. This curiosity accounts for the high popularity of biorhythms, psychics, numerologists, tea and palm readers, and astrology. Radio and TV talk shows, as well as newspaper and magazine columns featuring these topics, enjoy large participatory audiences.

Altruism.   Altruism is the generous urge to help others without any motive of self-gain. It is on this basic urge that the United Fund, Heart Fund, Salvation Army, and various cancer research funds base their appeals for financial aid and the Red Cross bases its appeal for blood donations. The desire to be altruistic also explains why such programs as the Peace Corps and VISTA have been so successful. Fortunately, many people feel a compulsion to help others—to do something for humanity.

Patriotism.   Many people who don't respond to other appeals may react generously when asked to help their country. This is especially true in times of war or other national disasters.

   Although our sense of patriotism reached a low ebb during and after the Vietnam War, a noticeable reversal of the antipatriotic mood was reported during the Reagan presidency. This fact is further documented by the increasing number of public and private colleges offering ROTC military training programs.

Identification of speaker with the audience.   Let's say you're going to speak to a gathering of farm workers about joining a union. If you once spent a summer picking lettuce or grapes, you should mention that experience in your introduction. Then you could relate to the farm workers, and they would more likely feel that you understand their day-to-day problems, and that you're concerned about their welfare. They would be far more inclined to accept your ideas

than if you had never experienced their long hours, meager pay, and spartan housing.

Belonging. We all belong to a family and feel loyal to it as well as to friends, schools, social clubs, political parties, and neighborhood organizations. Most of us feel a very strong loyalty to our profession and place of employment. These networks of loyalties and interrelationships strongly influence our actions and attitudes. Most people want to belong.

Adventure. Traveling to faraway, exotic places or experimenting with a new sport (scuba diving or hang gliding) are examples of fulfilling the desire for adventure. Some people feel a compulsion for adventure laced with clear-cut danger—for example, climbing a challenging mountain or exploring a fearsome glacier, big game hunting in Africa, diving perilously deep for ship wreckage or treasure, or sailing across the Atlantic singlehandedly. To exploit this urge for adventure, travel agencies publish vivid advertisements that show people climbing mountains or hiking across glaciers. Our history is distinguished by families and individuals with a penchant for adventure—from our early pioneer settlers to our pioneers in space travel.

Since all of these motives (needs, wants, desires) affect people in different ways, when you speak to persuade, you should try to appeal to your listeners through as many motives as possible.

Another phase of your overall strategy is to make it easy for your listeners to take the action you advocate. For example, if you're speaking to a neighborhood organization about better street lighting, don't ask them to send letters to the mayor, because they probably won't. Instead, make it easy for them: have a typed petition ready, circulate it immediately after you talk, and press them to sign it on the spot.

This very basic discussion of human needs, wants, and desires merely touches the surface of the vast, tremendously complex subject of human motivation and persuasion. It is a fascinating area with endless frontiers.

Who would imagine, for example, that even the *locale* (where the speech is given) of a persuasive speech could influence its outcome? Yet, this happened in the 1976 presidential primary campaign. Governor Jimmy Carter, a Southerner born and bred, won the black vote consistently, except in Maryland, and thereby won some crucial primary elections. One tactic distinguished Governor Carter from all of the other Democratic candidates—he spoke to black audiences in their churches.[5]

Remember this—to convince people, you should appeal to their minds and emotions; one reinforces the other.

> When listeners are convinced in their minds that what the speaker says is right, and when they feel in their "guts" (glands, muscles, nerve endings, viscera) that they very much want to engage in the action or movement he is urging, the combination of intellect plus emotions is all but unstoppable.[6]

---

5. *Boston Sunday Globe*, 11 July 1976, 33.

6. Communication and Leadership Program (Santa Ana, CA: Toastmasters International, Inc., 1971), 69.

A SAMPLE PERSUASIVE SPEECH AND ITS OUTLINE

Appearing in this section are a sentence outline of a persuasive speech and then the speech itself. For a detailed discussion of outlines, see Chapter 7; an informative speech is outlined in Chapter 11.

Title: Good News About Failure: To Fail Is Not to Be Defeated

Thesis Statement: Whatever the obstacles, you should never give up trying to achieve your personal goals.

I. Introduction: Two stories and a quotation about failure
   A. A businessman achieves fabulous success in business, marriage, and family life.
   B. President Harry S. Truman discusses his unhappy boyhood.
   C. Speaker quotes Saint Paul on importance of keeping on trying, of never giving up.

II. Body: Observations on failure
   A. We can avoid failure by saying nothing, doing nothing, being nothing. Speaker never failed in singing a solo, in playing in a tennis tournament, in getting his poems published, or in running for public office. He never failed because he never tried any of those challenges.
   B. Failure is a teacher. Before we learn to walk or play tennis or piano or to succeed in marriage, we fail many times.
   C. Failure need never be final: an apt quotation from old-time movie star Mary Pickford.

III. Conclusion: People who rejected failure and kept on trying
   A. Among the countless people—most of them unknown—who rejected their early failures, are Robert Frost, Albert Einstein, and Winston Churchill.
   B. "With God's help, we rise up from failure; afflicted but not crushed; perplexed, but not despairing; knocked down, but by the grace of God, never knocked out!"

Good News About Failure:
To Fail Is Not to Be Defeated

I. Introduction
   A. I think of two stories I've stumbled across in the last week or two. One was a newspaper feature about an unbelievably successful person for whom nothing ever went wrong. The article described a man who had made a fortune in computer hardware. On arriving home, he goes to his grand piano and plays Chopin while his attractive

wife puts the finishing touches on the gourmet French cuisine she has been preparing. Sometimes the man's playing is loud enough to disturb their fifteen-year-old son who has set up his own meteorology lab in the basement, says the article. The couple's daughter is away, being in a beauty contest at a local school. The whole article reads like the mimeographed Christmas letter your brother-in-law sends out.

B. About the same time, I read about an incident in President Truman's life after he had retired and was back in Independence. He was at Truman library, talking with some elementary-school students, and answering their questions. Finally, a question came from an owlish little boy. "Mr. President," he asked, "was you popular when you was a boy?" The President looked at the boy, and answered, "Why no. I was never popular. The popular boys were the ones who were good at games and had big tight fists. I was never like that. Without my glasses, I was blind as a bat, and to tell the truth, I was kind of a sissy. If there was any danger of getting into a fight, I took off. I guess that's why I'm here today." The little boy started to applaud and then everyone else did, too.

C. And so did I, as I read the story, for it is a reminder that all of us experience failure in different ways. That's why Paul's words in Corinthians have always hooked themselves onto my mind. "We are afflicted in every way, but not crushed; perplexed, but not driven to despair; persecuted, but not forsaken; knocked down, but not knocked out" (2 Cor. 4:8–9). Because such moments come to us, we acknowledge the bad times failure brings, and we look for good news.

II. Body

A. Then let's make some observations about failure.

Start by saying that *failure is something we can avoid.* That's good news, isn't it? Or is it? Failure is something we can avoid by saying nothing, doing nothing, and being nothing.

Let me brag on myself a bit. I have never in my life choked up while singing a solo. I have never lost a match in a tennis tournament. I have never had a poem rejected by a literary magazine. I have never been defeated in a race for public office. Inasmuch as I am one who loves music and tennis and poetry and politics, that's an amazing record. But you see, I have never sung a solo, or played in tournament tennis, or submitted a poem to a magazine, or run for public office. I have never failed at any of these things because I have never tried.

In life itself, the same options are open. Paul confessed that many times in his life he was afflicted, perplexed, persecuted, and knocked down. But many in Paul's day suffered none of these discouragements. Safely living tight little lives, they never offered themselves for any great new truth, and they lived and died with nothing more than kitchen failures and backyard defeats. What small battles most of us limit ourselves to: some successes, but at a very low level. Never any great commitment. Never a hard promise made. Never a challenging job taken.

B. Move on from there to note that *failure is a teacher*, the best one we'll ever have. Consider this: the only way you ever learned to walk was by failure. If your first step had waited until you were sure you would not fall, you would still be wearing high-topped white shoes with unscarred soles. The only way you ever learned to read, or add, or play the piano, or run an adding machine was by trying it and failing, and then trying again.

Last summer at Estes Park, in a court next to ours, some nine-year-olds were trying to play tennis. It wasn't going too well for them. One of the nine-year-olds swung at the ball and hit it clear over the fence just as his mother walked by. "Throw the ball to us, will you, Mom," the boy said. The mother replied, "Why did you hit it over the fence? You've had a tennis lesson!" It takes more than a lesson in tennis to learn how not to hit it over the fence. It takes long practice and frequent failure. You don't learn to hit it in until you've hit it out many a time.

Failure teaches us. If, in our work, something is going badly, something we need to learn is offering itself to us. There must be a better way to do this. In this situation, I am failing! What am I doing wrong, and where do I go from here? If, at home, things are going badly, we have the opportunity to learn, and to proceed stronger than before. Every marriage should expect moments of failure; the strong marriages are not those which never fail, but those which learn from their failures. Learning in marriage to treat all disasters as incidents and none of the incidents as disasters, the bond between husband and wife grows ever stronger.

Failure is a teacher, and it becomes an asset to us if we learn from it. We may learn that our present strategy won't work. We may learn that our goal itself wasn't good. We may learn that our inner problems interfere with our outer work. We may learn that we quit too soon. Whatever it is, failure teaches us if we will let it.

C. Therefore, *failure need never be final!* To fail is not to be defeated. Mary Pickford said, "If you have made mistakes, even serious ones, there is always another chance for you. What we call real failure is not the falling down, but the staying down." Someone tells of the young Methodist minister who went from seminary to his first church, and proceeded to fail miserably. The Bishop came out, talked with the laypeople, discovered that indeed, the young minister had botched the job completely. Invited to preach on Sunday, the Bishop publicly criticized the young man for his poor job. Everyone wondered what the young man would say the next Sunday, after having been publicly humiliated. He rose to the pulpit the next Sunday and said quietly: "I can sin, you can sin, and the Bishop can sin. I can make mistakes, you can make mistakes, and the Bishop can make mistakes. I could go to hell, you could go to hell, and the Bishop can go to hell!" No failure ever need be final!

In a bit of whimsy, Neil Postman quotes a letter written by a high-school senior who had received a letter of rejection from the college he wanted to attend. "Dear Admissions Officer," the student wrote. "I am in receipt of your rejection of my application. As much as I would like to accommodate you, I find I cannot accept it. I have already received four rejections from other colleges, and this number is, in fact, over my limit. Therefore, I must reject your rejection, and will appear for classes on September 18" (Neil Postman, *Crazy Talk*).

Crazy as it is, *I like that!* It may not have worked for that student, but it has worked and it works in many a life. That's just what Paul did. The world stamped "failure" on his hand, and Paul erased it. "Perplexed, but not despairing. Knocked down, but not knocked out." "*I reject your rejection!*"

III. Conclusion
   A. Any one of us can say that, too. So many have said it, and have risen from failure to real achievement. In 1902, the poetry editor of *Atlantic Monthly* returned a sheaf of poems to a twenty-eight-year-old poet with this curt note: "Our magazine has no room for your vigorous verse." The poet was Robert Frost, who rejected the rejection. In 1905, the University of Bern turned down a Ph.D. dissertation as being irrelevant and fanciful. The young physics student who wrote the dissertation was Albert Einstein, who rejected the rejection. In 1894, the rhetoric teacher at Harrow in England wrote on a sixteen-year-old's report card, "a conspicuous lack of success." The sixteen-year-old was Winston Churchill, who rejected the rejection.
   B. Go ahead and complete the list. "In 1982, John Doe failed in the effort to (and you fill in the blanks): keep a job, expand the business, make a good marriage, head a community project, be a good father." *Name your own failure.* How long the list might be! But John Doe rejected the rejection, and tried yet again. One of God's best gifts to us is the joy of trying again, for no failure ever need be final.

      Then sum it up with this. A small boy had been looking through a stationer's stock of greeting cards when a clerk asked, "Can I help you find what you're looking for, son? Birthday card? Get-well card? Anniversary card for mom and dad?" "Not exactly," said the little boy, shaking his head. Then he added wistfully, "You got anything in the line of blank report cards?"
   C. Life does; God does. Especially at the beginning of every new year those new report cards are available to us, and we ourselves fill

them in by how we respond to the D's and F's of life. With God's help, we rise up from failure; afflicted but not crushed; perplexed, but not despairing; knocked down, but by the grace of God, never knocked out! And that, my frequently failing friends, is good news, indeed!

SUGGESTED TOPICS FOR SPEECHES TO PERSUADE

1. Examinations for public school teachers should be mandatory as part of their evaluation process.
2. A public school education should not be for everyone.
3. There is (not) an equitable solution for the Mideast crisis.
4. Will there be a Social Security program when we retire?
5. Women should have the right to decide on a possible abortion.
6. Have we learned anything from the last energy crisis?
7. Can Detroit compete with Japan?
8. Is the strength of American unions beginning to wane?
9. All educational grants should be replaced by loan programs.
10. Most welfare programs should be replaced with workfare ones.
11. Why we must (not) reinstitute the draft.
12. Why a basic speech course should (not) be required for graduation.
13. We should (not) withdraw from the United Nations.
14. Prisons should be for punishment, not for rehabilitation.
15. All elected officials should be subject to recall.
16. All millionaires should pay some income tax.
17. X-rated movies should (not) be permitted on late-night TV.
18. Criminals are getting away with murder.
19. Why entrapment should (not) be illegal.
20. Since liquor and tobacco are legal, why not marijuana?
21. Everyone should be fingerprinted at birth.

22. In national elections, all polling places should close at the same time.

23. Grade inflation is watering down higher education.

24. Why public employees should (not) have the right to strike.

25. Gay couples should (not) be permitted to adopt children.

26. Cigarette smoking should be banned everywhere.

27. We should (not) have stricter immigration laws.

28. Convicted criminals should (not) be required to serve their entire sentences without parole.

29. The United States should (not) have protectionist laws to control foreign competition.

30. Women should (not) be given preferential treatment when employees are considered for promotion.

31. We should (not) support apartheid.

32. We should (not) negotiate with terrorists.

33. Americans who intentionally put themselves in jeopardy by traveling to world trouble spots should (not) expect protection from the government.

34. Public school days and the school year should (not) be longer.

35. Why should people of the opposite sex (not) be allowed to join private clubs or organizations where members are of the same sex?

Evaluation Guide for Persuasive Talks

Introduction	**Yes**	**No**
Did speaker attempt to win audience goodwill in first few sentences?	_____	_____
Did speaker identify with audience before starting body of speech?	_____	_____
Did speaker reveal understanding and knowledge of listeners' beliefs and attitudes in the first minute or two?	_____	_____

Body

Did speaker place most convincing arguments at the beginning and end of main body? _____ _____

Did speaker pay extra attention to leaders in audience because they "carry" others with them? _____ _____

Did speaker use evidence and reasoning to convince listeners? _____ _____

Did speaker achieve credibility with audience? _____ _____

Did speaker get the most possible "mileage" out of social, biological, and psychological needs and desires? _____ _____

Did speaker convince audience? _____ _____

Conclusion

Did speaker close with the strongest possible ending? _____ _____

Did speaker answer questions with poise and knowledge? _____ _____

Things to Discuss in Class

1. List a few topics for a persuasive speech that would affect members of your class. Explain what methods you would use to win their sympathy and motivate them to react the way you want them to.

2. Excluding the topics previously listed, give two topics for speeches to persuade.

3. Evaluate three TV commercials as to their intended audience and the persuasive appeal(s) used. Did the commercials accomplish their purpose?

4. Prepare a five-minute gripe talk about something at your school or place of employment. Present a solution to the situation and conclude by suggesting a form of action for your audience to take.

5. Give two examples of how you would persuade an audience using appeals to self-preservation and sexual attraction.

6. Give two examples of how you would persuade an audience using appeals to feeling and looking good and social acceptance.

7. Give two examples of how you would persuade an audience using appeals to acquisition of wealth and curiosity.

8. Give two examples of how you would persuade an audience using appeals to altruism and patriotism.

9. Bring to class three different newspaper or magazine advertisements and discuss the appeal(s) used to influence the intended audience.

What Do You Remember from This Chapter?

1. List a few purposes of talks to persuade.

2. Why is audience analysis crucial?

3. What is the benefit of anticipating questions and objections?

4. Name three ways to persuade people.

5. List several elements that contribute to a speaker's credibility.

6. Is credibility the sole requirement for persuading people? Explain.

7. Name several basic needs of individuals.

8. List at least five questions that you should ask yourself concerning an audience for whom you are planning a persuasive talk.

9. Regarding speech strategy, list at least five different audience situations you may encounter and describe a strategy for handling each one.

10. List three speakers you consider to have credibility and defend your choices.

11. Give three examples of deductive reasoning.

12. Give three examples of inductive reasoning.

13. Give three examples of causal reasoning.

Vitalize Your Vocabulary

When you communicate, you often use number words or number ideas, but did you ever wonder where the numbers come from? Most English number words derive from either Latin or Greek (L or G). For example:

Source Words	Meaning	Number Words
Semi (L)	half	semicircle, semicolon
Hemi (G)	half	hemisphere
Uni, from unus (L)	one	unit, union, unison, unilateral
Primus (L)	first	primary, primate
Monos (G)	single, solitary	monarch, monocle, monogamy, monolog
Sesqui (L)	one and a half	sesquicentennial
Bi, bin (L)	two	bigamy, binary, binocular
Tri (G)	three	tripod, triad, trilogy
Quadr, quadri (L)	four	quadrangle, quadrant, quadrille
Penta (G)	five	pentathlon, Pentagon, pentateuch
Quin, quint (L)	five	quintet, quintuplets
Decem (L)	ten	decade, decathlon, December
Deca, deka (G)	ten	decalogue
Decimus (L)	tenth	decibel, decimal
Centum (L)	100	centennial (see *Bi*), centipede
Mille (L)	1000	millennium
Kilo (G)	1000	kilometer, kiloton
Mega (G)	1,000,000, extremely large	megaton, megabuck
Myriad (G)	a large, indefinite number	myriad is used as an English word
Micro (G)	1/1,000,000, extremely small	microscope, microeconomics

13

Let thy speech
be short,
comprehending
much in a few
words.[1]

Saying a
Few Words

After reading and understanding this chapter, you should be able to:

- Make an announcement.
- Introduce a speaker.
- Present an award.
- Give a thank-you talk after receiving an award.
- Make a nominating speech.
- Give an installation speech.
- Propose a toast.
- Utilize a public address microphone.

Chapter Digest

Since you probably already belong to or are likely to join some organizations, you may be called on to introduce a speaker, present an award, nominate someone for office, make an announcement, or give a report. You may even

---

1. Ecclesiastes 32:8.

be asked to propose a short toast. If you're lucky, you may be elected toastmaster or function chairperson, and in that position you may present some or all of the special types of speeches explained in this chapter. As an active member of your organization, you may also be called on to respond to any of these speech situations.

This chapter briefly touches on these special-occasion talks from the standpoints of the introducer (function chairperson, toastmaster, master of ceremonies) and the person giving the response. Some examples of these talks are included.

GIVING A SHORT TALK

The odds are in your favor that, as you mature and start your ascent in the business or social community, you may be called on "to say a few words." Industry executives agree that there is no surer way for an employee to make his mark in the company than to display an ability to communicate effectively before an audience. The same holds true for your fraternal, civic, or other social activities, and you'll be amazed at the respect and admiration you earn when you can comfortably give a short talk.

There is no set of rules that encompasses all of the situations that may surround a special-occasion talk. Many factors impinge on the talk: your personality and position, the circumstances of the occasion, the time element, the type of audience, the main speaker, and the reason for the particular talk. All of these factors must be considered.

The most important characteristic of these talks is brevity. Usually the talk ranges from one to five minutes except for the toast, which is usually less than a minute. If you're the chairperson, your function is to be an intermediary between head table and audience. You're not expected to give a long-winded speech or to poke fun at the guest of honor. Your job is to move the proceedings along quickly and smoothly, with dignity and professionalism.

There are many types of special-occasion talks, ranging from announcements to sales talks to welcomes. This chapter deals with those talks that are most likely to be of immediate concern to you.

Once upon a time, in the days of the Roman Empire, a mob was gathered in the Coliseum to watch as a Christian was thrown to a hungry lion. The spectators cheered as the wild beast went after its prey. But the Christian quickly whispered something in the lion's ear and the beast backed away with obvious terror on his face. No amount of calling and foot stomping by the audience could get the lion to approach the Christian again. Fearlessly, he walked from the arena.

The Emperor was so amazed at what had happened that he sent for the Christian and offered him his freedom if he would say what he had done to make the ferocious beast cower in fear. The Christian bowed before the Emperor and said, "I merely whispered in the lion's ear: 'After dinner, you'll be required to say a few words.' "[2]

2. S. H. Simmons, *New Speakers' Handbook* (New York: Dial Press, 1972), 22–23.

MAKING AN ANNOUNCEMENT

At most organizational meetings, time is set aside to ask for help with a future event and to announce its time and place. Announcements should be short and carefully prepared, and they should include all pertinent information.

It's amazing how many announcements exclude an important bit of information—for example, the date or time of the event. Perhaps you can recall attending a meeting in which a committee chairperson announced an upcoming event, only to be asked, "What was that date again?"

Getting the Facts

If you're responsible for gathering information for an announcement, seek an authoritative source (the president of your organization, the chairperson of a committee, or the member designated by the chairperson). Get the source's phone number so that you can check information or any changes that occur before the announcement has to be made. In preparing your announcement, include as many of the five Ws (who, what, when, where, why) as possible and the H (how).

When you've prepared the announcement, check it for all details. Ask yourself:

1. What is being planned?

2. When and where will the event be held?

3. Will tickets be necessary? If so, how much will they cost?

4. Is the event open only to members?

5. What is the reason for the event?

6. Where will the proceeds go?

7. Who is responsible for the event?

8. Are volunteers needed? If they are, who should be contacted?

9. Do the day and date of the event coincide on the calendar?

10. If there's to be a speaker, who will he be?

Gather as much correct information as possible and present only vital information. Most organizations publish newsletters or bulletins that include additional details. Because of this, your announcement need not give telephone numbers of people to contact.

Delivering the Announcement

Delivering your announcement with enthusiasm can bolster interest and positive reaction from your audience. You may conclude your announcement by repeating key facts—for example:

> The Boston College High School Parents' Club will hold its annual May Festival on Saturday, May 18, from 9 A.M. to 4 P.M. on the school grounds. As you know, all proceeds will go toward the scholarship fund.
>
> We can still use some volunteers for an hour or two. Please check in with one of our volunteer coordinators, Mr. Joseph Robert or Ms. Deborah Grilli right after this meeting. We would appreciate a little of your time and effort.
>
> Remember, our annual May Festival will be held all day Saturday, May 18, right here on the B.C. High School grounds, and we need more volunteers. Thank you.

INTRODUCING A SPEAKER

The main problem with introducing a speaker is that, all too often, the introducer talks far too long. This situation was highlighted in an anecdote told by the late President William Howard Taft.

Once he presided at a meeting at which a number of distinguished guests were to give five-minute talks. The young chairman of the event rose to say a few words and rambled on for forty-five minutes. After he sat down, Chief Justice Taft stood up and said: "I remember once when I was in politics, we had a meeting at which there was to be one of these preliminary addresses. One guest captured and held the platform and when he finally finished, I remarked, 'I will now present Mr. So-and-So, who will give you his address.' Mr. So-and-So arose and stated, with some heat, 'My address is 789A 22nd Street, New York City, where my train goes in fifteen minutes. Good night.' "

If you're responsible for introducing a speaker, consider the following guidelines.

Be aware of your responsibility.   Your primary function is to prepare and motivate your audience to listen to the featured speaker. If you can instill such interest, you've done your job.

Be familiar with the speaker and the topic.   As soon as you know who the speaker will be, find out as much as possible about his background and the subject of the speech. If he is well known, information about him will be available through his press office or in newspapers. If he is not well known, call him for a profile.

If possible, try to meet the speaker before the event to ensure that your information is accurate and current and that you know the topic he will discuss. You don't want him to have to correct you during his opening remarks. Sometimes the title of the speech will suffice; at other times it may be appropriate to mention the subject matter.

Be brief.   How often have you heard an **MC** (master of ceremonies) say, "Our speaker this evening needs no introduction," and then extol him from birth to the present? If he needs no more than a short introduction, then give a short introduction and let him take over.

The length of your introduction should not exceed two or three minutes. No better example of brevity and simplicity exists than the introduction you've heard many times, "Ladies and gentlemen, the President of the United States."

Be careful not to embarrass the speaker.   Sometimes a chairperson can go to extremes in praising the speaker as one of the most brilliant, eloquent, and humorous orators of the day. This is embarrassing for three reasons: (1) the speaker very likely cannot live up to such an introduction, (2) he probably *realizes* that he cannot match the introduction, and (3) the chairperson may be preparing the audience for a resounding letdown.

Be natural.   If you're good at telling anecdotes and jokes or at being humorous, great. Nothing sets an audience more at ease and puts them in a receptive mood than a few laughs. It will benefit you to spice your introductory remarks with humor that directly links the speaker, the subject, and the occasion. However, if you're not a naturally humorous person, *don't try to be.* Humor in the wrong

Be brief in your introduction.

hands can be disastrous. As any professional comedian will admit, trying to make people laugh is a very serious business.

Be informative.   It's important to know and present a balanced blend of the following pieces of information: the speaker's background, the subject of the message, the specific occasion, and the audience. Ponder each of these items separately and completely when you're preparing your introduction.

Be careful not to make personal comments about the speaker's subject.   This is not the time and place to editorialize. When you introduce the speaker's topic to the audience, don't elaborate on the topic. That is the speaker's job. You may mention the importance of the subject, its relationship to the audience, and the speaker's knowledge of it, but leave the contents to him.

Be sure to pronounce the speaker's name correctly.   The most famous slip of the tongue was uttered by radio announcer Harry Von Zell when he proclaimed to the nation, "Ladies and gentlemen, the President of the United States, Hoobert Heever." Clearly, the announcer knew how to pronounce the name, but it just didn't come out that way.

If you're not positive about the exact pronunciation of the speaker's name, ask him how to pronounce it. If you have to, write it down phonetically.

Present the speaker to the audience.   If you feel that the speaker is not well known to the audience, you may mention his name several times during the introduction. If he is known to the audience and you want to use a dramatic approach, you may announce his name at the very end of your introduction. After you've presented him, face him, and in a warm, welcoming manner, wait until he arrives at the speaker's stand; then return to your seat. (You start the applause.) The following is an example of a speech of introduction.

> Good evening and welcome to our annual Media Awards Banquet. It is such a pleasure to see so many past recipients of these awards in our audience . . . a special welcome to all of you.
>
> It is, indeed, a rare privilege for me to have the opportunity of introducing our guest speaker for this evening.
>
> Dr. Joan Murray enjoys an international and distinguished reputation as a speaker, educator, writer, and communications consultant. She frequently appears as a guest on the nation's most popular radio and TV interview programs.
>
> During her tenure as chairperson of the Communication Department at Regis College in Weston, Massachusetts, Dr. Murray is responsible for developing media curricula in radio and television, public relations, photography, and motion picture production.
>
> Under her direction and leadership, the college's studio-classrooms, production facilities, and equipment represent the ultimate in state-of-the-art design and operation. Students enjoy individualized as well as small group learning experiences.
>
> Since Dr. Murray's many innovative approaches in media education and curriculum development have attained national prominence, she is a constant recipient of invitations to speak or conduct communication workshops not only in academe but also in private industry. As a matter of fact, she has just returned from a lecture tour in England, Germany, France, and Italy, where she discussed "International Communication," which is also her topic this evening.

We are extremely fortunate to have her here this evening, and I'm delighted to introduce our featured speaker, Dr. Joan Murray.

PRESENTING AN AWARD

In planning to present an award you should keep in mind the following key points.

Refer to the award itself.   It is important in your opening remarks to call attention to the award that is about to be presented. What is its significance; when and why was it founded? Who was its first recipient? Is it presented annually or only on special occasions? These are some questions to consider, and you may think of others.

Refer to the occasion.   This will prepare your audience for what is about to take place. You will attract the audience's attention and interest.

Refer to the recipient.   Explain why and how this individual or group was selected. Be sure to point out the recipient's achievements which led to this honor.

Refer to those whom you represent.   Mention if the award is being presented in behalf of a lodge, council, club, or company. The source of the award is of vital interest to the recipient and to the audience. The source certainly deserves praise. Express the sincere goodwill of the source and its satisfaction with the person chosen.

Make the presentation.   For the sake of building interest and including an element of mystery, you may wish to mention the name of the recipient last. Then, if the award can be handled easily, hold it up for all to see, read the inscription on it, present it, and congratulate the recipient. Then allow the recipient the opportunity to respond. The following is an example of a speech used in presenting an award.

> As you know, the highlight of today's annual dinner is the announcement of the CHEF OF THE YEAR. This is the highest honor that a member can receive because the honoree is selected by his or her peers of the Massachusetts Chefs de Cuisine by secret ballot.

This award is presented annually in memory of Peter Berrini, a well-known and respected executive chef and one of the original founders of the American Culinary Federation. It is presented to a member "for years of dedicated and distinguished service and for exemplifying the highest standards of character and unselfish devotion" not only to this organization but to the culinary arts profession as well.

This year's gold medal winner is a very special person. He is a member of the American Academy of Chefs, of which there are only 650 throughout the United States and Puerto Rico, and is a Certified Executive Chef, of which there are only 1500 nationwide. As a past president of the Massachusetts Chefs de Cuisine, he has held office for four consecutive years, the longest in the 14-year history of this organization. During his first term as president, he was personally responsible for the largest enrollment of new members of any chapter in the United States, for which he received a special national citation from the prestigious American Culinary Federation.

The eighth recipient of the CHEF OF THE YEAR award is a full professor and is department chairperson of the culinary Arts and Hotel/Restaurant Management programs at Bunker Hill Community College in Boston for both day and evening divisions. He is a food service consultant, lecturer, and writer. And you may have heard or seen one of his many appearances on radio and television programs. You can also say that this year's recipient practices what he teaches because he and his wife Claire recently opened a restaurant, called "Arthur's," in Weymouth, Massachusetts.

It's a distinct honor and privilege for me to announce that the members of the Massachusetts Chefs de Cuisine have unanimously voted Arthur P. Buccheri as CHEF OF THE YEAR.

RECEIVING AN AWARD

Sometimes when an award is presented, no formal reply is needed or expected. If that's the case, a simple, sincere "thank you" is sufficient. At other times a reply might be appropriate or called for by audience cheers of "speech, speech." If you're going to a function and there is the slightest possibility that you may be given an award, prepare a thank-you statement.

In preparing a speech of acceptance, use the following techniques.

Be honest. If the award comes as a total surprise, your facial expression may attest to the fact, but don't hesitate to express your surprise

Be generous in your praise, but . . .

orally. The audience will be more delighted. You should have no difficulty expressing your sincere gratitude. Sometimes a heartfelt "thank you very much" will suffice.

Call attention to the award.   Explain what the award means to you. (You might want to refer to others who have received the award previously.)

Be generous in your praise.   If you're accepting an award in behalf of a group or team, be sure to share the honor with them. If it was a singular effort and someone inspired you, don't keep it a secret. If appropriate, mention the future and how this honor may affect your efforts and plans. Don't forget to thank those responsible for presenting you with the award. It may also be appropriate to thank the individual who made the presentation. The following is an example of a speech to accept an award.

> You know, I can honestly say that I can't remember a single instance in my life when I was really at a loss for words.

There are two things I will always remember this evening for. One, I'm at a loss for words, and two, I'm deeply moved to receive this plaque naming me the recipient of your "Outstanding Member of the Year Award."

I know what this award represents, because I have actively participated in the voting for our first two recipients. It is indeed a thrill for me to join their elite company.

The honor you have presented me with this evening will always remain very special. I wish to thank the members of the nominating committee and each and every one of you for your most generous expression of recognition.

I will always cherish this award and the precious moments of this evening. Thank you very much.

MAKING A NOMINATING SPEECH

As you become more involved in organizations, whether scholastic, business, or political, you may have the opportunity to nominate someone for an office. If you belong to an organization, perhaps you recall a meeting when nominations for offices were called for. Someone from the floor, after being recognized by the chairperson, may say, "I would like to place in nomination the name of Mrs. Marcia Driscoll" or "I would like to nominate Mr. Vincent Shea." What you heard were *names* placed in nomination. Following are some suggestions to use if you want to nominate more than just a name but a person worthy of the office.

Describe the responsibilities of the office.   Mention the specific requirements attached to the office. Include its duties, importance, and broad responsibilities. (Remember that you want to build a powerful case for your nominee.)

Name the candidate.   In a voice so that all can hear *clearly*, announce your candidate and then explain to the gathering why he is the right person for the office. Mention the candidate's background, experience, and other offices held. How long has he been a member and did he serve on any committees? Now's the time to fire all cannons.

Place the name in nomination.   Conclude your nomination talk by formally announcing the full name of your candidate—for example, "Therefore, ladies and gentlemen, it is with a great deal of pride that I place in nomination for the office of president of local 2259 the name [loud and clear] of Jim Hurley." At this point your fellow supporters should explode with approval. The following is a sample speech to nominate a candidate.

> I am very proud to place in nomination for president of our alumni association the name of one of our most active members, Mr. Andrew Aloisi.
>
> We all know the demanding responsibilities that this office bears . . . leadership qualities, the talent to select chairpersons of important committees, the ability to look ahead, the gift to motivate, and certainly the love of his alma mater.
>
> Mr. Aloisi possesses all these attributes and more. During the last few years he has "answered the call" many times from this organization, and with distinction. As chairman of the membership committee, he was responsible for significantly increasing our active rolls. As program director, he brought many new and interesting events to this organization. Last year he was chairman of the Fund Raising Committee, and our coffers were swelled by the most successful year ever enjoyed by our association. He has also served with credit on our travel committee.
>
> Mr. Aloisi is a successful businessman and, at the request of this association, has generously made himself available many many times to talk and meet with recent graduates and help them in launching their careers.
>
> He is an executive with understanding and compassion and that special talent of being able to get things done. Those of us who have had the good fortune of working with Andrew know only too well his executive ability and devotion to his duties.
>
> This coming year we will be celebrating our 100th anniversary. It is a special occasion that promises to attract renowned educators and political leaders from all parts of the world. This special time warrants special leadership, and with that in mind I take great pleasure to place in nomination for the office of president of our alumni association . . . Mr. Andrew Aloisi.

GIVING AN INSTALLATION SPEECH

Congratulations, you've been elected to office. You've worked hard for the victory and you deserve it; however, you must now plan to make your first speech before the group. The following are some helpful ideas.

Express your gratitude. The first order of business is to express your sincere thanks for the vote of confidence bestowed on you, particularly by your supporters. You should also assure your non-supporters that you will represent them fairly.

Accept the challenge. You may wish to mention what the office is all about and enumerate some significant responsibilities. Explain that you accept all of the challenges the office has to offer and that you look forward to the coming term.

Admit that it's not a job for one person. Tell the group that getting the job done requires more than one person and that you're looking forward to working closely with the other officers and various committees. It's also appropriate (and could win goodwill) to refer to the past president in a complimentary fashion and indicate that you would like to call on him occasionally for advice.

Look ahead. The group will be anxious to hear something about your future plans. You can motivate your audience by outlining some of the steps you plan to take in the coming term. It is not necessary to detail every program, plan of action, or all you hope to accomplish. Brevity is important. You'll have many other opportunities to address the group. The following is an example of an installation speech.

> I wish to express my sincere thanks for the honor you have bestowed on me this evening. Our association is well known in the community not only for its active membership, but also for the many acts by its members in and for our community. It is a privilege to have been elected to its highest office.
>
> This organization—and we are all proud of it—achieved many milestones during the past year. It comforts me to know that I will have the full support and cooperation from our now past president, Stephen Rowley, as I begin my new term.
>
> Shortly, I will be calling on you for your assistance—to head committees, to become committee members, and to fulfill other important duties. I know your response will be as generous as it always has been.
>
> This organization, as any organization, is only as effective as the involvement of its members. We have one of the largest memberships of any organization in the state. And we have a record of accomplishments that speaks for itself.
>
> The two major goals I have established for the coming year are to increase our membership and to become more involved in our community. A high-priority item on our agenda will be the

establishment of a special fund-raising committee to help us further meet special community needs.

This will be a year of commitment, challenge, and participation. I will furnish that commitment. I will accept that challenge. I now ask for your participation.

Again, I thank you for your vote of confidence and the opportunity to serve you.

NOTE

Be careful not to say anything critical of the preceding year that will reflect unfavorably on your predecessor. Use good judgment and taste.

PROPOSING A TOAST

There are many occasions when proposing a toast is appropriate and desirable: births, birthdays, graduations, bar mitzvahs, weddings, anniversaries, promotions, and so on. The occasion could be a large gathering or simply an evening with a companion. No matter what the occasion, the toast should be brief, meaningful, and sincere.

A good exercise is to try to write down as many short toasts for as many situations as possible and keep the list handy for various occasions. Whenever you hear a clever toast, jot it down, perhaps rewording it to fit your own personality. The following are examples of toasts for various occasions.

Births

To Elliott . . . may you have the strength of your father, the patience of your mother, and, until that time, may you be as quiet as your teddy bear.

Birthdays

May the joy of this day be the forerunner of the many, many more to come. Happy birthday, Lloyd.

Graduation

As you leave the community of academe and enter the community of the business world, we wish you the very best for unlimited success. Congratulations.

Bar mitzvahs

To Craig, may the helping hand of God be always near as you leave boyhood and enter manhood. Shalom.

Weddings

To two beautiful people who have found each other, Howard and Rae, . . . may life shower on both of you torrents of love, health, and happiness.

Anniversaries

To Arthur and Sylvia, may the happy memories of yesterday and today be multiplied tenfold for all your tomorrows. Congratulations.

Job promotions

To one of your company's wisest investments from which it's bound to reap substantial dividends—your promotion. Good luck, Bob.

A toast to you

Here's to the student who may be called on to say
   A few meaningful words on someone's special day,
Be the request from a friend, a loved one, or boss,
   When you open your mouth, may you never be at a loss.

TESTING *1 . . . 2 . . . 3 . . . 4*

The chances are slim that you'll ever appear before a radio microphone (mike) or a television camera to express your views. It's far more likely that you'll appear before a public address (PA) microphone at a school, fraternal, or social gathering. Let's discuss some testing and speaking techniques you may find helpful.

Before you speak, you should test the mike to be sure it's working and at the proper level (volume). To test a mike, *speak* into it. The most common testing phrases are "Testing 1 . . . 2 . . . 3 . . . 4" and "Hello, testing. Can you hear me OK in the back of the hall?"

Above all, never test a mike by slapping it or blowing into it, because it is a very delicate, sensitive instrument. Doing either may damage it and annoy your audience.

Being the right distance from the mike is important. If you're too close, your voice will boom at everyone and your *P*s and *B*s (**plosives**) will sound like explosions. However, if you're far away from the mike, the audience will have to strain to hear you and may then tune you out.

The best way to know the correct distance from the mike is to test it. If the level has been set correctly, your mouth should be three to five inches away from the mike. If your voice is strong,

move back from the mike. If your voice is soft, move closer. It's important to listen to yourself and to look at your audience. You can hear yourself from the loudspeakers in the hall, and you can receive feedback from observing your audience.

When speaking over a PA system, be sure to slow your delivery so that every word can be heard clearly and distinctly. Otherwise, your words may sound jumbled. Because you'll hear yourself over the loudspeakers a split second after you've spoken, you shouldn't speak too rapidly.

Speak directly into the mike and don't move your head from left to right, or the audience will miss half of what you're saying. This guideline applies particularly to MCs who may be introducing head table guests. After you've introduced someone, you may look in his direction for a second or two; introduce the next person, speaking directly into the mike; then glance at him. Face the person you're introducing only if you can speak directly into the mike at the same time.

Above all, speak in your natural voice. For many people, this is the hardest thing to do. It seems that whenever people appear before a microphone, they try to lower their voice, sound dramatic, or start to over-e-n-u-n-c-i-a-t-e. Speak as you always do. Remember, the microphone is like a magnifying glass and will detect and amplify flaws in delivery.

Always treat a microphone with respect and always assume it is "on" (live). Otherwise, you could experience a few humiliating moments.

If you have to sneeze, cough, or blow your nose, be sure to turn your head as far away as possible from the mike. Finally, don't grab or hold onto the mike that you're speaking into. Doing so could produce an annoying hum or static over the loudspeakers.

Things to Discuss in Class

1. Get some news of an upcoming event either from your school newspaper or from the student activities center, and make an announcement of the event to the class.

2. Introduce a classmate who's prepared to give a talk.

3. Prepare and deliver a two-minute talk to present an award.

4. Prepare and deliver a two-minute talk after receiving an award.

5. Make a two-minute nominating speech.

6. Give a two-minute installation speech.

7. Give a short toast for a wedding, birthday, job promotion, bar mitzvah, or christening.

8. From your library research, find a good example of one of the special-occasion talks discussed in this chapter. Read it to the class, and explain the reason for your selection.

What Do You Remember from This Chapter?

1. What information should be included when you make an announcement?

2. Mention several valid sources of information for an announcement.

3. What is a common problem when someone introduces a speaker?

4. When you introduce a speaker, why should you be careful not to overpraise him?

5. Why should you try to inject some humor in your comments?

6. Name several elements to include when you present an award.

7. Name the important elements of a speech to nominate.

8. What information should an installation speech contain?

9. List several occasions when a toast would be appropriate.

10. How should you test a microphone for operation and level?

11. While speaking into a PA mike, how can you be aware of the right volume?

12. What is the most important characteristic of a special-occasion talk?

13. When giving an installation speech, of what must you be careful regarding the preceding administration?

Vitalize Your Vocabulary

Aviation and Space

aeronautics (n.)   the science and engineering involved in flight and in the design, construction, and operation of aircraft.

altimeter (n.)   an instrument that measures altitude.

amphibian (n.)   an airplane that can land and take off on land and water.

anemometer (n.)   an instrument that measures wind speed and force.

asteroid (n.)   any object that orbits the sun.

ceiling (n.)   the top limit of visibility for flying.

cosmic (adj.)   pertaining to the universe, as distinct from the earth.

fuselage (n.)   the body of an airplane.

gyroscope (n.)   a device that helps keep aircraft on course.

interplanetary (adj.)   between planets.

NASA (n.)   National Aeronautics and Space Administration.

orbit (n.)   the path of a celestial body or artificial satellite in space, especially a closed path around another body.

radar (n.)   a device for locating distant objects by reflecting high-frequency radio waves off of them.

re-entry (n.)   the return of a spacecraft to the earth's atmosphere.

retrorocket (n.)   a rocket fired from a spacecraft to slow or stop its forward motion.

satellite (n.)   a celestial body or human-made object that orbits another body.

stratosphere (n.)   an upper layer of earth's atmosphere.

supersonic (adj.)   faster than the speed of sound.

tachometer (n.)   a device that measures engine speed.

thrust (n.)   forward force created by the high-speed discharge from the rear of a jet or rocket engine.

14

Men are never so likely to settle a question rightly as when they discuss it freely.[1]

Let's Meet and Discuss It

After reading and understanding this chapter, you should know:

- The characteristics of a panel discussion, symposium, lecture, round-table discussion, brainstorming session, buzz session, meeting, and committee.

- The responsibilities of a panel moderator.

- The responsibilities of a panelist.

- The responsibilities of an audience.

- The responsibilities of a member attending a meeting and of a meeting chairperson.

- The main qualities of a group leader, or chairperson.

Chapter Digest

The environment, the consumer movement, health care, and education are just a few areas of public concern in which Americans are demanding and getting a voice. They are serving on more and more committees, forums,

---

1. Thomas Babington Macaulay, *Southey's Colloquies*, 1830.

panels, and symposia. They are interacting in groups to make decisions and to carry them out.

This chapter explains the more common types of group discussion: panel, symposium, lecture, round-table, brainstorming, buzz session, general meeting, and committee. These various groups consist of moderators, chairpeople or leaders, panelists or participants, and sometimes audiences. The significant responsibilities of these people are listed in detail. Also included in this chapter are diagrams of suggested seating arrangements for these major types of group discussions.

More and more Americans are becoming involved in community affairs. For example, in the past decade the consumer movement, spearheaded by Ralph Nader, has emerged as a vibrant force in our lives. As a result, consumers are being appointed to state and local regulatory boards and commissions. Parents are participating in advisory councils involving the operation of their children's schools. Concerned citizens are being selected as trustees and advisers to state-supported colleges and universities.

Perhaps never before have people shown more determination to "have a say" in events that affect them, their families, and their pocketbooks. They are a powerful force that can help return big government to grass-root levels.

More than just being present at hearings or large meetings in which they might ask a question or two, citizens are now becoming members of **symposia, panels,** and committees to communicate, interact, and make decisions. In the business and professional worlds you may be asked to, or may wish to, participate in a convention, conference, department or committee meeting, seminar, brainstorming or **buzz session,** or any one of the many other types of group communication.

Most small-group communication is either public (open) or private (closed). *Public* discussions take place before an audience, which may or may not be allowed to participate, whereas *private* discussions are open only to group members. (See Figure 14.1.) Federal and state legislation increasingly tends to favor public meetings.

The group's private or public status depends on certain considerations:

- How many group members will participate?
- What is each member's rank and influence?
- What is the subject to be discussed?

A Private/Closed Discussion

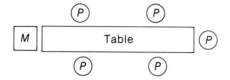

A Public/Open Discussion

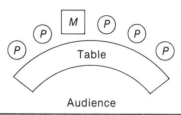

Figure 14.1
Suggested seating arrangements for a private/closed group discussion and a public/open group discussion are shown here. *M* signifies the moderator and *P* signifies the participants.

- Is the subject confidential?
- How soon must a decision or solution be reached?
- Will the decision affect a small group or a large group of people?
- When and where will the meeting be held?

THE PANEL DISCUSSION

The panel discussion is perhaps the most popular type of group communication and the one you'll most likely become involved in, either as a moderator, panelist, or audience member. A panel usually consists of four to six members and a moderator seated at a table and facing the audience. Figure 14.2 shows the customary seating arrangement for a panel discussion.

The primary purpose of a panel discussion is for the panelists to explore different aspects of a subject or problem by interaction. Each panelist expresses her views on the topic under discussion,

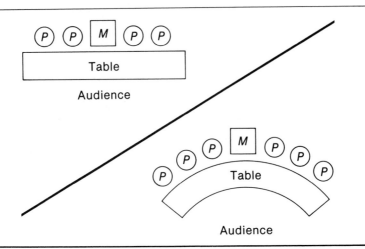

Figure 14.2
Shown here are two ways to set up a panel discussion. A semicircular arrangement is preferred so that panelists can easily see each other. *M* signifies the moderator and *P* signifies the panelists.

interacts with the other panelists, and then answers questions from the audience. The interaction among the panelists could result in a rather spirited, intellectually stimulating discussion. Whenever the audience is allowed to participate, regardless of the type of discussion, it is called a **forum.**

Responsibilities of the Panel Moderator

As a panel **moderator,** you have in your grasp the power to conduct either a smooth, meaningful discussion or one fraught with chaos.

1. Be sure that each panelist has a card, with her name clearly printed on it, on the table in front of her so that the audience will know her name. If the room is large and those in the rear have difficulty reading the names, you might put each panelist's name on the chalkboard directly behind her.
2. Greet the audience and introduce yourself.
3. Briefly tell the audience the topic to be discussed.
4. Inform the audience when they can question the panel.

Be tactful, but firm.

5. Introduce each panel member. You may also mention whether the panelist's position is pro or con.

6. Allow each panelist to make an opening statement of a minute or two.

7. After the opening remarks, allow the panelists to talk and question each other.

8. If interaction isn't immediate, be prepared to throw a question or two at the panelists to trigger discussion.

9. Remain impartial but be ready to question individual panelists if the discussion starts to lag or veer off course or if an opinion needs clarification.

10. Be sure to give each panelist a chance to express her views.

11. Be tactful but firm if you have a panelist who's monopolizing the floor. Try to spark some response from the more reticent members.

12. When you feel that the discussion has just about run its course, or if a time limit has been established, have each panelist summarize her views in a minute or two.

13. Present a summary of major ideas or concepts expressed from both viewpoints.

Be aware of the time element.

14. Open the discussion to the audience.
15. Call only on those who raise their hands. Again, be aware of time monopolizers. Accept only one question per person so that as many as possible may speak.
16. Don't hesitate to declare anyone out of order if the situation warrants.
17. When the time is up, thank the audience and the panel.

Being a moderator is an assignment that can be extremely rewarding when the result is a smoothly run interactional experience, followed by a spirited but orderly response from the audience.

Responsibilities of the Panelists

As a member of a team, your attitude and participation are vital to the overall success of the discussion.

1. Be informed and prepared to become totally involved in the discussion. In other words, do your homework.

Keep cool, no matter how heated the exchange.

2. Keep your opening remarks and summary to a minute or so.
3. If another panelist falters, come to her aid immediately by picking up the discussion and sustaining it. Perhaps the panelist just needs a minute or two to regain composure.
4. Have supporting material with you and be prepared to identify its source.
5. Don't monopolize the floor. Give others a chance to speak.
6. Don't interrupt a speaker. Let her finish before you start.
7. Be tolerant and understanding. Don't be overpowering and overbearing.
8. Be brief and to the point. Don't ramble.
9. Don't become personal and sarcastic.
10. Always respect the moderator and the other panelists.
11. Keep cool, no matter how heated the exchange becomes.

Responsibilities of the Audience

Psych yourself for a learning experience and be prepared to jot down questions to ask panelists during the question-and-answer period.

1. Give undivided attention to the discussion and to the participants' views.
2. When you wish to ask a question, raise your hand and wait for recognition by the moderator.
3. Keep an open mind until you've heard all of the views. Remember the words of engineer-inventor-author Charles F. Kettering, "Where there is an open mind, there will always be a frontier."
4. You may direct your question to the panel in general or to a specific individual.
5. Keep your question short and to the point; don't make speeches.
6. Don't question or enter a discussion with another member of the audience.
7. Don't antagonize or embarrass anyone.
8. Remember that you can disagree without being disagreeable. "We owe almost all our knowledge not to those who have agreed, but to those who have differed."[2]

THE SYMPOSIUM

A symposium usually consists of three to five members and a moderator. It differs from the panel discussion in that each participant of a symposium covers only one specific phase of the topic being discussed. The remarks should be well planned, prepared, and practiced before the discussion.

The symposium is very common at large conventions or business meetings in which experts are invited to speak on specific phases of a question or problem. The moderator introduces the participants and the subject and maintains control over the presentation. She

---

2. Charles Caleb Colton, *Lacon* (1825), 2.121.

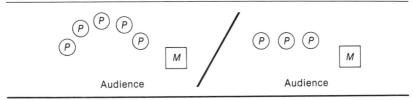

Figure 14.3
In these examples of symposia seating arrangements, *M* signifies the moderator and *P* signifies the panelists.

informs the audience of the procedure to be followed and whether there will be a forum after the talks. She should also be very much aware of the time element so that she does not interfere with other presentations on the program.

The seating arrangement of a symposium is similar to that of a panel discussion, except that the moderator may sit or stand on one side of the participants instead of in their midst. Figure 14.3 shows the arrangement.

THE LECTURE

The lecture panel is one form of public discussion in which a recognized authority on a specific subject presents a lecture and then is questioned by a panel. A variation is the *lecture panel forum* in which the audience is allowed to participate once the lecture and questions from the panel are over. Another variation is the *lecture forum,* in which the audience is allowed to ask questions of the lecturer after she finishes.

A chairperson presides over the lecture and introduces the guest lecturer, her subject, and the panel if there is one. She also states the format to be followed. Figure 14.4 illustrates the seating arrangement.

Figure 14.4
In this example of a lecture seating arrangement, *C* signifies the chairperson; *L,* the lecturer; and *P,* the panelists.

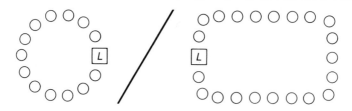

Figure 14.5
The choice of a seating arrangement for a round-table, or group, discussion depends on the number of participants. *L* signifies the group leader.

THE ROUND-TABLE, OR GROUP, DISCUSSION

The round-table, or group, discussion method is prevalent in classes where discussion and total group interaction are emphasized, as well as in many other settings. The unique feature of this discussion is that there are only participants; there is no audience. Circular seating allows for maximum informality and a sense of closeness.

The leader introduces a subject or question, calls on individuals to present their views, and then invites all members to express themselves freely. This is perhaps the most intimate form of group communication. The seating arrangement for a round-table discussion is shown in Figure 14.5.

The discussion is a learning experience for all participants if they make the effort to prepare and participate, keep an open mind, and are ready to inquire. The words of Joseph Joubert, French moralist and essayist, sum up this topic: "The aim of argument, or of discussion, should not be victory, but progress."[3]

THE BRAINSTORMING SESSION

Brainstorming is a creative, freewheeling, no-holds-barred approach to solving problems. Participants—usually five to ten in the business world and up to twenty in a class—should be given a few minutes

---

3. Joseph Joubert, *Pensées* (1842), 7.31, tr. Katherine Lyttelton.

There should be no criticism of an idea or its volunteer.

of silence to think and unleash their imaginations. They should spout anything and everything that comes to mind, while a recorder lists all of the ideas on paper or on a chalkboard. Quantity, not quality, of ideas should be emphasized.

The crucial principle behind brainstorming is this: no matter how preposterous an idea may sound, there must be no criticism or evaluation of it or its contributor. Participants must be free to say anything.

After about fifteen minutes of brainstorming, screen the ideas; then evaluate, expand, and refine them. Next, sift through the surviving list, focusing on the advantages and disadvantages of each; then finalize the list to the best two or three ideas.

Incidentally, brainstorming can be an excellent way to find speech topics.

THE BUZZ SESSION

This problem-solving process demands a knowledgeable discussion leader who is thoroughly familiar with the problem and who can conduct the entire discussion process. She explains the discussion procedure and the problem to the audience and divides the audience into clusters of four to six individuals. Each cluster functions independently and may take ten to fifteen minutes to come up with solutions. Someone in each cluster should record them.

At the end of the discussion period, the leader asks each cluster recorder to present a one-to-two minute summary of the cluster's recommendations. The responses are then combined and written on the chalkboard. The results are finally discussed either by a preselected panel or by the entire audience.

Buzz sessions are an outstanding mode of group communication; although some participants tend to clam up in big groups, everyone usually contributes to a buzz session. These sessions may have various formats depending on the people and problems involved, the time constraints, and the location.

THE MEETING

If you're an active member of a business, political, religious, educational, civic, or fraternal organization—congratulations. You're an activist and enjoy getting involved. On the other hand, maybe you would like to participate in an organization but you lack self-confidence. Becoming involved can be a gratifying, rewarding experience and can lead to unexpected opportunities.

Perhaps there's a local group that is in tune with your way of thinking; maybe a local issue has you so aroused that you feel compelled to sound off; perhaps you would like to volunteer for a worthy cause within your community. If you feel the desire to get involved, go for it.

Two components of any organization are meetings and committees. As a member, you're entitled to know the organization's constitution and bylaws; its officers; all of the working committees and their members; and the time, place, and agenda of each meeting. Of course, you also have the right to speak, to vote, and to run for elective office.

Most meetings use the following agenda:

1. Call to order.
2. Reading of minutes (an accounting of the previous meeting).
3. Committee reports.
4. Action on old or unfinished business.
5. Action on new business.
6. Announcements.
7. Adjournment.

Your Responsibilities When Attending a Meeting

1. **Be on time.**   Not only is it rude to be late for a meeting, but it can be disruptive. Continual tardiness can weaken your image and effectiveness among your peers.

2. **Be prepared.**   If you're planning to speak, be sure you've done your homework. Be clear, concise, and correct, and be sure to speak so that everyone can hear you.

3. **Be open-minded.**   Don't expect everyone to be agreeable to or ecstatic about what you have to say. Accept opposing views objectively.

4. **Be courteous.**   If you disagree with what's being said, don't interrupt the speaker. Wait for your turn to be recognized and don't get personal.

5. **Be attentive.**   Listen carefully to speakers so you'll understand what's being said. It's embarrassing to respond to or inquire about something that has already been discussed. Also, refrain from talking while someone else has the floor.

6. **Be serious.**   The temptation to be humorous at times can be overpowering but, generally speaking, keep your remarks sober and pertinent. Most people frown on a constant joker.

7. **Be sensitive.**   Be aware of other members' needs and anxieties and never try to advance your cause at the expense of others. Hurt feelings can leave deep scars.

8. **Be responsive.**   Offering suggestions and being sympathetic don't get things done. Organizations not only need talkers, they need doers. In order to pursue ideas or implement courses

of action, you should be prepared to offer your services. Perhaps you could volunteer to serve on a committee.

THE COMMITTEE

A committee is a small group consisting of five to nine members. (An odd number is usually chosen to avoid tie votes.) It is headed by a chairperson who establishes an agenda and keeps members on course. The organization's president may name the chairperson, or members of the committee may select their own. Committee members can be appointed or elected, or they may volunteer.

Organizations and action groups may have such committees as:

Entertainment	Health and safety
Fund raising	Building
Scholarship	Retirement
Membership	Student activities
Budget and finance	Taxation
Awards	Education
Political action	Nominations

Members of committees should exercise the same responsibilities as members attending a meeting and should ideally possess such qualities as the following.

Commitment. They should be dedicated individuals who can place the group's objectives and best interests above their personal feelings. Their presence and promptness can always be counted on. If they're going to be absent, they will notify the chairperson well in advance.

Intelligence and experience. They should be informed individuals who know how to track down information, digest it, and communicate it so that everyone can understand it. They can be counted on to have more than one perspective on the subject and to make positive contributions. If they plan to supply their colleagues with reports, memos, or other types of handouts, you can be sure they will.

Personality. They should be even-tempered persons who can take as well as give constructive criticism. They can disagree without becoming disagreeable, and their friendliness allows them to get along easily with other committee members. They are quick to compliment and to offer support.

Integrity. They should not intentionally belittle or degrade a colleague or her opinions and should be mindful of other people's feelings, especially when responding to a questionable viewpoint. They can be relied on for their honesty and ethics.

THE GROUP LEADER

Suppose that you have made your mark as an active and responsible participant in your organization, and you have just been selected to play a leadership role. It may be to conduct a large meeting or to chair a committee. For a large gathering (over twenty people), you would prepare and complete a premeeting checklist. (See Figure 14.6). Nothing can destroy the momentum and effectiveness of a meeting more easily than the lack of proper accommodations, equipment, and supplies. Investing the time to establish and check off such a list will pay dividends.

Also, as an effective leader you should be sensitive to the needs and demands confronting not only the group, but each member as well. You should be able to guide the group and, at the same time, be flexible enough to adapt to changing needs during the meeting. And, finally, you should radiate confidence and authority.

The following are some suggestions for acting as group leader.

1. Mention any rules of procedure.
2. Announce the topic and goal of discussion.
3. Help group members get to know each other (if size permits).
4. Encourage maximum participation.
5. Allow those with opposing views equal time to speak.
6. Encourage, but don't force, a silent member to speak.
7. Refer questions back to the group instead of answering them yourself.
8. Intervene when confronted with long-winded participants.
9. Ask questions to clarify meanings.
10. Ask questions that cannot be answered by just a yes or no.
11. Keep the discussion on track.

Figure 14.6

Premeeting Checklist

Reason for Meeting:
Day and Time of Meeting:
Name(s) and telephone number(s) of person(s) to contact in the event of problems:

Check When
Completed   *Comments*

Room (*Name or Number*)

Reserved	
Tables	
Chairs	
Sign designating room	
Nameplates	
Lectern	
Seating arrangement	
Refreshments	

Audiovisual Equipment

Public address system	
Tape recorder	
Presentation tapes	
Microphones	
Chalkboard	
Chalk	
Easel	
Flip Chart	
Overhead projector	
Other projectors	
Broad felt-tip pens	
Television monitor(s)	
VCR	
Screen	

Printed Material

Agenda	
Other handouts (list them)	

Supplies for Participants

Paper	
Pens or pencils	
Ashtrays	
Pitchers of ice water and glasses	

12. Be impartial, yet question logic and validity.
13. Avoid personality clashes.
14. Be complimentary whenever possible.
15. Don't permit private conversations while a person is speaking.
16. Don't allow a speaker to monopolize the floor.
17. List important points on the chalkboard if it would benefit the group to do so.
18. Watch the clock so you won't run out of time.
19. Take notes so that you can present a salient summary when the discussion ends.
20. Make announcements pertaining to a recommended course of action, information regarding next meeting, and so on.
21. Thank all participants and praise their contributions.

The position of group leader, or chairperson, is a responsible, challenging one that can also be rewarding and personally gratifying.

SUGGESTED TOPICS FOR GROUP DISCUSSION

1. The electorate should have the power to recall public officials.
2. Judges and/or parole board members should be held accountable for the actions of criminals on probation or parole.
3. Juveniles arrested for serious crimes should be tried as adults.
4. More money should be spent on domestic programs and less on foreign aid.
5. Able-bodied welfare and unemployment recipients should be required to work.
6. Financial aid to students should involve only loans and not grants.
7. Should we curtail our financial support of the United Nations?
8. Capital punishment, yes or no.
9. The Equal Rights Amendment.
10. Is our Social Security program obsolete?

11. Taxes on the middle class have reached confiscatory levels.

12. What can we do about the shortage of teachers?

13. Should corporal punishment be reinstated in the public schools?

14. Should the United States eliminate mandatory public education?

15. Are our colleges and universities suffering from grade inflation?

16. Can the United States attain full employment?

17. Is the United States headed for economic disaster?

18. Presidents of the United States should serve one six-year term.

19. How effective is student government on campus?

20. Should day care be available on campus?

21. What should the role of the United States be in the Middle East?

22. Should the United States be involved in Nicaragua?

23. Baseball players' salaries are right out of the ball park.

24. Should we have a national lottery?

25. Can the United States survive a 2.8-trillion-dollar national debt?

26. How effective is our military?

27. How does the U.S. space program compare with Russia's?

28. Should the United States renew diplomatic relations with Cuba?

29. Is "star wars" fact or fiction?

Things to Discuss in Class

1. Weigh the advantages and disadvantages of a strong discussion leader.

2. Assume the responsibility for selecting a small group and prepare a fifteen-minute panel discussion. Then, as moderator, present it to the class.

3. List three topics for each of the following:
    a. A panel discussion.
    b. A lecture.
    c. A symposium.
    d. A round-table discussion.
    e. A forum.
    f. A brainstorming session.

4. Assume that you are a panel moderator. Introduce yourself and briefly tell the audience the topic to be discussed. Then introduce each member of the panel and explain the format and ground rules.

What Do You Remember from This Chapter?

1. List several of the more common types of group discussion.

2. What is generally considered to be the most common type of group discussion?

3. How should a panel be set up for maximum impact?

4. Explain at least five responsibilities of a panel discussion moderator.

5. List and explain at least five responsibilities of a panelist.

6. List and explain at least five responsibilities of an audience.

7. What is a discussion called when the audience is allowed to participate?

8. Briefly explain the symposium.

9. How does the symposium differ from the panel discussion?

10. What is brainstorming?

11. What is a buzz session?

12. Name three qualities that a committee member should have.

Vitalize Your Vocabulary

Computers and Data Processing

access time (n.)   the time it takes a computer to locate a bit of data and deliver it to the user.

alphanumeric (adj.)   indicates a coding system consisting of letters, numbers, and punctuation symbols; a contraction of "alphabetic" and "numeric."

binary (n.)   a system based on the number 2 (rather than 10) that uses only the digits 0 and 1.

bit (n.)   abbreviation for "binary digit"; the smallest segment of information handled by a computer.

bug (n.)   a mistake in the design of a program or computer.

byte (n.)   a binary element string functioning as a unit, usually shorter than a computer word.

CPU (Central Processing Unit) (n.)   part of a computer that directs the sequence of operations and initiates the proper commands to the computer for execution.

debug (v.)   to find and correct mistakes in the design of a program or computer.

hardware (n.)   the mechanical, magnetic, electrical, and electronic components of a computer system.

input (n.)   information fed into a computer; may be instructions to direct the computer or data to be processed by the computer.

magnetic disk (n.)   a flat, circular plate with a surface that can be magnetized to store information in binary form.

output (n.)   information processed by a computer and fed to external devices that produce tape, cards, and so on.

peripheral equipment (n.)   physically independent machines that work with the central processor, such as high-speed printers, card reader-punches, magnetic tape units, and so on.

program (n.)   a series of instructions that tells the computer how to process data; (v.) to prepare such a program.

real-time processing (n.)   data processing performed during a business transaction; for example, an airline ticket agent may consult a computer about available seats while you wait.

software (n.)   programs designed to instruct a computer to carry out specific tasks.

time sharing (n.)   using a computer to process requests of many independent users at the same time.

15

To listen closely and reply well is the highest perfection we are able to attain in the art of conversation.[1]

What Do You Say After You Say "Hello"?

After reading and understanding this chapter, you should know:

- Some keys to good conversation.
- Some preconversational elements (factors, tips).
- How to improve your conversational ability.
- How to start a conversation.
- How to express sympathy and emotional support.
- How to talk on the telephone.

Chapter Digest

Almost all oral communication involves speaking face to face with one or a few persons. It's a daily activity in which you can improve a great deal if you try.

One of the keys to becoming a good conversationalist is to be genuinely

---

1. La Rochefoucauld, *Maxims* (1665).

interested in people. This interest is reflected by your attitude, eyes, smile, and handshake. Another key is to have many activities or hobbies and to be able to discuss them knowledgeably. Keeping up with the daily news in various fields by means of newspapers, magazines, and radio and TV broadcasts is a third way to help make you a more interesting person to talk with.

You can develop your conversational ability if you practice the suggestions given. For example, you should be sincere and listen attentively; you should not interrupt, monopolize, offend, complain, or pry; and you should not be a know-it-all.

There are also suggestions for initiating a conversation and keeping it moving—for example, how to introduce people and yourself, how to compliment people sincerely, how to discuss politics and religion, how to ask provocative questions, and how to express sympathy.

Since many people have trouble remembering names, we briefly discuss some psychological principles that can be applied to help you remember names.

Lastly, in today's fast-paced world, making contacts is a significant aspect of getting ahead, so there are suggestions that can help you advance your career.

So far, our emphasis has been primarily on how to prepare and deliver a talk confidently on a specific topic. Another more common but crucial aspect of communication is one that you engage in daily. It's a skill that you should master—the art of conversation.

You will engage in conversation countless times each day for the rest of your life. As far as making an impact on your daily life, there is perhaps nothing more important than the way you converse with people. At home; at work; at school; at a business, social or community gathering; in dealing with your spouse, your roommate, your children, or your neighbor; in interacting with your bank, utility company, or IRS agent; and in person or over the telephone, conversation plays a vital role in your life.

Conversational skill can be indispensable on the job. Let's look at an incident in the career of Sergeant Paul Crow, a homicide detective with the Daytona Beach (Florida) Police Department. He was investigating a case in which a woman had been stabbed to death. A second woman had been stabbed in a similar manner but had survived to identify her assailant. Sgt. Crow interviewed the suspect repeatedly, won his confidence and trust, and encouraged him to "open up." "Then he would go on and on," said the sergeant, "to get it off his chest. I had to talk on his level, laugh at his jokes, talk about things he knew about." In the end, the prisoner confessed to murdering twenty-seven women. He is now serving a life sentence.[2]

Think for a moment. Can you recall social or professional conversations that you wanted to leave or actually did leave because you felt the experience was a waste of time? Perhaps the person who spoke the most was boring and conceited and monopolized the conversation. Perhaps he was a tedious know-it-all or engaged in gossip.

SOME KEYS TO GOOD CONVERSATION

Some of the most delicious moments of life blossom in conversation. The art of swift and witty response is universally admired and enjoyed. Sarah Bernhardt, who reigned as the queen of the English- and French-speaking theater from about 1880 to 1920, was as skillful at dialogue offstage as on. In her later years, she lived high up in an apartment building in Paris. One day an elderly admirer arrived at her door, gasping for air after the long climb. When he recovered his breath, he asked, "Madame, why do you live so high up?"

"My dear," replied the divine Sarah, "it is the only way I can still make the hearts of men beat faster."[3]

You may recall conversations with people who were captivating, people who made you feel that you were part of the action and who listened to you with as much interest as you listened to them. If you're genuinely interested in others, the conversation stands an excellent chance of being interesting. There's nothing like a stimulating conversation; in fact, a good conversationalist is usually popular and well received. He knows how to communicate confidently with others. To be well liked, admired and respected and to feel that you're making a contribution to society, no matter how infinitesimal, is an unequaled experience.

You can become a better conversationalist, a more interesting person, and a more respected and admired individual. You can, that is, if you have the determination to work at it. And what's even

---

2. *Boston Sunday Globe*, 24 October 1982, 12–13.

3. *The Little, Brown Book of Anecdotes*, ed. Clifton Fadiman (Boston, MA: Little, Brown, 1985), 60.

You're not on a stage or under a magnifying glass . . .

better, you're not on a stage or under a magnifying glass but among friends. Every day you'll have a multitude of opportunities to practice, to experiment, and to evaluate yourself.

If you blunder, so what? In a few moments you'll have another chance. You won't be graded, criticized, or evaluated. You're free to progress as much as you want, at your own pace. You have your friends, even strangers, classrooms, home, work, the beach, social clubs, and meetings. The world is your laboratory in which to experiment.

Conversation begins even before you speak. As we mentioned in Chapter 3, your physical presence and expression transmit impressions, favorable or unfavorable, to those around you. Before engaging in conversation, consider the four following nonverbal elements.

Your attitude. You must look forward to conversation. It can be challenging, rewarding, and informative if you allow it to be. Have an open, unbiased mind and be ready to listen to all. Be eager to see what you can derive from this experience and what you can contribute to it.

Your eyes. Your eyes will reflect if you're genuinely interested. "The eyes have one language everywhere,"[4] and it's understood everywhere. Look people in the eye to communicate your friendliness and sincerity. If you're not interested, your eyes may transmit a negative impression.

Your smile. Can you think of a better way to communicate non-verbally with someone than with a sincere smile? Smiling can be contagious. Try it on the next acquaintance you see; you both may be surprised at the results.

Your handshake. Shake hands with a grip firm enough to convey a meaningful expression. If you're a strong person, don't use your strength for squashing knuckles. By the same token, people don't like a lifeless, dangling handshake.

When you can greet someone with responsive eyes, a friendly smile, and a warm, meaningful handshake, you've mastered the first step in learning to communicate interpersonally.

SUGGESTIONS TO IMPROVE YOUR CONVERSATIONAL ABILITY

Are there any secrets, special formulas, or rules that can make you a more effective conversationalist? No, but you must have a burning desire and a total commitment to effort. Let's look at some suggestions that can help you sharpen your conversational ability.

Be interested. The right attitude is a prerequisite for participating in conversation. Be interested not only in all of the topics but also in each participant. If you're not interested in the participants, they'll respond in the same way. So, when someone is speaking, focus your entire attention on him.

Have varied interests. One of the secrets of stimulating talkers is to have varied interests and to be knowledgeable about them. A

---

4. George Herbert, *Jacula Prudentum* (1651).

Try to avoid the "wet fish" handshake.

good conversationalist can discuss (with reasonable confidence) local, state, and national politics and knows something about the economy; sports; and the social, educational, and entertainment world. He reads the daily newspaper and a weekly news magazine, listens to news on radio and TV, sees movies, and reads books and magazines. He talks with people and *listens critically.*

Hobbies, travel experiences, sports, jobs, military service, and people you've met or work with are all possibilities for stimulating topics of conversation. If you make the effort to expand your horizons, you can become more interesting to others.

Be sincere.   In conversation, don't try to put on airs and don't bluff, lie, or brag. An insincere person usually ends up with himself as his only audience. There is no substitute for sincerity. Remember Lincoln's statement: "You may fool all the people some of the time; you can even fool some of the people all the time; but you can't fool all of the people all the time."

Be a good listener.   There is no greater compliment to a speaker than a listener's total absorption in what he is saying. Listen with your eyes, your ears, your mind—your total self—with intensity. You'll be amazed at how much you can get wrapped up in an individual and how much information you can acquire, which may ultimately enhance your contribution to the exchange. Listening is as important as speaking in the process of communication.

President Franklin D. Roosevelt once received an official visitor who immediately commented on one of the ship models on his desk. FDR took the bait and devoted most of the thirty-minute visit to discussing ships and the Navy. When the visitor left, the Chief Executive said to his secretary, "That man is one of the best conversationalists I have ever met."

Don't interrupt.   An easy way to turn people off or to anger them is to interrupt them often while they're speaking. It's a rude thing to do. The guilty person can't wait to finish someone else's story, to correct a speaker, or to announce a punch line prematurely. Interrupting is justified only when a speaker is boring his audience or becoming offensive (using profanity, bigotry, or insults). If you must interrupt, be as tactful as possible to avoid a scene.

In regard to interrupting people, here's a letter to "Dear Abby" that you or one of your classmates might have written.

> DEAR ABBY: I am dating a girl who has a very irritating habit. She interrupts me in the presence of others to correct my pronunciation of words. I wouldn't mind so much, but later when I check my dictionary, I learn that I was right and she was wrong. How should I deal with this? No names or initials, please, as this is a very small town.
>
> IRRITATED
>
> DEAR IRRITATED: If there are two girls in your town, date the other one.[5]

Don't flash family photos.   We all know one-track people who can discuss only one or two topics: their job, hobby or sport, house, car, or boat. It might have been interesting the first or second time, but the third time is boring.

Family and relatives can be boring topics, especially discussed by a person who can't wait to extract a wallet bursting with children's

---

5. *The Berkshire Eagle*, 10 June 1983, 39.

Family and relatives can be boring topics.

pictures. Winston Churchill felt that the subject of children was inappropriate for adult conversation. At one particular gathering, an ambassador said to him, "You know, Sir Winston, I've never told you about my grandchildren." The old warrior chomped on his cigar, dragged deeply, and exhaled, "I realize it, my dear fellow, and I can't tell you how grateful I am."

Don't drag on. Once your turn has come to talk, don't act as though it may be your last chance on earth and go on and on and on. If you have something to say, say it. Then give others the opportunity to express themselves; listen to them, and respond. That's the essence of conversation.

Unfortunately, long-winded speakers have always assailed our ears and taxed our patience. Early in the nineteenth century, General Alexander Smythe was noted for congressional speeches that droned on and on. Once he said to his rival, Senator Henry Clay, "You, sir, speak for the present generation, but I speak for posterity." Senator Clay, a brilliant orator, replied, "Yes, and you seem determined to speak until the arrival of your audience."

Don't be offensive.   There are many ways to offend people—for example, by making derogatory remarks about their dress, physical appearance, voice, accent, religion, or politics. These remarks cause two negative results: they anger the recipient and they brand the offender as a person to be avoided. It's far better to say nothing than to rub people the wrong way.

Don't be a constant complainer.   Everyone has problems and, as a rule, would rather not hear yours. A brief mention of your problem might be acceptable to your listeners, but don't dwell on it for the entire conversation. Some people always complain, no matter what the subject is. Since their negative attitude can be contagious, you'd be wise to avoid them.

Don't pry.   Nobody can be more offensive than one who persists in prying for personal information. Following are some typical questions:

- Why don't you have any children?
- Your drapes are beautiful. They must be expensive.
- And how old might you be, my dear?

A super reply was once returned by my wife (Mrs. AJV) when a busybody asked about the family income. My wife leaned toward the questioner and whispered, "Are you good at keeping secrets?" "Oh yes, certainly," was the reply, to which my wife answered, "So am I."

Don't be a know-it-all.   An obnoxious person in conversation is an expert on everything—politics, labor problems, social problems, religion, family affairs. No matter what the topic of discussion may be, he has the answers. Being knowledgeable is a tremendous asset when you participate in conversation, but sometimes discretion and good taste are higher virtues.

Disagree without being disagreeable.   Nothing is more stimulating than a conversation sparked with disagreement, provided it remains on a rational, friendly level. There is much to gain from hearing opposing viewpoints, plus the challenge of persuading or being persuaded. Whenever disagreement is introduced into a conversation, everybody's interest perks up. Don't shout or lose your temper if someone gets the better of you. If you feel embarrassed at losing an argument, perhaps you could have been better prepared. There will be a next time. No one likes to lose, but accepting it gracefully could earn you respect.

Don't exclude anyone. When you're involved in conversation, be sure to direct your remarks to everyone. Look at each person as you make your points. In this way you include everyone in your conversation. Then they'll be more apt to pay attention to you and to respond. Interest shown by eye contact, a nod of the head, and an occasional gesture toward an individual will do it.

Don't be shy. In every conversation there are speakers, listeners, and speaker-listeners. Perhaps you're the kind who'd rather remain in the background and just listen to what's going on. But that's only half the fun. If you tend toward shyness, you belong with the majority of the human race. (This topic is discussed in more detail in Chapter 1.)

TV commentator Barbara Walters was one of that majority. Some years ago she and her husband attended a Fourth of July party, where they were introduced to novelist Truman Capote. His book, *In Cold Blood*, had just been published and was zooming to the top of the bestseller list. ". . . I was yearning to talk with him about it," she confessed, "but I couldn't cross the barrier of my own shyness and my fear that Capote must be fed up with people asking about his work."[6]

If you're a listener or a speaker-listener, you may find that small groups (four or five people) are easier to break into than large groups (ten or more). The important thing is that you must *want* to engage in conversation. A good exercise is to observe good talkers in action and to adopt some of their methods.

There are situations in which a reluctance to speak up can be dangerous—even fatal. In February 1982 at Washington National Airport, two pilots of a Boeing 737, about to take off, saw snow and ice building up on the wings and engines even after their plane had been de-iced twice. Both pilots were deeply worried—the audiotapes revealed later—but instead of questioning the control tower about the advisability of takeoff, they said nothing. They crashed in the

---

6. Barbara Walters, *How to Talk with Practically Anybody About Practically Anything* (New York: Dell, 1971), xiii.

Potomac River, killing seventy-four aboard and four passing motorists.[7] It pays to speak up, even if you may be ignored.

As we said earlier, since the whole world is your laboratory, experiment with these techniques. You have a great deal to gain, and when you start to participate more in conversation, it will become easier and will do wonders for your self-confidence. Since improvement depends on active participation, the sooner you start, the better.

STARTING A CONVERSATION

Let's now look at some ways to help you start a conversation and keep it going.

"I'd like you to meet . . ." Assume that you're being introduced to a small group. Your introducer, if he's sharp, will mention something about you—your background, experience, or job—and perhaps even tell you some unusual tidbits about individual members of the group you're meeting. During this time you can decide to whom you would like to return for conversation because of a possible common interest.

"Hello, I'm . . ." If there's no one to introduce you, you should introduce yourself. Since nearly everyone at a gathering enjoys meeting the other guests, take a deep breath, approach someone, and introduce yourself. In addition to your name, give some information that might be interesting to the person and that might allow him to respond in kind. After a handshake, repeat his name aloud. Then you might say something about the host and hostess, your work, your home, sports, or the latest headline news. Then toss the ball to the other guest and see what he does with it.

"Excuse me, but didn't I hear you mention . . . ?" On occasion you may overhear a topic of interest from someone in a small group. Nothing could be more complimentary, at your first opportunity, than to approach the person with something like, "Excuse me, but

---

7. "We're Going Down, Larry," *Time*, 15 February 1982, 21.

"How do you like the weather?"

I couldn't help hearing you mention . . . That sounds fascinating. Could I ask you . . . ?" The fact that you're interested in someone enough to pursue his line of conversation will open the door for you, and a lively meeting could ensue.

"Say, I like your . . ."   Nothing is easier to accept than a sincere compliment. Perhaps you admire someone's jewelry, shirt, blouse, hairdo, or suit. If you do, say so. Again, since bringing positive attention to someone's abilities or possessions is highly satisfying, you're almost guaranteed an interested listener. Paying a genuine compliment is an excellent springboard for starting a conversation.

"Crummy weather we're having, eh?"   Discussing the weather can serve two purposes: it can fill in a silent period between people, and it can be an interesting subject if you're on top of the news. What about the drought in the Midwest and its effect on food prices and possible forest fires? What about the sinkholes caused by drought in Florida, the mudslides in California, and the torrential rains and dam burst in Colorado? How about the weather satellite? Is it doing its intended job?

"I never discuss politics and religion." Although some people will not discuss politics and religion, these subjects can lead to a stimulating, informative give-and-take. For that to happen, however, the participants must not become hot-headed, irrational, or belligerent. There perhaps has never been a time in our country's history when so much controversy surrounds so many political and religious issues. For that reason alone, we should talk over those subjects more than ever. Exploring them intelligently can be a beneficial experience that could lead to better understanding among people.

Play the role of interviewer. Although some people find this technique difficult, it can be most rewarding. It requires discovering someone who has an unusual life-style or profession, someone who may be quietly sitting in the background. Get the person to talk. This technique involves asking questions (how? what? why?) and could result in an exhilarating experience for all of those present.

A few years ago I (AJV) attended a large social gathering where I knew only the host and hostess. From talking with the hostess, I learned that one guest—the hostess pointed him out—was a senior design engineer in a company that produced and tested missiles. She added that he was not only brilliant and had a sense of humor, he could also translate difficult scientific concepts into common language.

At the first chance, I introduced myself to the engineer and started questioning him about his early start in mechanics and electronics, about some design challenges and solutions, about his travel overseas, and so on. As the conversation warmed up, more and more guests began to ask questions and contribute comments. When a lull occurred, I revved up the proceedings with another pertinent question. By the time the conversation ended three hours later, practically all forty guests had participated in this informative and sometimes entertaining experience.

An excellent way to learn this technique is to listen to radio and TV talk shows and to read interviews in the news media. Notice how questions are begun and followed up, how they're developed from answers, and how they're phrased so that they don't elicit one-word responses. Notice how interviewers leave a particular line of questioning and start another and when and how they wrap it all up.

"I never forget a face . . . but names?"   How often have you heard that? Some people can remember names but can't match them with faces; others can remember faces but can't recall names. One way to impress someone is to remember his name. To most people, nothing is more important.

Memory can be strengthened if you're willing to work at it. The following are some elements involved in developing your memory for names and faces.

1. *Attention.*   Whenever you meet someone for the first time, pay strict attention to the person, because you want to remember his name. Observe his facial features—eyes, hair, ears, dimple, nose—for something striking or peculiar that may make it easier for you to recall him later. During conversation, address him by name a few times; that will help you remember his name.

2. *Association.*   Is there any way you can associate the name with the person's features or occupation? Perhaps Miss Smiley has a beautiful smile. Perhaps Mr. Pearlman is in the jewelry business or his teeth resemble pearls. It's amazing how, with effort and imagination, you can associate a name with a physical feature, occupation, or hobby.

3. *Comparison.*   Perhaps a person has a name similar to that of a very good friend of yours. Visualize this person in comparison with your friend. Compare their features. Search for a resemblance or vast difference that might make it easier for you to remember your new acquaintance's name. Again, you may be amazed at what you can come up with.

4. *Repetition.*   When you meet a person for the first time, repeat the person's name as often as possible so that it is firmly implanted in your mind. Be sure that you hear the correct pronunciation of the name. If necessary, have it repeated and spelled; then you repeat it. Repetition is one of the keys to memorizing. But be sure to pay undivided attention to the person and the person's name. I (AJV) recall a rather embarrassing situation when I was introduced to a gentleman and, due to inattentiveness, I didn't catch his name and replied, "That's an unusual name; how do you spell it?" He obliged with "S-M-I-T-H."

MAKING SOCIAL AND BUSINESS CONTACTS

One of the more pragmatic aspects of life is making business and social contacts. Let's not kid ourselves; the more people we know, the more progress we may make in our career. You may have friends who were promoted or got jobs because they knew people. Others may have received certain benefits or special treatment because they have contacts.

Getting to know people is very important, but first you have to meet them. An excellent place to do this is at school. Try to get along with as many people as possible by being friendly and helpful and by keeping in touch. You never know who may be able to assist you in the near future or after graduation. If you're in a position to do someone a favor, do it. The day may come when you'll need a favor in return.

If you have a goal to achieve, make it a point to associate with people who can help you. Associate with people you admire and respect; some of their talents may rub off on you. Whether in your business or social environment, there are always key people, leaders who get things done. If you can help them in any way, volunteer. Do more than is expected, and that alone will set you apart from the masses. When people in authority can depend on you, you're building a future for yourself.

EXPRESSING SYMPATHY AND EMOTIONAL SUPPORT

Everyone occasionally finds himself in a situation when some comforting words or actions must be expressed. Perhaps a loved one or a friend has died, your husband was laid off work after fifteen years with the company, a close relative has just learned that she has a terminal illness, or the teenage son of your closest friend was arrested for injuring an elderly person while driving under the influence of alcohol.

Perhaps the most difficult situation to be confronted with is someone's death. How often have you heard people ask, "What do you say?" It would be impossible to list all of the appropriate things to say to cover specific situations, but the following suggestions may help make your presence a little more comforting and, at the same time, offer a grieving person some emotional support.

Be an active listener.   Listening attentively to a bereaved person can be very supportive and therapeutic. If the individual wishes to talk about the situation, listen with all the love and understanding at your command. Often, just listening without interrupting or pontificating can provide that person with the needed comfort. If he doesn't wish to talk and would rather be alone, respect that decision, but be sure to let him know that you'll be available whenever he feels like talking.

Empathize.   Be sure to communicate that you understand how the person feels by nodding or saying such things as, "I can understand your feelings," "I know what you're going through," "Yes, it is tragic," or "I know what you mean." It's important that the person feels that other people understand what he's experiencing and really care about him.

Express nonverbal support.   There are times when just touching is the most eloquent message that you can communicate to a distressed person. A hug, an arm around the shoulder, the squeeze of a hand, or a kiss says it all. If you honestly feel that you are at a complete loss for words, don't attempt any.

Don't platitudinize.   Sayings like "Well, everything happens for the best," "God works in strange ways," or "Think of the good times" are usually not what a grieving person wishes to hear. He needs your sensitive caring and understanding rather than your philosophizing. A sincere "If there's anything you need" or "If there's anything I can do, please let me know," or "I'll be in touch" can be very comforting.

Trying to think of just the right words to say to a grieving person can be quite uncomfortable and embarrassing—but it needn't be. You know the situation and the person(s) involved. As long as you are sincere with your expression of understanding, whether verbal or nonverbal, you can feel confident that your presence will be appreciated.

TALKING ON THE TELEPHONE

For most people, talking on the phone is an important means of developing and carrying on one-to-one relationships. Since you're not likely to speak on radio or appear on television, discussions of radio and television speaking are not included in this book. But talking on the phone is something you do regularly, perhaps many times daily, at home and on the job. The following are some suggestions to help you become more proficient at it.

Courtesy.   Always treat telephone callers courteously, not only because it's the right thing to do but because your response colors their impression of both you and your company or organization. If you've had a rough day and your nerves are rubbed raw, don't let your voice and words show it. That's easy to say but hard to do. If you're too pressured to talk at the moment, say so, get the caller's name and number, and tell him you'll call back in fifteen minutes, a half-hour, or whenever you can. But do what you said—call back.

Too many people today answer the phone "Just a moment, please," and then keep the caller hanging for three or four minutes. It's far more considerate and businesslike to get the caller's name and number and return the call a few minutes later. Courtesy and tact on the phone pay off in the long run.

Voice.   Your voice will come through more warmly if you remember that you're not talking to a piece of office equipment but to another human being. If you feel what you're saying and visualize the other person (see Oral Visualization in Chapter 5), you'll probably even use gestures like nodding your head, shrugging your shoulders, and smiling, and your voice will reflect that. As a result, you won't sound mechanical; you'll sound human.

For most people, the transmitter, or mouthpiece, should be held one or two inches away from the mouth and at the same level. If you tend to talk softly, keep the mouthpiece less than an inch away; if you blast, three or four inches would be better.

Pronunciation.   Don't chew gum, smoke, or clench a pencil between your teeth. Any of those actions will result in slurred words so that your listener may have to keep asking, "What did you say?" or "Pardon me?"

Always treat telephone callers courteously.

Brevity of calls.   At work it's a sensible idea to keep most of your calls short, say, five minutes or less. Plan your statement beforehand, and once on the phone explain the reason for your call and its importance. Then close with a few words on the course of action you or the other person is going to take. Avoid rambling endlessly; someone else, with an urgent message, may be trying to reach you or the person you're speaking with.

Expressions of goodwill.   Certain expressions "stroke" most people soothingly. Some of these are:

"Thank you."

"I appreciate that."

"I'm glad to help you."

"If you have any questions, be sure to call me."

When said sincerely, these expressions can build goodwill for you and your company.

Identification. At work, rather than answering with "Hello," you should immediately identify yourself and your department. Not only does this save time, but the caller will know that he has the right party and, in that case, will most likely identify himself. Whenever you make a call regarding a serious complaint or problem, be sure to note the date and the other person's name and number for future reference.

Security. Once you pick up the receiver, don't make side remarks to anybody nearby. Even if you cup your hand over the mouthpiece, the caller may hear information through the earpiece that he shouldn't know. In a social sense that could be embarrassing; in the business or professional world, it could be costly to your organization or to your career.

Memory aids. Always have a pencil and notepad near the phone so you can take messages promptly. Keeping on hand a list of frequently used numbers and emergency numbers can save precious time.

Taking messages. When you answer for someone who's not in the office, avoid statements like:

> "He's having coffee now."

> "He's late today."

> "He's in the men's room."

A more tactful approach would be to say, "He's out of the office. May I take your name and number so he can call you when he returns?"

Things to Discuss in Class

1. Before class, at the cafeteria, or at your next social function, select a person you've seen before but never talked with. Introduce yourself and engage him in conversation. Tell the class of your experience.

2. List the different sections of a newspaper and tell the class some news items you discovered in each section.

3. Listen to a radio talk program and take notes. Then tell the class

about the talk master and his line of questioning. Was he fair? probing? interesting? a good listener?

4. Try one or more of the techniques of starting a conversation discussed in this chapter and tell the class about your experience(s).

5. Tell the class how you feel about discussing politics and religion.

6. What methods do you use to remember names and faces? Share your methods with the class.

7. How do you rate yourself as a listener? Tell the class how you can become a more effective listener.

8. Your closest friend tells you that he didn't get the job that he wanted very much. Tell the class what you would say to comfort him.

9. List several "prying" questions, and suggest some suitable responses to them.

10. You're at a party, conversing with someone who doesn't agree with you. Suddenly, the other person becomes loud and disagreeable. Tell the class what your response would be.

What Do You Remember from This Chapter?

1. What are some ways of developing your conversational ability?

2. How can you become a more interesting person?

3. List several good conversational habits.   •

4. When is it permissible to interrupt someone?

5. Comment on this statement: Never discuss politics or religion.

6. Explain several ways to start a conversation.

7. What are some elements involved in memory development?

8. What is the key to making business and social contacts?

9. How can you disagree without being disagreeable?

10. When answering a question, should you look only at the questioner or at every member of the group? Explain.

11. Can you express sympathy nonverbally? Explain.

12.   When talking on the telephone, how far should your mouth be from the mouthpiece?

Vitalize Your Vocabulary

Electronic technology

alternating current (**ac**) (n.)   an electric current that reverses direction in response to a change in voltage polarity (positive or negative).

capacitor (n.)   an electrical device that can store an electric charge; a condenser.

charge (n.)   the amount of chemical energy stored in a battery and dischargeable as electrical energy, either positive or negative.

conductor (n.)   a material that allows electrical current to flow through; most metals are conductors.

direct current (**dc**) (n.)   an electrical current that flows in only one direction.

electron (n.)   the basic particle of an electrical charge (negative).

ground (n.)   in electrical circuits, a common point (which can be earth or some point on the metal case of a piece of electronic equipment) to which excess current can be harmlessly discharged.

insulator (n.)   a material that, under normal conditions, does not allow electrical current to flow through.

resistor (n.)   an electrical component that impedes flow of electrical current.

transistor (n.)   a device that much more efficiently performs the functions once performed by vacuum tubes.

voltage (n.)   the amount of energy available to move a certain number of electrons per second (current) from one point to another in an electronic circuit; unit of measure is the volt.

watt (n.)   a unit of electrical power.

wavelength (n.)   the length in space occupied by one cycle of an electromagnetic wave.

16

Too many job seekers expect other people to find a job for them. They don't do their homework. They don't evaluate what they have accomplished and figure out where their talent and experience might be most valuable.[1]

Let's Go
to Work

After reading and understanding this chapter, you should know:

- The most effective ways to find a job.
- How to set your job objectives.
- How to prepare a resumé.
- How to write an application letter.
- How to research a company before an interview.
- How to contact a company.
- How to prepare for a job interview.
- What to wear to an interview.
- How to handle yourself during an interview.
- How to discuss and negotiate a starting salary.
- How and when to ask for a raise.

---

1. *Business Week*, 23 March 1974, 73.

- Which questions may be discriminatory and illegal.

- How to follow up a job interview.

Chapter Digest

This chapter is a culmination of the authors' combined fifty-three years of business experience, especially in regard to job searching and interviewing. Applying the suggestions in this chapter should help make your job hunt more efficient and productive.

Your first step in finding employment is to determine your objective, without limiting your marketability to one type of job. Your second step is to prepare a one-page resumé that summarizes your education, experience, and capabilities. (Although resumés are primarily a writing task, this chapter on the interviewing process would not be complete without a brief mention of them, as well as of an application letter and a thank-you letter.)

Your third step is to get job interviews and to learn as much as possible about the companies that will interview you. Many ideas are given to help you land interviews and to find information on the companies.

The three phases of an interview—before, during, and after—are dealt with in depth. Numerous practical suggestions and cautions are presented, and they merit hard study. For example, there are many aspects of your life that an interviewer cannot legally ask about, and you need not answer such questions.

The last topics discussed are the importance of dressing correctly, negotiating a starting salary, and asking for a raise.

WAYS TO FIND A JOB

These are the most common ways to find a job:

1. A friend tells you there's an opening where she works and, if you're interested, she could set up an interview.

2. Someone tells you that Arthur's Restaurant is looking for waiters and waitresses. You telephone and are asked to come in for an interview.

3. You read an advertisement that representatives of a certain company will be in town, and if you're interested, call for an interview.

4. A close relative owns her own company and offers you a position—no interview required!
5. You contact your college placement office.
6. You contact state and private employment agencies.

No matter how you learn of a job opening, you are likely to be engaged in one or more interviews before you make a final decision. Just as in preparing a speech, the more you prepare for an interview, the better your chances will be.

SET YOUR JOB OBJECTIVES

According to a national expert on career planning, employers say that the number-one problem with people coming in for their first job is that they don't know what kind of position they're looking for.[2] On the basis of your education and experience, you should know what type of work you wish to pursue. It may be to your advantage to broaden your range of choices. If, for example, you're interested in becoming a police officer, don't confine your search exclusively to police departments. If there are no openings there, you may consider private investigation work or positions in a penal institution or in industrial and commercial security. By accepting a job in an allied field, you'll shorten your job-hunting time and make yourself more versatile.

During your job interview, you may be told that the position you're specifically applying for has been filled and asked if you would consider a related position. Even though you might be disappointed, it may be wise to consider the second option because (1) you may have a job and (2) after proving yourself, this may enhance your opportunity for upward mobility.

PREPARE A RESUMÉ

A **resumé** is a one- or two-page (preferably one-page) summary of your qualifications. It is your "ad," your foot in the door. It can either get you an interview or land in the wastebasket.

---

2. Peggy J. Schmidt, "That First Job: Finding It and Getting Ahead," *U.S. News & World Report*, 6 July 1981, 67–68.

A resumé serves a twofold purpose: (1) It is a significant communication between you and your potential employer. (2) It can be helpful when you're filling out a job application, especially for dates, a list of jobs held, and your social security number.

Whether you're offered a position might depend on how well you prepare your resumé. It is important that a resumé present all necessary, pertinent information clearly and neatly. The following elements usually comprise a resumé: personal data, job objectives, educational background, work experience, community activities, military service, and perhaps references.

Personal data. Give your name and address (include zip code), telephone number (include area code), date of birth (not required legally), and marital status (also not required).

Job objectives. Name the position you're seeking. If the position isn't specific, then be general.

Educational background. Include the schools you've attended and years of graduation, your major and minor fields of study, your degrees, any certificates or awards received, and activities you engaged in. Start with the most recent schooling first. If you ranked scholastically in the top quarter of your graduating class, state that fact; otherwise, don't.

Work experience.   List the more recent jobs you've held (full-time and part-time). Include dates, responsibilities, and any suggestions or improvements you contributed.

When describing your job duties in your resumé, use as many action verbs as possible, such as:

achieved	directed	originated
administered	documented	performed
analyzed	expedited	persuaded
coordinated	generated	planned
conceived	implemented	produced
conducted	increased	proposed
decreased	initiated	recommended
delegated	launched	reduced
demonstrated	managed	researched
designed	monitored	saved
developed	motivated	solved
devised	organized	supervised

Community activities.   You may list organizations and clubs to which you belong and any offices you held.

Military service.   This is especially important in an area related to your desired employment. Be sure to include the type of discharge or separation received.

References.   If you are asked for references, supply their names; otherwise, state that their names are available on request. Be sure to get permission from your references in order to avoid embarrassment. Give your references copies of your resumé so that they'll know your qualifications.

Once you have compiled your information, show it to someone who knows how a resumé should be set up and ask for constructive criticism. If you do not type well, have a competent typist type the resumé and then have clear photocopies made. A neat, well-typed resumé stands a chance of landing on the desk of the person who may hire you.

Production of your resumé can be a crucial factor. For example, presenting your resumé on pastel-colored paper instead of on plain white can increase *its* chances of being noticed and *your* chances of landing a particular job tenfold, according to Walter Lowen, one of the nation's leading personnel experts.

You can get excellent copies of your resumé by having a printing shop reproduce it through the offset printing method. The printer will have an ample supply of colored stock (paper) from which you can choose. Offset printing can produce at least fifty professional-looking copies. Generally, it's more advantageous to have too many resumés than too few. In any event, be sure to keep the original resumé in case you need to recopy it.

As mentioned earlier, resumés may take many formats; Figures 16.1 and 16.2 show two acceptable formats.

WRITE AN APPLICATION LETTER

When you mail your resumé, be sure to paper-clip a short **application (cover) letter** to it. This letter should tell your prospective employer two things: what you have to offer the company and why you feel you're qualified for the position.

The main objective of your application letter is to interest the reader to the point that she will invite you for an interview. Never start this letter with "To Whom It May Concern," "Dear Sir," or "Dear Ms.," unless you're answering a blind ad (an ad that instructs you to reply to a PO box number or address instead of to an individual). Remember, whenever possible, it's your responsibility to find out who will receive your letter. This information will also be useful in your follow-up phone call (see Figure 16.3).

RESEARCH THE COMPANY AND POSITION

Finding out as much as possible about a company and the position you seek can pay off for you during the interview. How old is the company? What products or services does it provide? What is its geographical area of sales? If it has branch offices, where are they?

Walter A. Bryant   Fall 1989
88 North Central Avenue
San Diego, CA 92111
(714) 555-1936

Job Objective   To work in the office of comptroller or treasurer of a small
                   manufacturing organization in order to qualify for general
                   management responsibilities.

Education
    1985 to 1989   Stanford University, School of Management
                   Received M.B.A. Degree in Business Administration, with
                   honors, June 1989. Concentrated on finance with strong
                   preparation in accounting and economics. Made Dean's
                   List. Was member of business club and debating team.
                   Financed expenses through outside work and fellowships.

    1981 to 1983   Bunker Hill Community College, Charlestown, MA,
                   Business Administration
                   Received Associate's Degree, June 1983. Majored in
                   Business Administration with several courses in
                   economics, including industrial organization and public
                   policy. Was president of Delta Kappa Epsilon. Financed
                   expenses partially through scholarship, summer jobs, and
                   part-time work as a sorter at the First National Bank
                   Computer Center, Boston, MA.

Experience   Barbara Calloway Investment, Inc., Weymouth, MA 02191
    1989 to   Security Analyst: Report to Director of Research. Duties
    Present   involve analyzing current stock issues and industry
                   trends, preparing weekly market letter for customers, and
                   writing reports on specific stocks or situations as
                   requested by partners. Am qualified as registered
                   representative by the New York Stock Exchange.

Summer Work   Summer jobs during college years included camp
                   counselor, construction laborer, and carpenter's helper.

Military Service U.S. Marine Corps
    1983 to 1985   On graduation from college, entered Marine Officer
                   Candidate School, Camp Lejeune, North Carolina. After
                   completing four-month program, was commissioned 2nd
                   lieutenant and assigned to U.S. embassy in Rome as

Figure 16.1
Sample resumé of a student with diversified experience

	security officer. I was responsible for a 15-man 24-hour security force assigned to protect the embassy and its grounds. Received commendation and was released from active duty in June 1985.
Interests	Interests include swimming, soccer, and gourmet cooking.
References	Available on request.

Is the company growing or standing still? (Refer to the text on research in Chapter 6.)

If you're looking for a specific position (for example, sales), you may want to know the present size of the company's sales staff. How much traveling is involved? How large is the average territory? As a new member of the sales staff, will you be selling the whole line of products or just a portion of it? What is the company's promotion policy—is it usually from within the company, or does the company bring in outsiders? What are your chances for advancement?

The more you know about the company and the position, the better you'll be able to respond during the interview. If you can't find all of the answers you'd like to have, when the right opportunity occurs during the interview, ask questions. This will demonstrate that you did your homework and are genuinely interested in the company.

Many sources of information are available about your prospective employer and the position you seek—for example, the public library and the college placement office and library, as well as company folders, newsletters, magazines, and annual reports. If possible, talk to employees, visit a brokerage office, and look through business publications and the business section of your newspaper.

CONTACT THE COMPANY

Now that you know the direction in which you're heading, it's time to contact the company and arrange an interview. You have two courses of action: conventional and unconventional.

Andrea S. Mintz   Spring 1989
45 Freedom Drive
Haddock, MA 02543
(617) 555-1936

Occupational goal

My immediate goal is to become a member of a corporate marketing
division, with the eventual aim of a management position.

Education

Carnegie Mellon Institute, M.B.A., 1989
Wheelock College, B.S., 1986
   Major: Marketing
   Minor: Psychology

Grades:
   Graduated both institutions with high honors

Extracurricular Activities:
   President of Speech Club
   President of Senior Class
   Member of Student Marketing Society
   Public relations director of campus day-care center

Work experience

Summer 1986–Fall 1987   American Telephone and Telegraph   I started as
   an intern in the management training program and after four months
   was promoted to assistant to the Director of the Northeast Marketing
   Division.

Summers, 1981–1985   Receptionist-secretary for the circulation department
   of *Redbook Magazine*, New York.

Figure 16.2
Sample resumé of a student with limited experience

Conventional.   You can mail your resumé and application letter
either to the personnel office or to the appropriate individual responsible for hiring. You can appear in person with your resumé to
inquire of possible openings, or you can telephone the personnel
office.

Unconventional.   Perhaps you have a friend already working for
the company who may be able to deliver your resumé and say some
good words on your behalf. Any action on your behalf by a contact

November 3, 1989

Mr. Albert W. Berger
Personnel Supervisor
Midwest Telephone Company
85 North Central Avenue
Chicago, IL 60603

Dear Mr. Berger:

In reference to your advertisement in the Quincy Sun on November
1 for a junior accountant, I am enclosing my resumé.

In college I majored in accounting and finance and ranked in the
top ten percent of my class. I also worked as an accountant for
three summers and part-time during my last two years of college.
I feel confident that my education and experience qualify me for
the position.

I would appreciate an opportunity to discuss this position with you,
and I will phone you in a few days to arrange an interview at your
convenience.

Sincerely,

Nancy Shea

Nancy Shea
37 Rangeley Street
Chicago, IL 60603

Figure 16.3
Sample application letter

within the company can expedite matters and give you an edge over
the competition.

Job Interviews

While job searching, your day could be considerably brightened by
a company's invitation to come in for an interview.

Try to learn as much as possible about the company.

Notification of Your Interview

You'll be notified of your forthcoming interview by telephone, by letter, or by your company contact. Be sure to write down the exact time, date, place (specific building, or office), and the correct name (and its pronunciation) of the person you're to meet. You'll find it useful to take along a pen and a small notebook.

You should put together some questions you may wish to ask at the appropriate time during the interview. Remember that it will be a conversation in which both of you will participate, even though the interviewer will most likely take the initiative, at least in the beginning. Your questions may run something like this: What exactly would my duties be? Is there a probation period, and if so, how long is it? When is the starting date? What are the company's prospects? What would be my chances for advancement? Does the company have an educational program for self-development? The interviewer may answer some or all of these questions during the interview, but if not, then ask them.

What Should You Wear to the Interview?

What you wear to the interview can play a significant role. As you learned in Chapter 3 (on nonverbal communication), you transmit messages even before you say a word. Your interviewer will receive an impression of you as soon as she sees you, and if you neglect your appearance, she may assume that you will neglect your work. Don't take chances with your image.

In a survey of over 100 top executives of major corporations, 84 percent said they turned down people who dressed improperly for job interviews; 96 percent answered that their firm's employees had a much better chance of getting ahead by dressing well; and 72 percent indicated they would hold up the promotion of a person who didn't dress properly.[3]

Guidelines for attire may vary from company to company or from one state to another, but generally it is wise to dress conservatively and not wear anything that would boldly call attention to you.

A woman should consider either a neutral-shade tailored suit with a neutral-colored tailored blouse, or a blazer and skirt with a pastel-colored tailored blouse. Wear a simple, well-groomed hairdo and avoid gaudy jewelry, excessive makeup, revealing clothes, and strappy shoes. Keep away from vibrant and clashing colors. Wearing a watch could signal your interviewer that you're aware of the importance of time.

A man should select a tailored, well-fitting, conservative suit in a neutral or dark color and a white or blue shirt with a regular or buttoned-down collar. His tie should be either striped or small-patterned, but conservative. Don't mix clashing colors, and avoid plaids

---

3. John T. Molloy, *Dress for Success* (New York: Warner Books, 1982), 36.

and checks. Don't overlook important "messages" from your grooming such as clean, manicured fingernails and polished shoes.

The Day of Your Interview

When the big day finally arrives, you'll probably be nervous—a normal reaction. Just remember that you've come a long way from your first talk in class. You've done your homework, you're confident, and you know what you want. You're ready. The following are some helpful suggestions:

1. Plan to arrive five or ten minutes early. Sitting in the reception area and reading or talking with the receptionist or secretary may relax you and may provide additional information about the company.
2. If you're asked to bring additional information (references or another copy of your resumé), put them in a briefcase, large folder, or manila envelope. Don't fold them or stuff them into your purse or pocket.
3. Be sure to have a pen or two in case you're asked to fill out additional forms, and don't forget a notebook.

The moment of truth has arrived. The secretary or receptionist announces, "Mr. Flagg will see you now. Go right in." Or the interviewer may come out to greet and escort you into the office. Your job interview has begun.

The interviewer plans to find out as much about you as possible. Since her task will be simpler if you're relaxed, the interviewer will most likely try to put you at ease quickly. After the initial introduction ritual (shaking hands firmly and offering you a seat), the interviewer may ask if you'd like a cup of coffee. When it arrives, if there's no napkin with it, tear a sheet of paper from your notebook and put the cup on it. By not placing your cup of coffee on the interviewer's desk or other furniture, you automatically gain a few points. Your notebook will serve additional purposes, as you'll see later.

The purpose of the job interview is twofold: (1) The interviewer has a position to fill with the best qualified individual in terms of education, intelligence, ambition, imagination, appearance, dependability, and moral character. (2) You want to convince the interviewer that you are that individual.

You're probably nervous.

Your Nonverbal Conduct During the Interview

What you do during the interview may be just as important as what you say and how you say it. Here are some points to ponder:

1. Maintain the **communication cycle.** Focus your eyes and mind on the interviewer and when she speaks, listen. If a reply is in order, respond. Total concentration will pay dividends.

2. Avoid distractions. The office may be laden with many interesting objects (on the interviewer's desk, on shelves, on walls, and so on). Although they may make for interesting conversation, remember that the primary purpose of your visit is to be interviewed, not to chat about curios. Obviously, if the situation calls for you to comment on an interesting piece, keep the comment brief. Don't digress from the main reason for your visit.

3. If you're sitting on a sofa or soft easy chair, don't relax into the contours or stretch out. While seated, don't fidget or change positions often because it can be distracting.

4. If you brought a briefcase or manila envelope, place it on your lap or beside your chair, not on a desk or table.

5. Keep your shoes away from furniture.

6. Don't smoke unless invited to do so, and before you light up, be sure that an ashtray is handy. (If the interviewer doesn't smoke, you should refrain from doing so during the interview. This gesture will very likely create a favorable impression.)

7. Don't play with your tie clip or tie, necklace, earrings, or other pieces of clothing or jewelry.

8. Keep hands away from your hair and face. Constantly brushing hair aside from your eyes may annoy the interviewer.

9. Don't chew gum or anything else. If for some reason you must take cough drops or throat lozenges, be sure to tell the interviewer. Don't distract her by clucking and slurping them.

10. If there's a confidential folder or papers on the interviewer's desk which look interesting, mind your own business!

The Verbal Side of the Interview

At this point you should review Chapters 5, 11, and 15.

Although you may be sitting during the interview, "be on your toes" for a question or two that might catch you off guard. It's not unusual for an interviewer to toss at you something like:

1. "O.K., Andrew, what can we do for you?"
2. "Why do you want to work for us?"
3. "Tell me something about yourself."
4. "Why should we hire you?"
5. "Tell me exactly what you're looking for."

A practical way to prepare for these questions is to ask yourself this question: if you were in the interviewer's place, what answers

Don't be too relaxed.

would impress you? The reason you may be confronted with such questions is that the interviewer wants to see how you handle yourself. Although most interviewers don't ask more than one or two such questions, you'd be wise to prepare answers to them, since there is no way of knowing which one she might ask. A popular approach is for the interviewer to ask a question about current events. A person who's interested in what's happening in the world will probably be interested in the company she works for and in the job she is doing.

Here are some other topics and questions you should be prepared to answer:

1. Place of birth and where you grew up.
2. Schools attended, courses of study, favorite subjects.
3. Why you selected the schools and what extracurricular activities you engaged in.
4. Do you want to continue your education?
5. Did you work while going to school and to what extent?
6. Military service and present status.

7. What do you know about the company?
8. Your immediate and long-range goals.
9. Do you know anyone who works for the company?
10. Present occupation. Why you left other jobs.
11. Have you ever been fired? If so, why?
12. What specific job do you want?
13. A question or two about politics and current events.
14. Do you have any hobbies?
15. Do you like to travel?
16. Are you willing to relocate?
17. Are you involved in community activities and to what extent?
18. What can you do for the company?
19. How much money do you need to start with?

Let's Talk Money

For some strange reason many people, including some employment counselors, consider the discussion of salary during an interview as risky and questionable. It shouldn't be because most people work for one reason—to earn money.

Most companies usually classify positions with specific job descriptions, including minimum and maximum salary ranges. It's only natural for an employer to try to hire someone for as little as possible. That is business.

During your first interview, the chances are slim that the subject of salary will emerge. If the company is interested in you, they'll ask you to return for a second interview; then they may offer you the position and announce the starting salary. At this point you can either accept the figure or try to negotiate a higher one. If you feel confident and have good vibes about the situation, then shoot for the higher salary.

Let the person know that you want the job, that you can do it well, and that you would be an asset to the department and the company. There's nothing wrong in asking if the salary offered is entry level or if the position carries a minimum and maximum salary range. You could state that, based on your academic credentials and previous job experience, you were hoping for a higher starting salary—and name a figure.

"With all of the lovely fringe benefits we offer, you'll find you have very little need for money."

Some individuals may find it more comfortable, if they're offered a position and a figure, to simply ask, "Is the salary negotiable?" If the answer is no—then, that's it. Obviously, whatever strategy you choose will depend on how much you want and need the job.

During your negotiations, explore the company's policy regarding raises, promotions, vacations, medical and dental coverage, and other fringe benefits, such as tuition reimbursement and profit sharing, (if they haven't already been discussed). There's a good chance these may more than compensate for a lower starting salary.

And be careful not to close the door on yourself. Don't say things like "Although I would like the job, I must have more money" or "I couldn't take the job at that low figure." Always leave room for possible negotiations.

Questions Which May Be Illegal or Discriminatory

Since passage of the Age Discrimination in Employment Act of 1967, Title VII of the Civil Rights Act of 1964, the Equal Pay Act of 1963, and executive orders related to such legislation, an interviewer must be very cautious about her questions.

Any questions pertaining to age, sex, color, race, religion, or national origin could be discriminatory and unlawful. Other topics which may be illicit include questions about your marital status, spouse, dependents, credit status, home ownership, personal savings, experiences with the law and litigations, questionable experiences while in the military; present salary, bondability, and health problems or handicaps. If such questions are asked and the applicant is not hired, the applicant could file a complaint at the local office of the Commission Against Discrimination or the Equal Employment Opportunity Commission. Prior to a job interview, it would be wise to make an appointment with your school's Career Development or Job Placement office for guidance in this ticklish area.

The Interviewer's Approach

The interviewer will probably use one of the following approaches.

1. She may do most of the talking and questioning to see how you respond. She will observe your poise, patience, and immediate reaction to questions, as well as how well you handle difficult ones.

2. She may say very little so that the burden of sustaining the interview will be on you. This approach is the most difficult for the new job seeker, but the interviewer may be looking for someone who is determined and well prepared and who can communicate intelligently.

3. She may employ a give-and-take technique in which both of you contribute a somewhat equal amount to the conversation.

Some Additional Tips to Follow During the Interview

The way in which you behave, verbally and nonverbally, during the interview may or may not clinch the job for you. The following tips may help ensure your success.

1. Try not to respond to questions with one- and two-word

answers. Occasionally, however, a yes or no answer is perfectly acceptable.

2. Your answers should contain only the information sought by the question. One exception would be some valuable information that would benefit your cause and that you hadn't yet had the opportunity to mention. If the questioning allows you to slide in the information without being too obvious, do it. For example, if you were asked about part-time employment and you wanted to mention that you paid for 80 percent of your education, you could say something like "Yes, I feel that working while going to school is worthwhile. For some of us it is a necessity. I've worked nights and weekends during the school session and full-time during the summers. Not only did this work enable me to complete my education, but the experience was invaluable, especially for the position I'm now seeking."

3. Look for nonverbal signs. If the interviewer takes her eyes away from you and looks around the office or at some things on her desk, perhaps you've been rambling on without substance. If she looks at her watch or gathers papers together, she may be about to terminate the interview. If the interviewer tilts back in her chair while she's still looking at you, that could mean that she's interested in your response. Therefore, you should keep going.

4. Be honest in your answers and opinions because the interviewer is a pro who can spot phony talk.

5. When answering tough questions, it's permissible to pause a second or two to gather your thoughts. Then look the interviewer straight in the eye and respond as confidently as possible.

6. Never offer confidential information about a competitor for whom you worked. It could weaken your chances for employment because the interviewer may feel, and rightfully so, that you might reveal company secrets while in her employ. If you have any business or professional secrets, keep them locked up. If your prospective employer enters on this delicate area, she could be testing your integrity.

7. Don't criticize former employers. If you've had an unpleasant experience on a job, admit that it may have been a personality conflict and share some of the blame.

Look for nonverbal signs.

8. If you've ever been fired and are asked why, there's no better approach than to be honest. Personnel specialists in the same area usually know one another on a first-name basis. If the interviewer doubts the truth of some of your statements, she can easily phone the personnel director of your former employer and check you out. It's far better to tell the interviewer the reasons for the firing and then convince her to give you the job which you feel you deserve.

9. Don't beg for the position. Don't say, "I'll do anything just to get my foot in the door" or "I'll work for nothing to get a start." Your interviewer may feel that if you're willing to work for nothing, that's all you may be worth. No respectable employer expects anyone to work for nothing.

10. The last thing you need is an argument. If you find that you must disagree, be as tactful and as brief as possible. On the other hand, don't always agree just to be sociable.

11. If you're being considered by other companies, don't pressure

your interviewer by comparing conditions and offers. Negotiate terms at your second meeting. If you play games during your initial interview, you could lose.

12. Keep your options open. There's always a possibility that the interviewer might feel that you're better suited for another available position rather than the one you're applying for. Listen closely to all aspects of the other position because it may prove more challenging and rewarding than the original one.

13. If you're offered a position then and there and you have no doubts or questions, accept it and ask when you can start. If you have some doubts or would like to compare some of the other offers, then thank the interviewer for the offer but explain you'd like some time to think it over. Ask if you could call her in a few days, and regardless of your decision, be sure to call her at the appointed time. Requesting time to think over acceptance of a position is common. If the interviewer wants a definite answer immediately, you're faced with a major decision. Before the interview you might think about such a possibility so that you'll be prepared if a decision is expected. An immediate answer, however, is rarely requested. Almost all companies will give you a few days to decide.

14. If you feel that the interview is not going well and that you're really blowing it, *don't give up*. Do you best and keep your cool. Many people tend to underrate themselves and be too self-critical. Have you ever taken an exam and felt that you did poorly, only to be pleasantly surprised later? It could happen again. Even if you did botch the interview, so what? You've gained valuable experience, and you'll have other opportunities.

15. No matter how much at ease your interviewer sets you, don't get overly chummy. Remember, putting you at ease and in a relaxed mood is one way the interviewer can see the real you. Always refer to the interviewer by Mr., Miss, Mrs., or Ms. Reply with a "yes sir" or "yes ma'am."

16. Be alert not to oversell yourself. If, either by facial expression or by words, the interviewer shows that she's impressed with your qualifications, leave it at that. Don't ramble on and on about your abilities.

17. At the end of the interview you should be told when a decision will be made. If the interviewer doesn't tell you, ask. It's a reasonable request.

18. Before you leave, smile, shake hands (but only if the interviewer extends her hand first), and thank the interviewer for the chance to discuss the job.

Tips for Following Up the Interview

Now that the interview is behind you, can you sit down and relax? No, not yet. There are still things to do. For example:

1. At the earliest opportunity after leaving the office, take out your trusty little notebook and jot down notes and impressions you wish to remember. Since you may be invited back for a follow-up interview, these notes can play an important role at future meetings. In fact, keeping notes on all interviews should help you compare offers and make a final decision.

2. Should you send a thank-you note to the interviewer? Why not? It'll give you favorable attention and another opportunity to make a subtle pitch—"after having the opportunity of speaking with you and learning more about the company and the position, I'm more convinced about wanting to work for your company and making a contribution to it." Figure 16.4 shows an acceptable thank-you note.

3. Would a telephone follow-up be proper? Certainly. Showing your further interest by a short phone call will, more often than not, make a positive impression. Do one or the other— a note or a phone call—but not both.

4. If you didn't receive an offer, *don't get discouraged*. The more interviews you have, the more experience you'll acquire, and just by the law of averages, you're bound to find a job. Although the legendary Babe Ruth chalked up an enviable home run record, he also struck out often. It takes no talent to quit, but if you believe in yourself and your abilities and are determined to succeed, then you eventually will.

Your college placement office is there to help you and your

116 King Street
Avon, MA 02173
July 24, 1989

Mrs. Frances Adler, R.N.
Supervisor, Department of Nursing
Shalom Hospital
Boston, MA 02116

Dear Mrs. Adler:

Thank you for the opportunity to meet with you today to discuss one of the openings on your staff.

The position appeals to me very much and sounds exactly like what I'm looking for. I am more eager than ever to join your staff.

I appreciate your kind comments regarding my qualifications and look forward to hearing from you.

Sincerely yours,

Evelyn Elisav

Evelyn Elisav

Figure 16.4
Sample thank-you letter

career. Get to know the director and members of her staff. They have a great deal to offer you, but it is *you* who must take the initiative and it is *you* who must sell yourself. Good luck.

HOW ABOUT A RAISE?

Let's assume that you've been on the job eight to ten months and haven't received a pay increase. You feel that you should be getting more money and you decide to ask for a raise, but how and when should you do it?

Before you ask for a raise, be sure you've done your homework. Be prepared to justify your request with documented facts and figures. Being on time, never being absent, and doing a good job are not valid reasons for a raise. These qualities are expected of you and

Find out what mood your boss is in.

may very well prompt your boss to declare, "That's what you're getting paid to do."

On the other hand, if, during a special project, you've often stayed late in order to finish the job on time, if you're always willing to assist others to benefit the company, if you have established an impressive sales record, if you have exceeded your quota or your department's expectations of you, if you have displayed leadership qualities, if you have willingly accepted additional responsibilities, if you have either implemented or suggested to management ways to increase productivity—in other words, if your performance is above and beyond what is normally expected of you, then you would have a powerful case for a raise. But be sure to document all of your facts and be prepared to state the amount of increase you feel you deserve. Be confident and realistic with your request or you may find yourself negotiating a starting salary with another company.

It may be worthwhile to find out what mood your boss is in before approaching her for a raise. Clearly, your chances would be better if she were in a positive frame of mind. If you know that someone plowed into her new car on the way to work, postpone your visit.

Things to Discuss in Class

1. If you haven't already done so, visit the placement office at your school and become familiar with its function.

2. Either from your audiovisual library or from the placement office, get and study a videotape or film on interviewing procedures and demonstrations.

3. Visit your school's placement office, gather the latest information on types of questions that should not be asked in an employment interview, and discuss them in class.

4. Select a company that you'd like to work for and conduct some research on it. Discuss your findings in class.

5. Assume that you're presently working and you feel that you deserve a raise. Tell the class how you would approach this topic and what you would say to your boss.

6. Select a personal subject that you feel would be very inappropriate to discuss with an interviewer. Explain to the class how you would handle this delicate situation if the interviewer raised the subject.

7. If the interviewer asked you questions about your previous employer, explain to the class what your response should be.

What Do You Remember from This Chapter?

1. What is a resumé and why is it important?

2. What is an application letter and what is its purpose?

3. When you research a company, what information should you look for?

4. What would be appropriate dress for a man (woman) to wear to a job interview?

5. Should you prepare some questions to ask the interviewer? Explain.

6. List some important tips to keep in mind relative to conduct during the interview.

7. What are some questions you should be prepared to answer that could catch you off guard?

8. What areas of questioning during an interview could be discriminatory and illegal?

9. What's a good policy to follow regarding criticism of former employers?

10. List several things to think about and do after the interview.

11. List three ways to find a job.

12. Explain two ways to contact a company to arrange for a job interview.

Vitalize Your Vocabulary

Words from Native Americans

From dozens of native American dialects many words have entered the English language. Here are some of the more common ones:

barbecue	papoose	squaw
canoe	pecan	tepee
cougar	potato	tobacco
hickory	pow-wow	toboggan
hominy	raccoon	tomahawk
moccasin	skunk	wampum
moose	squash	wigwam

Some less well-known native American words are:

calumet (n.)   a pipe smoked as a token of peace.

caribou (n.)   deer found in the arctic regions of North America.

caucus (n.)   a closed meeting of members of a political party to decide on policy and to select candidates for office.

chautauqua (n.)   an annual summer recreational and educational program.

mackinaw (n.)   a short double-breasted coat of heavy woolen material, often plaid.

maize (n.)   corn.

peyote (n.)   a drug derived from cactus.

sachem (n.)   the chief of a tribe or the head of an organization.

sequoia (n.)   giant redwood trees of California.

Communicate with confidence.

There are hundreds, possibly thousands, of native American names of places in the United States—for example:

Allegheny	Niagara
Buffalo	Oklahoma
Chicago	Oneida
Dakota	Penobscot
Kalamazoo	Potomac
Kennebec	Saratoga
Manhattan	Scituate
Mashpee	Seneca
Massachusetts	Susquehanna
Milwaukee	Tallahassee
Mississippi	

Chargoggagoggmanchauggauggagoggchaubunagungamaugg (The name of the largest recreational lake in Massachusetts. The Nipmuck Indians gave this lake the longest name of any waterway in the world.)[4]

---

4. *The Boston Herald*, 19 January 1988, 7.

Appendix A
Basic Evaluation Guide

	Yes	No
Before Talk		
Did speaker walk to the front of class quietly and confidently?	☐	☐
Was posture acceptable?	☐	☐
When name was called, was there an oral reaction (groan or sigh)?	☐	☐
Was overall appearance appealing?	☐	☐
If speaker carried notes, were they inconspicuous?	☐	☐
Did speaker briefly pause, look around at audience, and then start to speak?	☐	☐
During Talk		
If speech had a title, was it mind-teasing?	☐	☐
Did speaker greet class?	☐	☐
Did speaker constantly look at audience?	☐	☐
Were speaker's notes hidden?	☐	☐
Could entire class hear speaker?	☐	☐
Did speaker pronounce words clearly?	☐	☐
Did speaker use gestures?	☐	☐

	Yes	No
Did gestures seem natural?	☐	☐
Was introduction brief and to the point?	☐	☐
Did speaker remain frozen in one position?	☐	☐
Did talk follow a plan?	☐	☐
Was talk connected by transitions?	☐	☐
Did speaker make subject interesting?	☐	☐
Was speaker aware of audience reaction?	☐	☐
Was conclusion brief and to the point?	☐	☐
Did speaker seem to enjoy giving talk?	☐	☐
Was speaker's voice expressive?	☐	☐
Was speaker animated?	☐	☐
Did speaker do anything distracting?	☐	☐

After Talk

	Yes	No
If audience asked questions, did speaker handle them with confidence?	☐	☐
If some questions were difficult to hear, did speaker repeat them before answering?	☐	☐
When answering, did speaker look at questioner as well as other members of audience?	☐	☐
Did speaker return to seat confidently and sit down quietly?	☐	☐

Overall Effect

	Needs improvement	Passable	Good	Very good
Posture	☐	☐	☐	☐
Movement	☐	☐	☐	☐
Eye contact	☐	☐	☐	☐
Enthusiasm	☐	☐	☐	☐
Voice delivery	☐	☐	☐	☐
Language	☐	☐	☐	☐
Understandability	☐	☐	☐	☐
Overall presence	☐	☐	☐	☐

Additional comments:

Appendix B
Speeches to Study

The following two speeches were given by men who spoke with confidence and effectiveness. The first speech, delivered by President John F. Kennedy in Berlin in 1963, ranks among the best of this century. Kennedy had gone to Europe to support democracy and freedom and to strengthen our commitment to Western Europe. He spoke to the people and reached them most effectively. The title won audience goodwill and interest because it is in German. His entire speech—note how short it is—appears below, and our comments on each numbered paragraph appear following it.

"Ich Bin Ein Berliner"

1. I am proud to come to this city as the guest of your distinguished Mayor, who has symbolized throughout the world the fighting spirit of West Berlin. And I am proud to visit the Federal Republic with your distinguished Chancellor who for so many years has committed Germany to democracy and freedom and progress, and to come here in the company of my fellow American, General Clay, who has been in this city during its great moments of crisis and will come again if ever needed.

2. Two thousand years ago the proudest boast was *"civis Romanus sum."* Today, in the world of freedom, the proudest boast is *"Ich bin ein Berliner."*

3. I appreciate my interpreter translating my German!

4. There are many people in the world who really don't understand, or say they don't, what is the great issue between the free world and the Communist world. Let them come to Berlin. There are some who say that communism is the wave of the future. Let them come to Berlin. And there are some who say in Europe and elsewhere we can work with the Communists. Let them come to Berlin. And there are even a

President John F. Kennedy, West Berlin, June 26, 1963.

few who say that it is true that communism is an evil system, but it permits us to make economic progress. *Lass' sie nach Berlin kommen.* Let them come to Berlin.

5. Freedom has many difficulties and democracy is not perfect, but we have never had to put a wall up to keep our people in, to prevent them from leaving us. I want to say, on behalf of my countrymen, who live many miles away on the other side of the Atlantic, who are far distant from you, that they take the greatest pride that they have been able to share with you, even from a distance, the story of the last 18 years. I know of no town, no city, that has been besieged for 18 years that still lives with the vitality and the force, and the hope and the determination of the city of West Berlin. While the wall is the most obvious and vivid

demonstration of the failures of the Communist system, for all the world to see, we take no satisfaction in it, for it is, as your Mayor has said, an offense not only against history but an offense against humanity, separating families, dividing husbands and wives and brothers and sisters, and dividing a people who wish to be joined together.

6. What is true of this city is true of Germany—real, lasting peace in Europe can never be assured as long as one German out of four is denied the elementary right of free men, and that is to make a free choice. In 18 years of peace and good faith, this generation of Germans has earned the right to be free, including the right to unite their families and their nation in lasting peace, with good will to all people. You live in a defended island of freedom, but your life is part of the main. So *let me ask you, as I close,* to lift your eyes beyond the dangers of today, to the hopes of tomorrow, beyond the freedom merely of this city of Berlin, or your country of Germany, to the advance of freedom everywhere, beyond the wall to the day of peace with justice, beyond yourselves and ourselves to all mankind.

7. Freedom is indivisible, and when one man is enslaved, all are not free. When all are free, then we can look forward to that day when this city will be joined as one and this country and this great continent of Europe in a peaceful and hopeful globe. When that day finally comes, as it will, the people of West Berlin can take sober satisfaction in the fact that they were in the front lines for almost two decades.

8. All free men, wherever they may live, are citizens of Berlin, and, therefore, as a free man, I take pride in the words *"Ich bin ein Berliner."*

Here are our comments, numbered according to paragraph, on the speech President Kennedy made on that summer's day:

1. JFK's pride in visiting Berlin and his compliments to the Mayor and Chancellor further intensify his hold on audience goodwill and interest. His assurance of American military aid, if necessary, gives his listeners a feeling of security.

2. His knowledge of history enables him to compare Berlin with Rome. He identifies with his listeners by using their language.

3. Here is the President of the United States, the most powerful man in the world, poking fun at his German accent and at the same time complimenting the interpreter. Europeans are not used to this kind of humor from heads of state.

4. The President builds up powerful emotional impact through repeating "Let them come to Berlin." Again he relates to the audience by repeating that statement in German.

5. The President admits that democracy has its faults, but it does not have to erect walls to keep people as prisoners. Another compliment to West Berlin. Now JFK reaches out emotionally and touches people—husbands and wives, brothers and sisters, families.

6. Germans have earned the right to be free, to unite their families, and to live in peace. These ideas appeal to West Europeans. Note the transition to the conclusion. "So let me ask you, as I close, . . ." and the emotional buildup using parallel construction, "beyond . . . to . . . ." The President expresses hope for a better tomorrow.

7. He builds his conclusion on the idea of a better future.

8. Another compliment to Berlin. An extremely moving conclusion in German words, the title of the speech. Note the conciseness of the last paragraph.

The second speech we present for you to study was spoken not *by* a President but *to* a President. Rarely in American history has a citizen been honored at a White House ceremony by a President, and then turned around and lectured the President on ethics and morality. This astounding event occurred in April 1985 when President Ronald Reagan presented the Congressional Gold Medal, our highest civilian award, to Professor Elie Wiesel.

Although the professor survived Hitler's Holocaust during World War II, his mother, father, and sister were among the six million Jews murdered. As chairman of the U.S. Holocaust Commission, Professor Wiesel is the nationally recognized literary conscience of the Holocaust. He directed his remarks at the international controversy ignited by President Reagan's decision to visit a German military cemetery where some Nazi SS troops are buried.

Wiesel's emotional thoughts and delivery, although critical of the President, were in such good taste that he earned worldwide respect and admiration. Below are excerpts from his speech; our comments on each numbered paragraph follow.

On Receipt of the Congressional Gold Medal

1. This medal is not mine alone. It belongs to all those who remember what SS killers have done to their victims. It was given to me for my writings, teaching, and for my testimony. When I write, I feel my invisi-

ble teachers standing over my shoulders, reading my words and judging their veracity. While I feel responsible for the living, I feel equally responsible to the dead. Their memory dwells in my memory.

2. What have I learned in the last 40 years? Small things. I learned the perils of language and those of silence. I learned that in extreme situations, when human lives and dignity are at stake, neutrality is a sin: it helps the killers, not the victims.

3. I learned the meaning of solitude: We were alone—desperately alone. Leaders of the free world knew everything and did nothing—nothing specifically to save Jewish children from death. One million of them perished. If I spent my entire life reciting their names—I would die before finishing the task. Children . . . I have seen some of them thrown into the flames . . . alive. Words? They die on my lips. I have learned the necessity of describing their death—at least their death.

4. I have learned the fragility of the human condition. The killers were not monsters. They were human beings. Good parents. Obedient citizens. Some had college degrees with a passion for the arts or philosophy. Did their education prevent them from committing murder? Evidently not. I have learned that the Holocaust was a unique and uniquely Jewish event—albeit with universal implications. Not all victims were Jews; but all Jews were victims. Dachau's first inmates were German anti-Nazis; but Treblinka and Belzec and Ponar and Babi-Yar were designed to serve as a sacrificial altar for the entire Jewish people.

5. I have learned the guilt of indifference: The opposite of love is not hate, but indifference. Jews were killed by the enemy but betrayed by their so-called allies who found political reasons to justify their indifference.

6. But I have also learned that suffering confers no privileges: It depends upon what one does with it. This is why survivors have tried to teach their contemporaries how to build on ruins. How to invent hope in a world that offers none. How to proclaim faith to a generation that has seen it shamed and mutilated. The survivors have every reason to despair of society: they did not. They opted to work for humankind, not against it.

7. Mr. President, we are grateful to this country for having offered us haven and refuge. Grateful to its leadership for being friendly to Israel—for we are grateful to Israel for existing. Grateful to Congress for its continuous philosophy of humanism and compassion for the underprivileged. As for yourself, Mr. President, we are grateful to you for being a friend of the Jewish people, for trying to help the oppressed Jews in the Soviet Union and for your continuing support of the Jewish state.

Elie Wiesel accepting the Congressional Gold Medal from President Ronald Reagan.

8. Mr. President, am I dreaming? Is this but a nightmare? This day was meant to be a day of joy for me, my family and our friends. Why then is there such a sadness in my heart?

9. Allow me, Mr. President, to touch on a matter which is sensitive. I belong to a traumatized generation; to us symbols are important. Furthermore, following our ancient tradition which commands us to "speak truth to power," may I speak to you of recent events that have caused us much pain and anguish?

10. We have met four or five times. I know of your commitment to humanity. I am convinced that you were not aware of the presence of SS in the Bitburg cemetery. But now we all are. I therefore implore you, Mr. President. In the spirit of this moment that justifies so many

others, tell us now that you will not go there. That place, Mr. President, is not your place. Your place is with the victims of the SS. We know there are political and even strategic considerations—but this issue, as all issues related to that awesome event, transcends politics and even diplomacy.

11. There was a degree of suffering and loneliness in the concentration camps that defies imagination—cut off from the world, with no refuge anywhere, sons watched helplessly as their fathers were beaten to death; mothers watched their children die of hunger. And then there was Mengele and his selections, terror, fear, isolation and torture.

12. Mr. President, you seek reconciliation. So do I. And I, too, wish to attain true reconciliation with the German people. I do not believe in collective guilt—nor in collective responsibility. Only the killers were guilty. Their sons and daughters are not. I believe we can, we must work together with them, with all people to bring peace and understanding to a tormented world that is still awaiting redemption.

1. This speech is extremely persuasive because it is saturated with speaker credibility. He is sincere, tactful, respectful, and friendly. His character and reputation are impeccable and throughout his delivery he displays poise and self-confidence. The introduction contains short, powerful sentences that are easily understood.

2. Wiesel recalls what he has personally learned in the past by stressing the importance of speaking up when lives are at stake.

3. He introduces a shocking statistical statement followed by vivid and descriptive narrative.

4. Concrete examples are cited with which we can associate as he stresses the point that education has little to do with morality.

5. He tells of his experience with indifference.

6. In strong language Wiesel introduces the element of hope, stressing that the survivors of the death camps have hope for the future of society.

7. He generously praises the person whom he is lecturing (the President) by stating that the survivors are grateful to the United States, to Congress, and to the President.

8. Again he directly addresses the Chief Executive by directly asking a few poignant questions that penetrate to the heart of the matter.

9. Wiesel now addresses the President on a most sensitive matter—"to speak truth to power," which is the President, as he recalls recent events.

10. The professor delicately suggests a diplomatic way out to the President. In very eloquent, emotional words he implores the President to stand up for good, not for evil, and to cancel the trip.

11. In graphic and easy-to-visualize language, Wiesel mentions shocking statements of Nazi evil.

12. Wiesel concludes his talk by clearly stating that both he and the President want the same thing and have the same objective—to seek reconciliation with the German people and to work with all people for peace and understanding.

Appendix C
Suggested Speech Topics

If you're having difficulty coming up with ideas on what to talk about, here are a number of suggestions to aid you in your selection.

More Topic Suggestions for a Demonstration Talk

1. How to bathe a new baby.
2. Police equipment.
3. How to read a champagne label.
4. How to use a casting rod.
5. How to change a flat tire.
6. Recreational use of a home computer.
7. Auto antitheft devices.
8. How to play cribbage.
9. Salt water fishing.
10. How to shingle a roof.
11. Making a shadow box.
12. Selecting sports equipment (football, hockey, skiing).
13. How to replace brakes on a car.
14. How to set a table.
15. How to fold napkins creatively for a dinner party.
16. Finger painting.
17. How to decorate a cake.

18. How to transplant a plant.

19. Various types of dancing.

20. Wrapping presents and making bows.

21. How to lower a ceiling.

22. How to make candles.

23. Making ceramics.

24. How to create ornaments with stained glass.

25. How to make paper flowers.

26. How to make Christmas decorations.

27. How to make a pillow.

28. Découpage.

29. Karate.

30. Various types of collections (coins, stamps, Hummels).

31. Firefighter's equipment.

32. How to manicure.

33. How to make animals from balloons.

34. How to decorate a candle.

35. Planting an indoor garden.

36. How to make dolls from rags.

37. How to make a Caesar salad.

38. Structure of court system.

39. How to make a Christmas wreath from pine cones.

40. Performing card tricks.

41. Scuba diving and equipment.

42. How to quilt.

43. How to tune a piano.

44. How to solder.

45. How to identify counterfeit bills.

46. How to wood-carve signs.

47. How to draw cartoons.

48. Flower decorating.

49. How to eat a lobster.

50. What to look for when buying a house.

More Topic Suggestions for an Informative Talk

1. What needs to be done to get Amtrak back on the right track?

2. How to cut vacation costs.

3. Exercise might be a fast track to the grave.

4. How healthful is exercise?

5. What are natural foods?

6. The great American health kick.

7. Buying a VCR.

8. The American dream of home ownership is now a nightmare.

9. How to avoid being ripped off by unscrupulous auto mechanics.

10. The health dangers of the summer sun.

11. Planning an economical family vacation.

12. Is the U.S. ready to fight a modern war?

13. What is happening down on the farms?

14. Why all the fuss about our nation's prisons?

15. The press has too much freedom.

16. What is a conservative?

17. What is a liberal?

18. How to hunt for a job.

19. Why so many national lawmakers have called it quits.

20. Whatever happened to our synefuels program?

21. How to eat well and stay healthy.

22. Degrees from diploma mills.

23. Is Congress for sale? (Powerful lobbying groups).

24. How to buy a house.

25. Selecting a type of home mortgage.

26. The tragedy of Amerasians. (Result of our Far East wars)

27. What is a financial planner?

28. More crime and less punishment.

29. Psychic phenomena.

30. What's ailing our present health system?

31. Why do banks charge so much for basic services?

32. ESP.

33. Are political pollsters getting out of hand?

34. The Soviet obsession for American high technology.

35. The high cost of supporting our former presidents.

36. The increase of child abuse cases.

37. Defense fraud.

38. What federal entitlement programs are citizens entitled to?

39. Lloyd's of London.

40. A better way to pick our presidents.

41. How Russia makes psychiatry a weapon.

42. Why Soviets are far behind in computer technology.

43. Where will the jobs be through 1995?

44. The functions of the World Bank.

45. Hang gliding.

46. A trip to Disney World.

47. Toxic waste.

48. America's illiteracy problem.

49. Canada—our northern neighbor.

50. Whatever happened to the meaning of our Monroe Doctrine?

51. Make your home more energy efficient.

52. How automobiles can be made safer.

53. The various types of medical insurance.

54. Selecting the college of your choice.

55. The high risk of marriage.

56. The high cost of seeking and keeping public office.

57. The popularity of home equity loans.

58. Why the stock market crashed in October, 1987.

59. Who can contract the AIDS virus?

60. Our national debt is out of control.

61. How secure is Social Security?

62. The status of nursing home care.

63. The popularity of automatic teller machines.

64. A day in the life of a lobbyist.

65. Breathing can be dangerous to your health (air pollution).

66. Travel by air balloon.

67. The basic philosophy of the Democratic party.

68. The basic philosophy of the Republican party.

69. The basic philosophy of the Libertarian party.

70. Religion by television.

71. Our polluted waterways.

72. Why union membership is on the rapid decline.

73. The plight of the homeless in America.

74. Innovative ways to finance a college education.

75. How wearing seat belts can save lives.

More Topic Suggestions for a Persuasive Talk

1. Spouses of political candidates should (not) be required to make their financial statements and tax returns public.

2. The Miss America Pageant is (not) sexist.

3. Greece should (not) be made the permanent site of the Olympic Games.

4. The United States should (not) become involved in Central American politics.

5. The United States should (not) impose quotas on the import of foreign cars.

6. Auto repair mechanics should be licensed.

7. Countries boycotting the Olympic Games should (not) be penalized.

8. The incredible waste in the military.

9. The United States should (not) use military force to keep Mideast oil flowing.

10. A United States President should serve only one six-year term.

11. The Environmental Protection Agency is (not) effective.

12. A college education is more important than ever.

13. Why the ERA should (not) become law.

14. Why farmers should (not) be paid for not planting.

15. The presidential primaries should be shortened.

16. Women have yet to enjoy pay equity.

17. Why we should (not) have a national drinking law.

18. Our military budget should be increased (slashed).

19. Our fishing fleets are going down for the third time.

20. How a politician can personally oppose abortion but support freedom of choice.

21. The electoral college should take a sabbatical.

22. Presidents should be elected by popular vote.

23. Foreign cars are (not) made better than domestic ones.

24. America is ready for a woman president.

25. Why you should leave home without your credit cards.

26. Let's get politics out of the Olympics.

27. The United States military machine needs oiling.

28. Campaign donations by PAC's should (not) be limited.

29. We should be prepared to fight in the Persian Gulf.

30. You should have a will.

31. We must prevent our maritime fleet from sinking.

32. Our political nominating system needs an overhaul.

33. Big business mergers are (not) good for the consumer.

34. We must (not) try to improve relations with Cuba.

35. Smoking is (not) dangerous to nonsmokers.

36. We should (not) have a national balanced budget.

37. We must (not) place tighter curbs on FBI stings.

38. The government should (not) allow "double dipping."

39. Cigarette (liquor) advertising should be banned.

40. The government should (not) bail out banks in trouble because of unwise foreign loans.

41. Wearing seat belts should be the choice of the public and not the government.

42. A National Health Insurance Plan is long overdue.

43. More student discipline should be returned to the schools.

44. Tipping should (not) be allowed.

45. You should give to fund drives.

46. All colleges should (not) have fraternities and sororities.

47. Voting in America should (not) be mandatory.

48. Why you should (not) buy a small car.

49. Why you should (not) buy a big car.

50. Why we should have air bags in cars.

51. The United States should (not) reinstate the draft.

52. The jury system should (not) be abolished.

53. The rewards of a liberal arts education.

54. Why all students should study a foreign language.

55. Why Japanese products are (not) superior to American products.

56. Why teachers should (not) be able to strike.

57. Presidential campaigning should be limited to six months prior to the national election.

58. A candidate's private life should (not) remain private.

59. Public tax money should (not) be used to aid private education.

60. We should (not) spend less in foreign aid and more on domestic programs.

61. Deregulation is (not) hurting our country.

62. Many baseball players' salaries are out of the ballpark.

63. The government should (not) abolish all grants for student loans.

64. All politicians should (not) serve only two terms.

65. The courts should (not) be allowed to grant anyone immunity.

66. The president should (not) be allowed to veto a line item in a budget.

67. Nuclear power plants are (not) safe.

68. We need more low/moderate housing.

69. America needs more day care centers.

70. Public higher education should be free to all who qualify.

71. Public employees should (not) have the right to strike.

72. The breakup of AT&T was (not) a big mistake.

73. How you can literally die for a cigarette.

74. Hostile business takeovers should not be legal.

75. Our country is suffering from too much deregulation.

Glossary

abstract words words that derive their meaning from personal interpretation and opinion; the opposite of concrete. (Ch. 8)

announcement a short statement of an event including all pertinent information. (Ch. 13)

application letter a letter which usually accompanies a resumé telling the employer what you have to offer the company and why you should be hired. (Ch. 16)

articulation movements of lips, tongue, jaw, and soft palate that convert vocal sounds into speech. The most common faults among college students are running words together and omitting word endings. (Ch. 5)

assertive able to express true feelings and opinions honestly and comfortably, and able to say no without feeling guilty. (Ch. 1)

audience analysis finding out as much as possible about the makeup of an audience. The more you know about the members of the audience the more effectively you'll be able to communicate with them. (Ch. 8)

audiovisual aids material that helps a speaker clarify and reinforce his or her message; photographs, cartoons, objects, videotape, and so on. (Ch. 10)

body language see *nonverbal communication*. (Ch. 2)

bibliography a listing of authors and sources of information on a particular subject. (Ch. 6)

body (of speech) the central part of a speech, which contains the key information, ideas, or emotions to be communicated by a speaker to the audience. (Ch. 7)

brainstorming a stimulating exercise using the imagination for the purpose of generating as many ideas as possible. (Ch. 6)

buzz sessions small groups of people who gather to try to solve a common problem. All of the participating groups collectively present their proposed solutions. (Ch. 14)

card catalog a file of cards listing all books in a library by author's name, title, and subject and indicating where they may be found. (Ch. 6)

causal reasoning establishing a relationship between causes and effects. (Ch. 12)

chairperson or **chair** one who presides over a meeting, panel, forum, round-table discussion, or symposium; a moderator or discussion leader. (Ch. 14)

clichés expressions that have been around and used for so long that they have become virtually meaningless. (Ch. 8)

codes messages or methods of communication. (Ch. 3)

communication in this book, the interpersonal exchange of ideas and feelings between speaker and listeners. (throughout text)

communication cycle the activity in which a person speaks and another listens and responds to the speaker. (Ch. 16)

compact disc a recording on a disc from which sound is reproduced by a laser beam instead of a needle. (Ch. 2)

conclusion (of speech) the ending of a speech, which often sums up the main points or stresses the major idea. A conclusion should contain no new material. (Ch. 7)

concrete words words that pertain to objects you can see; tangible things. (Ch. 8)

consonant a speech sound produced by a partial or total stoppage of the air stream—for example, the letters *t, k, f, b, p.* (Ch. 5)

credibility the degree to which a speaker and/or his or her message is considered believable. (Ch. 12)

deductive reasoning making deductions or drawing conclusions. It involves moving from a general principle to a specific principle. (Ch. 12)

delivery the way a speech is given; it can be read, memorized, or spoken extemporaneously (with or without notes after preparation beforehand). Delivery may also refer to the use of the voice. (Ch. 9)

demonstration talk a talk intended to show how to do or how to make something or to explain how something functions with the use of audio/visual aids. (Ch. 10)

diction pronunciation and enunciation of words: clarity, intelligibility, and distinctness are essential in public speaking. (Ch. 5)

diphthong a voice glide produced in one breath. The sound may be a blend of two vowels. (Ch. 5)

duration length of time that vowel sounds are held. (Ch. 5)

empathy the ability to experience another person's feelings; "putting yourself in the other person's shoes." (Ch. 9)

enthusiasm interest, animation, emphasis, and excitement conveyed while speaking. (Ch. 9)

enunciate   to pronounce every syllable of a word clearly and distinctly; to articulate. (Ch. 5)

evidence   facts and/or expert testimony to support a person's position or statements. (Ch. 12)

extemporaneous   researched, thought about, outlined, rehearsed, and then delivered with or without notes. (Ch. 9)

eye contact   a communicative two-way relationship in which a speaker constantly looks at the listeners and reacts to their feedback (cheers, boos, facial expressions, gestures). (Ch. 2)

forum   a public speaking situation in which members of the audience are allowed to participate by asking questions or making comments. (Ch. 14)

gestures   movements by hands, arms, head, shoulders, or body to emphasize or clarify spoken thoughts and emotions. (Ch. 2)

identification with audience   associating oneself with the ideas, opinions, and feelings of listeners, usually in an attempt to persuade them. (Ch. 12)

impromptu talk   a talk given on the spur of the moment, without prior notice or time for preparation. (Ch. 9)

inductive reasoning   the reverse of deductive reasoning; starts with specific examples or cases and ends with a general conclusion based on the examples or cases. (Ch. 12)

inflection   a change, up or down, in vocal tone or pitch. (Ch. 3)

informative talks   communication in which the chief aim is to share knowledge and understanding with the audience. (Ch. 11)

interpersonal communication   a verbal or nonverbal exchange of ideas, knowledge, and feelings between two or more people. (throughout text)

interview   oral communication between two people or by a panel questioning an individual for the purpose of eliciting information. (Ch. 16)

introduction (of speech)   the part of a speech in which the speaker usually explains the purpose and scope of the speech and, at the same time, tries to win audience interest and goodwill. (Ch. 7)

kinesics   the study of body movements, such as posture, facial expressions, arm movement, and so on. (Ch. 3)

lectern   a speaker's stand with a slanted top that supports the notes (if any) of a speaker; a lectern may rest on a table or floor. See *podium*. (Ch. 2)

lecture   an exposition of a given subject to a group for the purpose of disseminating information. (Ch. 14)

listening   making an effort to hear and understand a speaker's statement. (Ch. 4)

loaded words   words concerning race, religion, politics, or personal character which can produce overpowering, negative reactions. (Ch. 8)

manuscript   copy that is written out word for word. (Ch. 9)

MC   master of ceremonies (Ch. 8)

moderator   a group leader whose basic responsibilities include introducing the members of a panel and its subject, presiding over a smooth and fair discussion, bringing a discussion to a close, and allowing questions from the audience. (Ch. 14)

modes of communication   certain elements which communicate messages, often nonverbally—for example, facial expressions, eye contact, gestures, objects, space, time, touch, and paralanguage. (Ch. 3)

monorate   the tendency to speak each syllable, word, phrase, and sentence at the same rate of speed. (Ch. 5)

monotone   the tendency of a voice not to move far up and down the tone scale, thus resulting in very little expression. The voice sounds flat, dull, and boring. (Ch. 4)

motivation   an inner drive, impulse, or incentive that causes a person to do something or to act in a certain way. (Ch. 4)

nervousness   an emotional state characterized by tension or fear. (Ch. 2)

nonverbal communication   the transmission and reception of messages, knowingly or unknowingly, other than by spoken words: through facial expressions; eye contact; posture; and gestures by hands, arms, head, shoulders, and body. Also known as body language, silent language, and soundless speech. (Ch. 2)

notecards   3-by-5 or 5-by-7 cards on which key ideas are written or printed to aid a speaker's memory. (Ch. 6)

oral visualization   conveying a message by feeling, experiencing, or reliving the ideas and emotions one wishes to communicate. (Ch. 5)

outline   a plan of a talk that lists the topics and subtopics, plus their major and minor backup points. (Ch. 7)

pacing   creating an interesting rate of delivery and variety that will hold your listeners' interest. For example, you may slow down or speed up your delivery, or you may use pauses. (Ch. 5)

panels   discussion groups of three to six or more people, led by a moderator or chair, who explore a subject. The purpose is to inquire, deliberate, and enlighten, not to argue and persuade. Audiences usually ask questions after the panelists have spoken. (Ch. 14)

paralanguage   how you say it as opposed to what you say. Some elements of paralanguage, or vocalics, are the quality of the voice, its pitch, rate of delivery, inflection, emphasis, and pauses. (Ch. 3)

pauses momentary silences in speaking. They can stress a point, separate ideas, and give a speaker time to organize his or her thoughts. (Ch. 3)

pause, vocalized a distracting hesitation filled with vocal "static" such as *ah, er, like, right, you know,* and so on. It is caused by habit, nervousness, or both and can be cured by conscious effort. (Ch. 9)

persuasive speaking speaking that tries, by logical reasoning and emotional appeals, to convince listeners to change their opinions, to hold fast to them, or to perform an action recommended by the speaker. (Ch. 12)

pitch the highness or lowness of a voice. Normal pitch should allow a speaker to comfortably raise or lower his or her voice for varied expression. (Ch. 5)

plagiarism the act of taking ideas and opinions, or actual wording, from another and passing them off as one's own. (Ch. 6)

plosives initial sounds produced by the sudden release of breath, such as *k, p,* and *t.* (Ch. 13)

podium an elevated platform or stage, not to be confused with lectern or speaker's stand. (Ch. 13)

prolongation extension of the duration of a vowel sound. (Ch. 9)

proxemics the study of space as a mode of communication. (Ch. 3)

public address (PA) system an electronic amplification system used in halls or auditoriums so that speakers can be heard by a large audience. (Ch. 13)

rate of speaking the average number of words spoken in one minute. The average person speaks between 130 and 160 words a minute. (Ch. 5)

reasoning the forming of conclusions based on known or assumed facts; the use of reason. (Ch. 12)

resumé a written statement of a job applicant's work objective, employment experience, education, and other qualifications. (Ch. 16)

round-table discussion a meeting in which several people sit at a table and, under a moderator or chair, discuss a given topic. See *forum, panel discussion,* and *symposium.* (Ch. 14)

self-image what and how one thinks of oneself. (Ch. 3)

silent language see *nonverbal communication.* (Ch. 2)

soundless speech see *nonverbal communication.* (Ch. 2)

speaking apprehension see *nervousness.* (Ch. 2)

speaker's stand   see *lectern*. (Ch. 2)

special-occasion speeches   speeches given under special circumstances and for a particular reason: presenting or accepting an award, nominating a candidate for office, making an announcement, and so on. (Ch. 13)

speech tension   see *nervousness*. (Ch. 2)

stage fright   nervousness felt by the vast majority of speakers, both before and during speaking. (Ch. 2)

symposia   meetings in which participants speak on specific phases of the same question. Then the participants question one another or answer questions from the audience. (Ch. 14)

thesis statement   a sentence that states the main purpose of a talk. (Ch. 14)

transitions   words, phrases, or sentences that smoothly connect parts of a talk. (Ch. 7)

transparency   a positive film or slide with an image that is visible when light shines through it; usually projected onto a screen. (Ch. 10)

videocassette recorder (VCR)   a magnetic tape instrument that records audio and video signals; the recording can be played back any number of times. (Ch. 7)

vocalics   see *paralanguage*. (Ch. 3)

vocal volume   the loudness or softness of a speaker's voice. (Ch. 5)

vowel   the strongest sound in most syllables; the letters *a, e, i, o, u,* and occasionally *y*. (Ch. 5)

Index

Photo Credits

Unless otherwise acknowledged, all photos are the property of Scott, Foresman and Company.

page 14	Jim Whitmer
page 34	Jim Whitmer
page 58	Jean-Claude LeJeune
page 74	Wide World
page 142	Owen Franken/Stock Boston
page 164	Manuel Ceneta/Black Star
page 184	NASA
page 188	United Nations
page 208	Cynthia Johnson/Gamma-Liaison
page 232	Peter Jordan/Gamma-Liaison
page 260	Bob Daemmerich/Click/Chicago Ltd.
page 280	Paul Conklin/Monkmeyer Press Photo Service
page 324	Stacy Pick/Uniphoto
page 357	John F. Kennedy Library
page 361	Diana Walker/Gamma-Liaison